ACCLAIM FOR ANN JONES'S

Looking for Lovedu

"A spellbinding travel memoir."   —*Elle*

"Lively . . . [and] provocative."
                              —*The Women's Review of Books*

"A startling glimpse of modern Africa. . . . Jones is
both a dauntless adventurer and a wise observer."
                              —*Publishers Weekly*

"Entertaining and enlightening."
                              —*St. Louis Post-Dispatch*

"[Jones] peoples the journey with characters no package tourist would ever find. . . . It is her descriptions
of people that raise this above mere travelogue."
                              —*London Daily Express*

"An elegant, ambivalent travelogue."   —*Outside*

"An honest and illuminating study that portrays the
process by which the investigation of a continent
becomes the examination of the self."
                              —*Kirkus Reviews*

"A lively trip into the heart of Africa."   —*US Weekly*

ANN JONES

Looking for Lovedu

Ann Jones received an M.A. from the University of Michigan and a Ph.D. from the University of Wisconsin. Her travel essays and photographs have appeared in many newspapers and magazines, among them *The New York Times, Condé Nast Traveler, Town & Country, Women's Sports & Fitness, Outside, National Geographic Traveler,* and *Spur.* She is the author of five other books. Ann Jones lives in New York's Hudson River Valley.

Looking for Lovedu

Looking for Lovedu

A WOMAN'S JOURNEY
ACROSS AFRICA

Ann Jones

VINTAGE DEPARTURES
VINTAGE BOOKS
A DIVISION OF RANDOM HOUSE, INC.
NEW YORK

FIRST VINTAGE DEPARTURES EDITION, JULY 2002

The Library of Congress has cataloged the Knopf edition as follows:
Jones, Ann, [date]
Looking for Lovedu : Days and nights in Africa / by Ann Jones.
p.   cm.
ISBN 0-375-40554-2 (alk. paper)
1. Africa—Description and travel.   2. Jones, Ann, 1937–   I. Title.
DT12.75.J66 2001
916.04'329—dc21   00-055933

Vintage ISBN: 0-375-70533-3

Author photograph © Fran Moore
Book design by Anthea Lingeman

www.vintagebooks.com

Printed in the United States of America
10 9 8 7 6 5 4 3 2 1

"Would you tell me please which way I have to go from here?"
"That depends a good deal on where you want to get to."

—Lewis Carroll, *Alice's Adventures in Wonderland*

Contents

Acknowledgments   xi

Map of Africa   2

THE MISSION   5

LOVEDULAND   14

PREPARATIONS   24

READ HISTORY   32

OFF THE EDGE   42

PARAMETERS   49

CONVOY   60

SAHARA   68

THE ROAD TO BAMAKO   79

THE ROAD NOT TAKEN   93

REAL AFRICA   100

WHITE BREAD   109

NO CONDITION IS PERMANENT   116

NOT A GREAT COUNTRY   122

FEMINISTS AND *FONS*   133

MALARIA AND MISSIONARIES   140

STUFFED   151

MIRACLES   157

CONVOY II   165

LES ROUTES DU ZAÏRE   170

SURVIVAL   182

CIVILIZATION   190

WAITING FOR TO GO   202

HOME AND AWAY   210

AFRICAN TRAVELER   215

TWO CAMPS   223

UJAMAA   232

WHAT YOU SEE   239

AFRICAN HERITAGE   246

THE RAIN QUEEN   253

Acknowledgments

No expedition is done solo. I owe thanks to everyone who pushed this one along: David Kleinman; Christa Brantsch; Alex Andrews; John Gould of UTC and his colleagues Sheila MacGregor, Ashanti Sheth, and Jonathan Oakes; the late Wayne Muggleton; the family of Celia Muhonjo; Lucinda and Tristan Voorspuy; and especially my friend Diane Ebzery, Executive Director of African Portfolio. And thanks to all those trusting companies that gave us great gear and services: Basic Designs, British Airways, Camptime, Canon, Cascade Designs, Coleman-Peak, Compaq, Cricket USA, Eagle Creek, Eddie Bauer, Ex Officio, GSI Outdoors, Grundig, Kodak, Leatherman Tools, Lonely Planet, Lowe Pro, 3-M, Magellan, Mont Bell, Nikon, Outdoor Research, Petzl, Polaroid, PUR, REI, Teva, Thorlo, Toyota Kenya, Travelsmith, Trimble Navigation, Vasque, and Wisconsin Pharmacal.

I've been lucky to have a loyal band of supporters: Morris Dye at AOL and Trish Reynales at Microsoft's Mungo Park, who edited my original dispatches and photographs from the road; Tom Passavant and Susan Shipman at Diversion, Linda Gardiner and Ellen Cantarow at *Women's Review of Books,* and Larry Habegger and Lucy McCauley at Travelers' Tales, Inc., all of whom published essays about the expedition; my agents Charlotte Sheedy, Octavia Wiseman, and Abner Stein; and the sporty girls, Fran Moore and Nell Schofield, who were with me to the end. Hannah Wallace helped with initial research. Valerie Martin, Phyllis Grosskurth, Bob McMullen, and Richard West added insight and encouragement. Joan Silber, Maxine Kumin, Jean Grossholtz, Alison Baker, Mary O'Neil, and African historian Eugenia Herbert generously commented on various drafts of the manuscript; and my editor, Victoria Wilson, brought her critical intelligence to bear. I am deeply indebted to all of these colleagues and friends, and to Patricia Lewis and Mary Clemmey, who kept a light in the window for me during my travels.

Among many books that increased my knowledge of Africa, I found these particularly helpful: *Africa: The Biography of a Continent,* by John Reader; *In My Father's House,* by Kwame Anthony Appiah; *The Scramble for Africa,* by Thomas Pakenham; *King Leopold's Ghost,* by Adam Hochschild; *Season of Blood,* by Fergal Keane; and *We Wish to Inform You That Tomorrow We Will Be Killed with Our Families,* by Philip Gourevitch. For deepening my understanding I am indebted to the work of many African thinkers and writers, notably Chinua Achebe, Wole Soyinka, Nelson Mandela, Jomo Kenyatta, Yoweri Museveni, Buchi Emecheta, Ama Ata Aidoo, Fatima Mernissi, Bessie Head, Nadine Gordimer, Amos Tutuola, Meja Mwangi, Ayi Kwei Armah, Sembene Ousmane, Mariama Ba, Mercy Amba Oduyoye, Ngugi Wa Thiong'o, and Ken Saro-Wiwa.

I cannot adequately acknowledge the generosity of the Africans who welcomed us to their continent and helped us on our way. My gratitude to them is beyond calculation. As is my gratitude to my traveling companions—Caro and Celia, and my peerless friend Kevin Muggleton, who doesn't mind being the villain of the piece as long as he can be amusing. My most profound debt is to the woman who started it all. Through every mile I've been mindful of Liz Knights, my beloved friend and editor at Victor Gollancz in London, who first encouraged me to write about my travels, saw me off to Africa, and slipped away herself to parts unknown before my return. She left to me and to all who loved her the priceless example of how to live bravely, with a full heart.

Looking for Lovedu

JONES / MUGGLETON

JONES ALONE

JONES / CARO

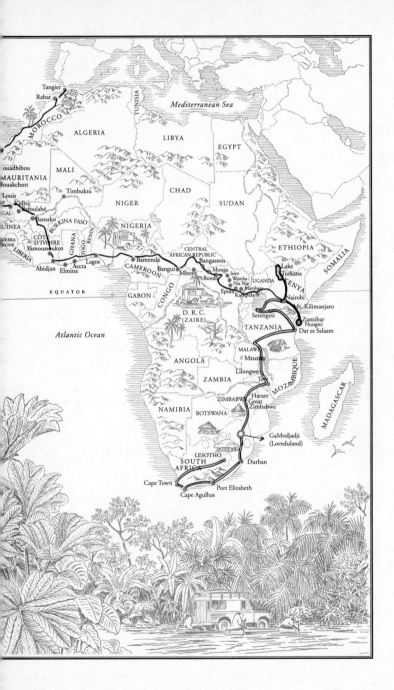

THE MISSION

The Queen was an afterthought. Long before we heard of her, we hatched the scheme in Africa—in Zimbabwe, on the Zambezi, in a canoe. In the long white afternoon, the intensity of the sun propelled us, lightheaded, into a reedy little backwater to rest. We drew the four canoes together, and Dave, our guide, opened a cooler and pitched us bottles of warm Coke. I dipped my bandana in the river, wrapped it around my eyes, smarting from the glint of sun on water, and lay back against the thwart, half dozing, embraced by my friends' banter. Images of the African morning played upon the inside of my eyelids: Elephants showering in the shallows at the river's edge. Crocodiles lying like logs against the banks, innocent and sinister. A flight of carmine bee-eaters darting from their nests in the riverbank, flinging themselves like rubies over the bright water. Now, as heat enveloped us, pressing our bodies as a lover might, everything grew still as all that had gone before and all that was to come converged upon this single suspended moment that was both dream and reality: Africa.

Of course we couldn't bear perfection. Who first pitched dream trips into the silence I can't recall, but my companions leaped upon the subject, describing half a dozen places that might be better—more beautiful, more exciting, more perfect than this. It's the subject that always comes up among travelers: Where do you *really* want to go? Someone spoke of Timbuktu: of camels and drifting coppery dunes, and blue-robed masked men slim as swords. Another spoke of rain forests along the Congo: of furtive okapis and tiny Pygmies hunting with nets, and women who make houses out of leaves. Someone spoke of the Skeleton Coast: of ships flung inland among desert elephants, and lions prowling among seals on the beach. And then a British voice was saying: "I've always been keen to drive all the way through Africa." This was Kevin Muggleton, a photographer from pastoral Wiltshire. He spoke offhandedly with an easy tantalizing laugh. Not even Muggleton could seriously make this proposition: to drive from one end of Africa to the other. But his voice carried a decidedly un-British edge of enthusiasm that drew me out of this moment—relaxed and contemplative in a green canoe on a blue river in the heart of Africa—and flung me by the sheer force of its vitality into an uncertain and adventurous future. "It's classic," Muggleton said. "You know, the old 'Cape to Cairo' sort of thing." That's all it took. Later I stumbled upon the Queen and used her as a good excuse, but in fact I decided everything in that moment.

When I was a kid, my father's idea of a good time was to get in the car and drive somewhere. Anywhere. Anything to escape the malicious carping that passed for family life in our house. "Want to take a little ride in the jalopy, kiddo?" he'd say to me when tension sucked the air from our kitchen, and off we'd go in the old green Ford for a few hours or a few days. Even in winter we'd roll down the windows for a faceful of wind. We'd go where my father felt like going and head home when he was laughing again and felt like going back. Maybe he had a plan all along, but he never let on. To me and my dog, Lady, this aimless wandering was bliss. When I grew up I labeled it "travel" and kept at it, which is how I came to be lazing in a canoe on the Zambezi in the first place.

I lifted my bandana and squinted up at Muggleton in the next canoe. He was young, big, tall, lean. He'd grown up in Hong Kong, a military brat, gone to boarding school in England, and after Sandhurst done a stint as an officer in the British equivalent of the Green Berets. Later he'd started a video business in Victoria Falls, and once, for the hell of it, he'd walked through South America. If ever a man was qualified to go anywhere, Muggleton was it. He had the right attitude for the job too, perhaps because he was one of the last known male descendants of Prophet Muggleton, the seventeenth-century English sectarian who taught that "God takes no notice of us." That dogma left the younger Muggleton self-reliant and endlessly amused by the human comedy, if also somewhat slack in his moral scruples.

"Me too," I said.

Muggleton grinned.

"Great news," he said. And then he asked me: "Do you want to take a little ride?"

Everybody laughed. I laughed. I closed my eyes against the light and mulled it over. We'd been on the river for days—we being four American journalists; Diane, the travel executive who'd invited us on a press trip; Dave, the guide; and Muggleton. We'd run into Muggleton, an old friend of Diane's, in Victoria Falls just after most of the journalists confessed to her that they'd significantly exaggerated their experience in canoeing. We were scheduled to leave for the Zambezi, a big river full of crocodiles and hippos, and Diane was desperate to bring her journalists back alive. She asked Muggleton to come along. He was a man who could paddle his own canoe.

That was supposed to give us an experienced paddler in the stern of each of our four canoes: Dave in the lead canoe, Muggleton, a journalist named George, and me. About George. He was young, like Muggleton. But that was all they had in common. George was a feature writer from a Midwestern daily, on his first trip to Africa—his first trip, I believe, outside the United States. He called Africa "The Dark Continent," intoning the phrase in a deep booming voice, pausing ever so slightly between the words for emphasis, utterly untroubled by the racist history and implications of the label. George had done some research on Africa. He'd read Bartle Bull's big glossy book on safaris. He'd studied the extravagant exploits of several Victorian adventurers. He'd read up on Tarzan and the man-eating lions of Tsavo. He knew that The Dark Continent was a place of prodigious peril, fraught with dangers, yet his reading had taught him that a man could face those dangers and surmount them. A man like Sir Richard Burton, for example, or David Livingstone or Henry Morton Stanley. A man could be a hero. (My own hero was Mary Kingsley, who had contrived to explore West Africa without shooting a single local resident, but I could tell she wouldn't figure in George's fantasy.)

George wore the hero's clothes. He'd assembled a natty khaki safari outfit—all tabs and flaps and epaulets—such as Robert Redford wore in *Out of Africa,* such as even Denys Finch Hatton himself might have worn had he been able to avail himself of permanent press. He wore a Leatherman Super Tool on his belt and a large sheathed knife like the one Tarzan whips out of his loincloth when caught unawares by a crocodile. Even the strap securing his safari hat under his chin spoke not of sissyhood but of forethought and preparedness. When we walked down to the canoes to begin our river trip, George carried his paddle at the ready like an elephant gun.

That's when he turned to Dave and boomed: "If hippos attack and overturn your canoe, is it better to swim for shore on the surface or underwater?" The question astonished me. Could a person really *plan* a thing like that? I wondered. Where did forethought cross the line into fruitless worry? But George had been asking questions like that all along, directing them at Dave, the expert. "Are there any man-eating black mambas around here?" he asked on the manicured lawn of our hotel in Victoria Falls. "If a lion attacks, is it better to climb a tree or make a run for it?" "When elephants charge your Land Rover, should you stay in the vehicle?" Dave was a pro—unflappable and unsurprised. But this time, when George asked for help with his hippo-escape plans, I saw Dave glance up quickly, stifling a smile and careful to avoid catching the eye of Muggleton, who was bent double over his paddle, rolling his eyes and miming hysterical laughter.

"In a case like that," Dave said, straight-faced, "you should just swim, George. Just swim." Then, watching as George stepped boldly into his canoe and almost overturned it, Dave added: "When we're on the river, George, why don't you keep right behind me?"

With another journalist named Bob in the bow, I was designated to pilot the third canoe, right behind George and his bowman, Kenny. Muggleton, with Diane in the bow, was assigned to bring up the rear. Dave peeled off from the bank, and Muggleton pushed George's canoe off into Dave's wake before jumping into his own boat. I slipped into line behind George and watched his canoe begin to weave. I could hear him booming out to his partner, Kenny, "Paddle on the left. No! Paddle on the right. Faster!"—all the while shifting his own paddle from one side of the canoe to the other. Dave swung about and tactfully offered us all a quick refresher course on basic canoe strokes. Muggleton sidled his canoe up beside mine. I knew without looking that he was fairly shaking with repressed laughter.

"Could you let us see that one again, Dave?" he called. "That's a bloody tricky stroke."

. . .

So that's how we went down the river—with Dave always looking over his shoulder, keeping one eye on George; me hanging back every time George's canoe took another wide swing abreast of the current; and Muggleton hanging in beside me, cracking jokes behind a mask of sublime innocence while Diane watched out ahead for hippos and held her breath. "I wish I could make those little circles," Muggleton would say as George's canoe spun aimlessly, out of control. "How does he do that?"

Following Dave's lead, we kept close to shore, and each time we came upon a pod of hippos lazing on a sandbar, we moved closer still, to hug the riverbank and scoot past them at a safe distance. The biggest hippos grunted and roared and opened enormous jaws in a threatening display of armament. When they thought we'd come too close, they rose up and charged as we sped through the narrow passage between them and the bank. Hippos are big and fast, and from the human point of view the most dangerous wild creatures in Africa. At that critical moment, when they considered shifting gears from intimidation to serious attack, we needed speed and luck on our side. "Dig in!" Dave would sing out, and we'd dig.

Once, when we cut it close, something happened to George. Maybe he panicked. Or maybe he saw an opportunity at last to be a hero. In any case, he undertook to steer. As we drove forward, George's canoe sheared off from the line and wobbled along a new trajectory toward the threatening hippos. From the bow, where Kenny perched, utterly exposed, like an offering being delivered to the river gods, came a strangled cry: "George! Oh my god, George!" Kenny snatched his paddle from the water and held it in front of him like a spear, at the same time twisting about to aim his full-throated scream at George. The canoe lurched under his weight and spun until it faced upstream, where it hung just out of reach of an onrushing hippo until the current sucked it suddenly downstream, backward, to safety.

That evening we made camp on the riverbank. As we gathered around a campfire for our nightly ration of maize meal and stew, everyone congratulated George and Kenny on their narrow escape. "I could see right down that hippo's throat," Kenny kept saying. "I mean, I could see his tonsils. I could count his goddamn cavities." The sun falling behind the convoluted mountains of Zambia on the far shore shone on the water, and the great river wound a bloody path into the darkness downstream. In a moment the river silvered, a strip of tinsel in the deepening dark. Then it was gone, vanished into the African night.

George's voice boomed out of the darkness: "Say, Dave, what time do the malaria-carrying mosquitoes come out?"

"They'll be along any time now," Dave said.

"Is it best to put on insect repellent and get inside your tent?" George asked.

"Good plan, George," Muggleton chimed in. "Good man."

Later I was awakened in the night. Under cover of darkness, the great river horses—the hippos—had come out of the water to graze among our tents. All around me I could hear their slow soft munching, and from the tent next to mine, a sharper sound—the high keen rasping sobs of Muggleton struggling to stifle a fit of laughter.

I mention George because his ineptitude helped seal my decision to go for a ride with Muggleton. Poor George posed a danger to himself and others on a simple camping trip, but his incompetence amplified by contrast the easy strength and capability of Muggleton. His deadly seriousness pointed up Muggleton's freewheeling wicked wit. Next to George, Muggleton seemed peerless: a man you could count on to get the job done and keep you laughing all the while. Bitsy was with us too, the only other female journalist on the trip. In the first days she'd fallen off a horse and doctored herself with enough Valium and Prozac to precipitate total collapse and a night in the Victoria Falls hospital, watched over by Diane. On the river, unable to paddle at all, she sat huddled under her safari hat in the bow of Dave's canoe, popping pills and periodically replenishing her sunblock, while Muggleton and I, side by side, guided our canoes downriver. Just as Muggleton was not George, I was not Bitsy. In our superiority we became conspiratorial and daring. It didn't occur to me to wonder what might happen when Muggleton reached the limits of his skill, or how heartlessly he might laugh when I reached the limits of mine. And I don't think it occurred to either of us that in our overland journey across Africa, we wouldn't be traveling by canoe. We shrugged off such reasonable reservations, and by the time we returned to Vic Falls, we had reached an understanding. We would go.

· · ·

A couple of months later Muggleton, Dave, and Diane showed up at my New York apartment and we walked over to Milady's Bar in SoHo for breakfast. Diane, who runs her travel business out of New York and Harare, had brought Dave to the States to publicize Zimbabwe at an adventure-travel conference. Muggleton, who had a near-fatal crush on Diane, had appeared uninvited for a visit. We talked over vehicles and routes for our trans-African expedition and points along the way where Dave or Diane might join us. Anything seemed possible.

"What do you think it will cost?" Dave asked.

Muggleton shrugged. "We'll get sponsors," he said. "They'll pay us."

"Why?" Dave asked. "What for?"

"For making the bloody expedition," Muggleton said. "Why not?"

"No offense, mate," Dave said, "but we drive around Africa all the time. Nobody pays us for it. We *live* there. If you want to call your trip an expedition, don't you have to have a mission or something?"

"Right," Muggleton said. "A mission." He turned to me. "A bloody mission."

That very afternoon we found one at the Museum of Natural History. We took the subway uptown, hoping that in the African sections of the great museum we would find inspiration. There, in one of the cavernous halls of African animals, some drummers and dancers from East Africa were performing. I stood among the little crowd, mostly schoolchildren with their teachers, and let the *boom-boom-boom*ing of the drums carry me away. The dancing women, wrapped in red, shuffled and swayed as if blown about by the rise and fall of a fine hot wind. Behind them lions prowled in the yellow grass of a diorama.

After the dance I traipsed after Muggleton, who was wandering slowly through the Hall of African Peoples. And there I came upon a glass case containing a display of artifacts associated with the lives of Bantu women: pots, pandanus mats, beer strainers woven of grass. Reading a caption neatly lettered on a card affixed to the case, I was struck suddenly by a tiny dependent clause buried deep in the middle of the paragraph. Somehow I'd missed this sentence on previous visits to the museum, but now it stopped me.

> *Except for a few tribes like the Lovedu,*
> *where women rule, they seem unimportant*
> *in political life.*

Did some mad feminist lurk in the back rooms of the museum, writing subversive signs? Or could it be true? Women, perhaps, like the dancers I'd seen? Tall. Serene. Splendid. Could there be such a place?

I dragged Muggleton over to the exhibit. "Read that!" I said. "There's our mission." I felt inspired. Triumphant. "We'll go looking for Lovedu. We'll find the tribe where women rule. We'll pay homage to the Queen. There *must* be a queen."

Muggleton read the caption again, his forehead creased with concern.

"This queen business," he said. "You're not looking for some ancient matriarchy, are you? Some feminist la-la-land?"

I hesitated only a moment, pondering the tenderness of the masculine ego. "Well, yes and no," I said. "I don't have an axe to grind, if that's what you mean. But I admit I'm very curious to see a land 'where women rule.' Wouldn't you find it interesting to hear from the Queen?"

"I have a queen," he said. "And Mrs. Thatcher."

"Point taken."

Muggleton studied the grass mats in the display case as if he might find a clue encoded in the woven designs. "Can we visit some other tribes as well?" he said. "Pygmies perhaps? Or Masai? Or Ndebele?"

"Of course," I said. Why was he suddenly so serious? So hesitant?

"I'd rather like to visit some tribes where men still have something to say."

"No problem," I said. "How can we miss them? Men always have something to say."

Muggleton didn't smile. What had become of his irrepressible sense of humor?

"You're not going to go all wobbly on me, are you?" he said. "You're not going to wind yourself up for that mystical hoo-ha?"

"What are you talking about?"

"All that new-age born-again life-changing nonsense you bloody Americans are always going on about. You know. Spiritual growth."

"No, no, Muggleton. I promise. I never grow."

"You're sure you're not going in search of your true self?"

"I *am* my true self!" I said. "Anyway, all that transformation stuff is just a literary cliché. Somebody takes a trip, has some 'peak experience,' and comes back a new person."

"What rubbish!"

"It's wish fulfillment," I said. "It's what a lot of travelers hope for. But in real life it doesn't happen. People come back from exotic holidays talking about how it changed their lives; but there they are—same house, same job, same relationship, same tax loopholes. So what's changed?"

"Exactly," Muggleton said. "So let's just make an expedition."

"C'mon, Muggleton," I coaxed. "You heard Dave. We've got to come up with an official purpose to justify the journey. And what could be better than this? *Looking for Lovedu.*" I pronounced it "love-dew," making it sound like some kind of romantic elixir. (It was months before we learned to say correctly: "low-BAY-doo.")

"Looking for Love-Due," Muggleton echoed. "It does have a certain ring."

We shook hands on it. Our mission was agreed.

LOVEDULAND

Muggleton returned to London to study overland routes and weather charts while I finished a semester of college teaching. I dispatched my student assistant, Hannah, to gather information about the Lovedu, but she e-mailed back dispiriting news from the stacks: "I have found few references to this tribe in books and anthropological journals. Even professors of African history and anthropological scholars can't direct me to sources that might shed some light on this Lovedu tribe." She found an alternate spelling: Lobedu. But nobody could shed light on them either.

I did some cursory research, turning up precious bits of information. I learned that the tribe was indeed headed by a queen, an illustrious rainmaking queen bearing the name Modjadji. She was praised as "Transformer of the Clouds" and blessed with the power to call down life-giving waters from the sky. The royal line, some said, was founded four centuries ago by a princess named Dzugudini. So slight are the historical sources and oral traditions recounting the story of Dzugudini that it may be no more than legend, but it is a good story nonetheless. It seems that Dzugudini was the daughter of a great *mambo* who lived somewhere to the north in what is now Zimbabwe, and he in turn was one of the sons of an even greater ruler of the Mwene Mutapa empire, a confederation of city-states of the Karanga people, who controlled the region of the lower Zambezi, or what is now Zimbabwe and Mozambique. At the time, the Karanga lived north of present-day Harare, but they were said to remember an earlier home at Great Zimbabwe, the magnificent stone-built city raised in the twelfth century to crown the granite hills on the southern edge of the Zimbabwean plateau, just where it slopes away southward toward the Limpopo River and South Africa. Sometime around the year 1600, it seems, the unmarried Princess Dzugudini was found to be inconveniently pregnant and unwilling to name the father of her child. The great *mambo* was not pleased. With her mother's help, Dzugudini fled the kingdom, taking along her newborn son, Makaphimo, and the sacred charms of the rainmaker, stolen from her father's court. Far to the south, beyond the Limpopo on the edge of the great escarpment known to the Zulus as Quathlamba—"The Battlement of Spears"—in the northeastern corner of what is now South Africa, she set herself up as a rainmaking queen and established a dynasty that would culminate in the succession of Modjadji queens: a dynasty of single mothers.

I learned too that Lovedu society, under the rule of the Modjadji queens, placed the highest value on traditionally "feminine" ideals: appeasement, compromise, cooperation, helpfulness, tolerance, generosity, peace. European invaders pronounced the Queen "devious" and "evil" because they couldn't get around the skillful diplomacy she practiced to avoid a fight; but among Africans, even Shaka, the fierce Zulu warrior-chief, paid her homage as a wise ruler and powerful magician, and he left her people alone. She needed no army, for she alone possessed the power to bring life-giving rain to her people and to withhold it from their enemies, an ability to discriminate that put her far ahead of all other southern African rulers, not to mention the feeble Christian god, who was said to make rain fall upon the just and the unjust alike. It was from the Zulus that the popular British novelist H. Rider Haggard learned of the Rain Queen whom he celebrated in the fictional account *She,* published in 1887. Haggard dubbed the queen "She Who Must Be Obeyed." Her own people knew her as "She Who Does Not Fight." The most powerful queen in southern Africa made rain, not war. Here was a ruler after my own heart.

At last Hannah unearthed the one and only firsthand anthropological account of the Lovedu tribe. Published by Oxford University Press in 1943, *The Realm of a Rain-Queen: A Study of the Pattern of Lovedu Society* was the work of South African anthropologists Eileen Jensen Krige and her husband, J. D. Krige. They reported that Queen Modjadji II (or Mujaji II, as the Kriges spelled it) had once ruled an area of fifteen hundred square kilometers and was renowned throughout southern Africa. The name "Lovedu" was interpreted to mean the country where cattle and wealth and even sisters and daughters of foreign chiefs were forever lost, given as offerings to supplicate the great Rain Queen. In the 1890s, however, armed Boer settlers stripped the Queen of her lands, and by the time the Kriges visited the Lovedu in the late 1930s, the tribe of thirty-three thousand people was confined to an area of less than 400 square kilometers, a tiny island of monarchy in the midst of the country we know as the Republic of South Africa. But even then, according to the Kriges, Modjadji III continued to govern "without official husband to cramp her authority." South African Prime Minister Jan Smuts, who happened to be J. D. Krige's uncle, also called on Modjadji III, then sixty years old, and was impressed by the "air of authority" that marked her as "really" a queen. She was said to be possessed of powerful magic. She was said to be mysterious, inaccessible, immortal—even divine. Her divinity was apparent in the rain she showered upon her people: a manifestation of celestial grace. But this divinity was also the glitch in her job description. Being so superior to the average human, a Lovedu queen could not lose her life to mere mortals or to natural causes. Instead, she had to take her life herself in ritual suicide, as Modjadji II did in 1894. (She used the old family recipe for poison, in which the chief ingredient is crocodile brains.) But first she trained her successor to rule by the divine right for which she would pay with her life.

Feared for her power and famed for her duplicitous diplomacy, each Lovedu queen lived in seclusion with her wives. Yes, *wives.* What distinguished the Lovedu from other Bantu tribes, it seems, was that women as well as men could hold property, and what else is a wife but a piece of property? Wives came as gifts to the Queen, like cattle or corn: as tributes, offerings, bribes. At her capital, wives did for the Queen, their husband, what ordinary Lovedu wives did for theirs: they hoed her fields, brewed her beer, cooked her food, and kept her in domestic comfort. (Only sexual service seems to have been excluded from the job description.) The Queen used her wives in trade and diplomacy like any other commodity. To her *indunas,* or district headmen, she allocated wives to bind them in kinship. To would-be conquerors she offered wives and fields: a chance to settle down in peace. In this way, anthropologists say, the Lovedu queens built alliances and knit the realm into a family. A Boer trader and mercenary who came later to the Transvaal described Modjadji III as a powerful unscrupulous madam, little better than a bordello keeper, who pacified intruders with beer and girls, and dealt diplomacy by seduction. Accustomed to shooting Africans, he considered the Queen's pacifist tactics "immoral."

Yet the Lovedu people lived in peace and prospered. They were hard-working farmers who cultivated a healthful variety of crops: maize, millet, sorghum, groundnuts, pumpkins, beans, and sugarcane. They kept cattle and goats, not for food but as objects of wealth that passed from hand to hand as gifts, strengthening the closely woven social web. (The Kriges believed the Lovedu had a true "genius" for social life.) They supplemented their vegetable diet with termites, ants, grasshoppers, and other insect delicacies; and once, during a famine in the 1850s, the Queen rained down locusts upon her people, not to plague but to nourish them. The Lovedu were highly skilled botanists who knew and used five hundred different plants for food, medicine, or material for making houses, household objects, tools, apparel, and works of art. The Kriges said that this "direct reliance on nature," this perfect correspondence of environment and culture, made the Lovedu profoundly different from "us"—by which they meant white Europeans. That and their sense of values, which to the European sensibility seemed perversely "topsy-turvy."

The Lovedu aimed in life for maturity, self-sufficiency, and independence, and they despised ambition, competition, aggression, exploitation, and all forms of coercion. According to the Kriges, who use the word "success" as any American might, "Moderate success is credited to industry, but immoderate success may be suspect; he who reaps much more than his neighbours is in danger of being looked upon as an enemy in league with anti-social forces." To the Lovedu it was better to give than to sell. Better to ask for what you needed than to buy or steal. And he who had but did not give what another needed and asked for committed a great offense. Lovedu wealth was not based on trade; cattle and land passed from one household to another as gifts, and security lay in faith in reciprocity and the equivalence over the long term of services and obligations. By contrast, what the Lovedu called "bizmis"—the new European cash economy—seemed to them a world of subterfuge, commercial exploitation, and selfish desire for immediate personal gain: conduct far beyond the pale of decency. The Lovedu were deeply shocked to find that beer, which in Loveduland was a kind of liquid appreciation, a freely offered feast that transformed work into celebration, was *for sale* in the white man's store. And holier-than-thou Christian missionaries, with their collection plates and commandments and self-righteous ambitions for personal salvation, seemed to the Lovedu to be utterly depraved.

Something else that set the Lovedu apart from "us" was the high status enjoyed by women—"the strongest pillars of the social structure," according to the Kriges. Like many other African people then and now, Lovedu women and men led quite separate lives, going about their daily activities mainly with members of their own sex. Everyone worked at farming, but generally spiritual life and ritual were the province of women, while politics and law fell to men. Nevertheless, many important political positions were held by women. They could be *indunas*. They could be appointed by the Queen to critical diplomatic posts, mediating between her and the *indunas* or foreign emissaries; most such officials in fact were women, though some were men, and all of them were called "Mothers." Like the Queen, women could take wives, provided they had enough cattle to make appropriate gifts to the right people. (Marriage arrangements were not simple exchanges of cattle for brides, but part of an elaborate circle of gift-giving that underlay and supported the complex network of family and society; like all other social relationships, marriages were founded upon mutual agreement.) Many women did have cattle to give, especially older women who had become doctors, craftswomen, or artists. After marriage both men and women had extramarital affairs, an arrangement the Kriges describe as "a realistic concession to the impossibility of completely conditioning so primeval a force as sexual attraction to the purposes of the social structure." But among the Lovedu that primeval force most often swept young men into the arms of old women, for even in matters of sexual attraction Lovedu ideas and European ideas were (as the Kriges put it) "completely reversed." Topsy-turvy. To the Lovedu a mature, wise, self-sufficient, independent, powerful old woman was hot stuff.

All these topsy-turvy beliefs and practices had their roots in the curious way the Lovedu brought up their children. They were entrusted to the care of grandmothers, whose policy was to placate and pacify but never force. Infants were never alone but carried everywhere on Grandmother's back or Mother's—to the fields, the forest, the dance. Soon enough they were on their own, hanging out with their age-mates, coming and going as they pleased. If they wanted something, they had only to ask for it. There were never any rules or regular hours. Nothing like bedtime. Or toilet training. Or troublesome refinements like the European insistence that children keep clean. Even tribal initiation ceremonies were mild; there was no reason to coerce boys to "manly" valor or military discipline, and girls were not subjected to the genital mutilation widely practiced elsewhere in Africa. Children learned by observing adults, and by age five boys were herding cattle and studying bush lore. By age seven or eight, girls could perform every household task. Boys and girls alike were often praised and hardly ever punished, unless they were quarrelsome. In that case all parties to the squabble were punished equally; there was never any question about who was in the right, for quarrelsomeness was by definition a grievous fault—one the Lovedu were amazed to see in the bullying, combative, mean-spirited behavior of European children, who simply couldn't play amicably together. Perhaps the Kriges had those bad European kids in mind when they said that parenting among the Lovedu was a lot "easier." It seemed effortlessly to foster harmony and tolerance while giving the greatest scope to individuality and self-expression. The only things permissive Lovedu parents insisted upon and rewarded in their children were those qualities valued among adults: generosity, unselfishness, and the ability to live in peace with others.

In 1652, half a century after Princess Dzugudini established Loveduland, agents of the Dutch East India Company landed far to the southwest, at the Cape of Good Hope, and set up a supply station there called Kaapstad. People settled there to service and to sell fresh produce to company ships bound for India, and gradually a colony grew. For the next 150 years settlers pushed north and east from the Cape, overrunning San hunters and Khoi herdsmen and waging war against the Bantu, whose lands stood in their way. (Farmland was what they were after, and they came to be known as "farmers"—*boers*.) Then in 1806 Britain seized the Cape Colony, and in 1834 declared an end to slavery. Kaapstad became Cape Town. Whereupon, six thousand disgusted Afrikaans-speaking, staunchly Calvinist Boer residents—who regarded themselves as God's elect—set out with six thousand African slaves to follow their brethren north and east on a Great Trek to a promised land. That's how Loveduland came to stand on the late-nineteenth-century map in the middle of the independent Boer South African Republic of Transvaal. That's how armyless Queen Modjadji II came to surrender peaceably to General Joubert, commander of Boer forces in the Transvaal, in 1894, and why soon afterward she committed ritual suicide. Whether what happened next resulted from the Queen's suicide or merely certain meteorological conditions is a matter of opinion. For three years drought stalked the countryside, plaguing the Boers and killing a third of the Lovedu people.

Boer farmers had already found a new source of wealth—immense gold deposits discovered at Witwatersrand in 1886—and by 1899 the little Boer republic of Transvaal was the richest state in all Africa. How could the British resist what had long been their dream: to unite all of South Africa as a dominion of the British Commonwealth in the name of a great white queen who lived far away in a rain-drenched land and made empire in any weather? Boers and British alike had wiped out Zulus and Matabele and imprisoned their kings, but now British forces under General Kitchener defeated the Boers. Considering that more than twenty-six thousand white European Boer women and children died in British concentration camps during the Anglo-Boer War of 1899–1902, you can see that black African Lovedu people never had a chance against the British Empire.

The European world struck at the heart of everything Lovedu valued in life. They considered the white man's world incomprehensible, hostile, disruptive, and capricious. To combat it, they used the only weapon they had: secrecy. They retreated into the jagged battlements of the escarpment, protected on the south by the barrier the Boers called Drakensberg (Dragon Mountains) and on the north by the Limpopo River. To drive European settlers from the lowveld to the east, they counted on two bloodsucking allies: the malaria-carrying mosquito and the deadly tsetse fly that spread sleeping sickness to people and cattle alike. But Europeans imposed taxes, to be paid in cash, and for the first time young Lovedu men had to migrate to towns or European farms to sell for money the labor they had always given freely to one another. (Traditional Lovedu work parties were collective, beer-fueled social events; people labored together without bosses, time constraints, or pay, and got the work done.) Yet Lovedu social structure stood firm even against this assault, maintained as it always had been by women and older men. Christian missionaries too assailed the Lovedu, whom they never liked. They complained of Lovedu lack of discipline, inefficiency, unwillingness to follow orders, suspicion, ingratitude, and, worst of all, begging. Lovedu were always asking for things. They had a lot of other nasty habits too that set the missionaries' teeth on edge: casual nakedness, secrecy, beer-drinking, dancing, drumming, polygyny, same-sex (though apparently not homosexual) marriage, adultery, rainmaking, witchcraft. And they married their cousins. In half a century of Christian endeavor, the missionaries converted only about three percent of the Lovedu—a troublesome lot who deliberately violated rain taboos and made more work for the Queen. Nevertheless, when the Kriges studied Loveduland late in the 1930s, they believed that Lovedu culture was still substantially intact, although they said that hostility was "fierce" between Lovedu and European farmers who "with the best intentions . . . ejected Lovedu squatters from their ancestral lands in order to re-employ them as wage-earners." The Kriges worried about this hostility. They wanted the Lovedu to "respond better" to European settlement and at the same time maintain their own traditions, living happily on the Lovedu Reserve. After all, they said, this was "the spiritual foundation of the segregational structure" of modern South Africa. Seated beside Lovedu campfires in the soft African evenings, the Afrikaner Kriges said they felt a "sense of homeliness and quiet joy," but even these sympathetic anthropologists, it seems, had apartheid all the time in their hearts.

After the Second World War, only a few years after the Kriges published their account of *The Realm of a Rain-Queen,* that realm began to change more rapidly. The war stimulated research on tropical diseases; once malaria and sleeping sickness were brought under control, European farmers swarmed into the Lovedu lowveld, pushing Lovedu farmers back into the overcrowded reserve. Where 72 Lovedu per square kilometer lived in 1936, 160 lived in 1970. The land could no longer feed the people, and the people were forced to buy maize from the European farmers who had stolen their fields. Men lost their traditional occupations, for there was no longer land for them to clear and cultivate; and when Europeans seized the iron mines and prohibited tree cutting, Lovedu men could no longer build traditional houses and enclosures or make tools, crafts, or even ceremonial masks. For hoes and machetes and cooking pots they had to go to the white man's store—and pay cash. Following a pattern painfully familiar throughout Africa, men deprived of their traditional occupations and in need of cash for trade and taxes left their homes in greater numbers to work and live for weeks or months at a time at European farms and mines and distant cities, on the Witwatersrand and in Pretoria. The older, more equitable division of labor went askew as women took up all the work of the home village. Still more cash was needed, and by the 1970s Lovedu women were entering the European cash economy too, as day laborers and domestics on nearby white farms. Lovedu farming suffered, and with it Lovedu health. They were unable to rotate their crops on limited land, or to grow and gather the variety of foods they'd once consumed. Their diet shrank and became unbalanced and made way for disease: bilharzia, malaria, tapeworm, dysentery, tuberculosis. The land suffered too as old fields wore out and the depleted soil washed away, silting up the streams. One thing led to another, and when the white government claimed jurisdiction over tribal courts, imposing a Western adversarial system of "justice" where once disagreements had been resolved by open discussion and consensus, the Queen is reported to have said: "Is there nothing left to us?" The Lovedu had entered the modern world.

And then what? Had the great wave of Western capitalist imperialism swept them away? Had they been "civilized" by British schoolbooks or "modernized" by American TV? Had they been "developed" and "globalized" past recognition and plunged into poverty by some perverse project of the World Bank, or adjusted into oblivion by the International Monetary Fund? Or did they still dwell in the ancient cycad forest high on the escarpment, clinging by their fingernails to their topsy-turvy ideals and holding high above the rising tide their beautiful black queen? I pondered what I'd learned of Loveduland, studied the Kriges' sketchy maps of the territory, and did some mental calculations. Surely Modjadji III, who was about sixty years old when Jan Smuts called on her in 1940, must have ended her reign long ago. Was it possible that her designated daughter or granddaughter still ruled? The books and scholars I consulted had no answers, and the shabby little theories they set forth left me disheartened. I kept colliding with experts whose scholarly objectivity wasn't up to the job of contemplating a powerful black queen. Nineteenth-century Europeans who never actually saw the secluded Queen Modjadji II said she was light-skinned, probably descended from European women who had fallen victim to the white slave trade. H. Rider Haggard attributed the fair complexion of his She to Arab ancestry. The Kriges, who actually saw a black Queen Modjadji III (as photographic evidence indicates), said nevertheless that she was light-skinned. By way of explanation, they repeated rumors that the Lovedu capital had been visited by a Portuguese Don Juan. A couple of anthropologists I interviewed assured me of the "fact" that Lovedu queens were fair-skinned descendants of white European traders, and in any case filled only a symbolic office. A curator at the British Museum assured a colleague who inquired on my behalf that Lovedu queens were actually men in drag. What could I do but go and see for myself?

Muggleton was faxing me computer-generated route maps: big, loopy lines, like the track of some indecisive snake, superimposed on the outline of Africa. Black dots designated the location of tribes Muggleton had chosen to visit, the tribes where men had something to say: Bushmen in the Kalahari, Himba in northern Namibia, Mbuti Pygmies in Zaire, Pokot and Masai in Kenya, Ndebele in Zimbabwe. Another, bigger dot in the northeast corner of South Africa marked the dwelling place—if they were still there—of the legendary Lovedu. Our ultimate destination. Our objective. The land where women rule. The land of the serene and powerful daughters of She Who Does Not Fight. Across the top of this magnificent map Muggleton had lettered in some stylized script big and bold enough to embody the spirit of our enterprise: *LOOKING FOR LOVEDU*. This was to be our quest.

PREPARATIONS

How do you prepare for an expedition? Read up on exploration, and you notice right away that it's a masculine pursuit. It's not that there haven't been plenty of intrepid women travelers and observers of the world, even in the nineteenth century—women such as Mary Kingsley, Isabella Bird, Mary Gaunt, Marianne North, Fanny Bullock Workman, Ida Pfeiffer. But none of them claimed to be the first to stand here or there on the face of the earth or to "discover" territory they could plainly see was already occupied by other people (though of a different race), so their daring and often valuable exploits fade, uncelebrated and largely unremembered, while history reserves the title "Great Explorer" for men. Luckily for them, almost every Great Explorer had a useful wife at home. The wife helps the Great One plan. The wife helps him order supplies. The wife helps him pack. Then while he's away the wife takes care of the house and kids. She takes care of his aged parents. She takes care of his business too—answers the mail, pays the bills, puts little notices in the papers so the public won't forget him, occasionally prods the Royal Geographical Society to send out supplies or mounts a public subscription for more funds for his expedition. When things go wrong, it's the wife who hounds officials to send a search party. It's the wife who sees to it that a monument is erected to honor the intrepid, though inconveniently lost, explorer. It's the wife who ushers his letters and journals through to publication after first expunging every sign of ill temper, bad judgment, and fear. Think of Sir John Franklin, lost in the Canadian Arctic, and Robert Falcon Scott, dead in Antarctica after having struggled—too late—to the South Pole. Without their wives, history would know them—if history remembered them at all—as failures, bunglers, and, but for the lives lost, almost comic in the scope of their incompetence. Instead, in Britain at least, they are national heroes, brilliant men martyred in the cause of exploration and empire.

Between us, Muggleton and I had not a single wife. When it came to planning our expedition, gathering our equipment and supplies, and soliciting official sponsors, we were on our own. And pressed for time. Summer was upon us, and we had to be under way by September, according to Muggleton's calculations, to hit the cool dry season in North Africa and get across the Congo Basin before the rains set in.

Still, our venture didn't exactly present the logistical demands of Stanley's Anglo-American Expedition to the Congo, which set off from Zanzibar in 1874 with 356 people, including forty-six women and children, bearing sixteen thousand pounds of arms, equipment, and goods. They marched in a column so long that buglers were needed to signal when to stop. Our expedition was just the two of us. Besides, Muggleton said he was well connected. In England he milked his Old Boy network for the loan of an overland vehicle, some tires, some gas— and came up empty. Frustrated, he went round to the used-car lot and bought an army surplus 1980 Series III Land Rover, cheap. The body was painted the glowing blue of morning glories, and the top a creamy yellow. He scoured the scrap yards of Wiltshire, where he lived, for secondhand jerry cans and sand ladders—those heavy planks of perforated steel plate that you jam under the tires to help them crawl out of sand or mud. He painted the sand ladders a matching morning-glory blue and bolted them on the roof rails like a decorative edging of rickrack. (Much later, after the Land Rover had slumped in ruins like a heap of scrap, Muggleton confessed his regret that he had not painted the bumpers blue too.) He had a huge steel security box—meant to conceal our valuables: cameras, computer, cash—fabricated and welded to the chassis just behind the front seat. Then he covered the interior of the vehicle, box and all, with industrial carpet—like the rickrack ladders, a homey touch. He bought some secondhand tools, a high-lift jack, two spare tires, an electric tire pump, a Michelin map of Africa, and a guide to Land Rover repairs, heavily illustrated with complicated drawings. He was ready.

We learned later, when we met them along the way, that most independent travelers who make transcontinental road trips in Africa spend at least a year or two planning their journeys. They search out the right vehicle, modify it for comfort and utility, add on, strip off, build in, fine-tune. They make trial runs. They check out all systems, then check them again. When they set off at last, they are thoroughly and efficiently equipped with every essential—finely detailed topographical maps, for example—and with such creature comforts as tiny folding tables, camp chairs, and cutlery. But we were eager to go. We had no time for refinements of preparation, and no wife to tidy up the details. So it wasn't until we were well under way that we discovered some of the things we might have done, or might have done differently. Mired in the Sahara, we grasped the impracticality of Muggleton's charming arrangement of sand ladders. They were lovely up there, edging the roof where he had bolted them securely in place. But in an emergency— which is the only time you use a sand ladder—there they were: high overhead, locked down by bolts now corroded and wedged with particles of sand. Once freed, after a sweaty thumb-jamming struggle with wrench and hammer, the saw-toothed panels of heavy steel plummeted to the ground, gouging paint and steel and flesh as they fell.

If we'd had a wife to worry about wifely things—what to eat, for example, or where to sleep, or where to stow a tiny folding table—I might have flown to England to help Muggleton prepare the Land Rover. But as he raced over the British army test-driving range in Wiltshire, readying himself for the challenges of the road, those other concerns—the wifely ones—fell to me. A good wife I was neither willing nor able to be, but somebody had to take up the slack in the loose arrangement we called "plans." Muggleton insisted we must be prepared for anything, so I made a list of all the equipment we might need for "anything" and called up the manufacturers. After all, I thought, we'd gone to the trouble of finding a purpose for our trip. Why not see if Muggleton's theory was right, that people would actually help us to make the journey? As a rule, I travel light, and like any other traveler, I purchase whatever equipment I need. But I'd done the calculations: the cost of equipment suited to hard conditions—tents, sleeping bags, boots, heavy-duty clothing—added to the cost of the Land Rover, insurance, and *carnet de passage* we'd already bought, put the journey out of sight. It was time, I thought, to trade on my credentials.

Muggleton's Old Boy network had let him down, his buddies being still too young and cloutless to dole out expensive favors on the strength of a public-school tie. And I had no such network. My old school was a huge public university, and my old friends were immersed in the arts or still working valiantly for social change, out organizing in the boondocks. I knew not a single person in the corporate world, but I did have some experience that might count as qualifications. I'd been a traveler all my life, impelled by feelings first roused on those Dakota roads in my dad's old Ford: the desire to learn how people live and how we might all live more generously, with more fresh air. I'd written about my travels and made photographs, and when I made a list of all the travel stories I'd done over the years, I seemed—on paper anyway—to be somebody.

So I did what big-time explorers do. I faxed my credentials to the marketing specialists of all the best manufacturers. Then I got them on the line and offered them an opportunity to put their products to a tough test. "The Muggleton-Jones Expedition will travel across the heart of Africa," I said, "in search of the great Rain Queen of the Lovedu. And you have an opportunity to become one of the distinguished sponsors of this expedition." To my amazement, contributions poured in from corporate giants. Nikon sent two pairs of binoculars worth more than we'd paid for the Land Rover. Kodak sent hundreds of rolls of film. Cascade Designs sent sleeping bags and air mattresses. Ex Officio sent the most durable clothing on the planet. Eagle Creek sent an assortment of duffel bags and backpacks, one in every color, with instructions to give them away at the end of the journey to Africans who helped us. 3-M sent an immense supply of heavy-duty Ultrathon insect repellent, wrapped in enough tiny single-dose foil packets to litter the road through the Congo from one end to the other. Coleman-Peak sent tents and stoves and lanterns, and in a gesture I found particularly touching, extra glass chimneys for the lanterns, just in case we should break one. Each day the UPS man climbed the stairs to my fourth-floor walk-up with more boxes. "Holiday?" he asked. I tore open the packages and gaped at expensive yuppie treasures: boots, jackets, high-tech shirts and pants, bivy bags, knives, headlamps. Without asking me anything but my mailing address, Compaq sent me a new laptop computer. I thought of sending everything back with apologies for my pretensions, but as the goods accumulated—thousands upon thousands of dollars worth of state-of-the-art gear—I convinced myself that these high-powered corporations must know more than I about sound business practices.

I donned my new traveling outfit and shoved a pile of boxes aside to get a look at myself in the full-length mirror on the back of my closet door. There stood a stranger clad from head to toe in oversize khakis, like a little Boy Scout playing dress-up in his scoutmaster's uniform. My shirt, made of some crisp pseudo-cotton fabric and lined with sleazy white micro-mesh, bulged with pockets: zippered pockets, flapped pockets, buttoned pockets, Velcroed pockets, and secret pockets. My trousers, made of a slightly heavier version of the same high-tech fabric, were also pocketed, in front and behind and on the thigh and at the knee, under heavy-duty knee patches. My trousers were secured by a tan twill belt fitted on the inside with a long zipper, concealing a security slot suitable for tightly folded cash. My jacket sported three ranks of pockets down the front and an assortment of flaps and button-down and Velcro tabs that could be used to attach to the person whatever odd bits of gear might overflow. This garment also featured detachable sleeves, so that even in weather too warm for a jacket, I could still wear the pockets. On my feet I wore heavy trekking socks under bulbous Gore-Tex hiking boots. On my head I wore a khaki baseball cap embellished with a Land Rover insignia. I stared into the mirror: I, a New Yorker with a New Yorker's pizzazz, a New Yorker who wore nothing but black. The little beige Boy Scout, chubby with pockets, stared back.

What was I doing, dressing up in this pseudo-military uniform and going off to the bush with a man I scarcely knew? He'd look great in such gear. He'd look like a hunter. A commando. A hero. He'd look like Stewart Granger in *King Solomon's Mines.* Whereas I looked like Stewart Granger's chunky little boy. The manufacturers had sent me women's sizes, but sized to the dimensions of Xena, Warrior Princess. What I would need badly in this whole macho venture, I thought, was female company.

Quickly I sent a fax to two Australian colleagues, Nell and Fran, a writer and photographer, respectively, who were my frequent traveling companions. We like to play at being intrepid together. Or at least game. We met years ago on assignment on a voyage to Antarctica. Pinned down in our cabins as the southern ocean kicked up a Force 9 gale, we passed the time together reading about the fantastic career of the British explorer Sir Ernest Shackleton. In 1914 he set sail in the *Endurance* with twenty-eight men and sixty-nine sled dogs bound for Antarctica, where he intended to walk from one side of the continent to the other. He'd tried previously to reach the South Pole, but fell short by 745 miles as a member of Robert Falcon Scott's 1901 Antarctic Expedition, and by only ninety-seven miles on his own expedition in 1907. But the pole had been conquered in 1911 by Norwegian explorer Roald Amundsen, leaving nothing for Shackleton to attempt but a transcontinental traverse. Anything less, Shackleton told his wife, would be "not much." That's the way these boys think: What's the point of going anywhere if you can't get there first?

Poor Shackleton failed again when his ship was beset by ice, though the long grueling process by which he saved himself and all his men is one of the greatest tales of leadership and endurance in the history of exploration. Officially, by that "first man" standard of discovery, Shackleton was a failure, but he performed such incredible feats to maintain the loyalty, spirits, and lives of his men that he remains a hero to those for whom exploration means camaraderie and the freedom of the road.

From our point of view, he had only one great shortcoming: he wouldn't travel with women. When Shackleton first issued a call for volunteers for the 1914 expedition, he received more than five thousand applications. One of them was from "three sporty girls," as they described themselves, who were willing to undertake any adventure and even to don men's clothes. Shackleton turned them down flat. Our spirits sank when we read about that rejection as our ship pitched toward the white continent, but by the time the icy shoulder of Antarctica appeared off the starboard bow, we had christened ourselves "three sporty girls" and vowed to uphold the honor of those departed sisters who would have been intrepid if only Shackleton had given them a chance.

Now, undertaking this expedition with Muggleton, how could I forget my sporty sisters? I was certain I would need them. Like Shackleton, Muggleton was a big strong bear of a man. I knew I could trust his strength and resourcefulness in any emergency. I knew if I fell through the ice in my sleeping bag in the middle of the night, that he'd rush to yank me one-handed from the jaws of death, as Shackleton had done for one of his men. But would he grow resentful of the fact that

I couldn't do the same for him? Muggleton was half my age and twice my size, and he possessed skills I had never acquired. Thanks to his upbringing in a family of boys and his military training, he was adept at auto mechanics, celestial navigation, martial arts. He was qualified in automatic weapons. I, on the other hand, had only a few Camp Fire Girls' honor beads—and these new state-of-the-high-tech-camping-art khaki clothes. In a pinch I could handle a boat, a horse, a truck, a rifle, and I could survive outdoors, but mostly I'd traveled all my life on the strength of street smarts and a woman's skills: observation, conversation, a conciliatory smile, and a sixth sense attuned to auras, bad vibes, and other intimations of disaster. In my lucid moments, I knew that wouldn't be enough.

I sent Nell and Fran another fax, including the map Muggleton had made and the loopy itinerary he had designed. I sent them his warning too: that every day we would face great challenges. Besides the dodgy political conditions that enveloped whole countries, we would be up against great extremes of nature: the hottest spots in the world and some of the wettest. "We'll drive through desert, jungle, river valleys, mountains, snow, rain, scorching heat," Muggleton had cautioned. "Every day we'll pit wits against the elements." I had asked him for examples of the wit-pitting he anticipated, and he'd sent me a list of formidable situations, such as struggling with sand ladders in the Sahara, digging through hip-deep mud in the Congo, sitting for days by the roadside hoping for help. Well, I thought, there's nothing there nearly as daunting as crossing the southern seas in winter in an open boat, as Shackleton did, and this last bit—sitting by the roadside—was something the sporty girls could handle with style. I passed along Muggleton's warning and urged Nell and Fran to join us in the expedition. From Australia came a long silence.

"Don't you want to come?" I faxed again. Another long silence. Then Nell faxed back: "Darling, I'm sure the Queen is perfectly charming, but couldn't we just rent a car in Johannesburg some fine afternoon and drive out to see her?"

That was it, then. I was on my own with Muggleton. Never mind. I jammed everything into the flashy duffel bags and hired a Checker cab to haul it all to JFK. "Sleep-away camp?" the cabbie said. The man at the ticket counter at British Airways, the airline that had offered us free tickets, checked in my mountain of "expedition baggage" without the slightest hesitation. "Your luggage receipts, madam," he said. "Good luck on your expedition!" He stapled fourteen coupons to my complimentary first-class ticket. We had received the imprimatur of the corporate world. And single-handedly I had amassed as much baggage, I thought, as even the most experienced and dedicated wife. As the lights of New York City slipped away beneath the plane, it occurred to me that the first great division of labor of the Muggleton-Jones Expedition had fallen along gender lines. In the back of my mind, I filed this horrible thought: when neither party has a wife, it's the woman who gets to play the part.

READ HISTORY

On the plane, settling in to watch khaki-clad Michael Douglas track the man-eating lions of Tsavo through the African bush, I thought about our expedition. All right, so ours was no venture into the unknown, no journey of discovery. Everything in Africa had been "discovered" and made known long ago, though Westerners—Americans in particular—still like to think that Africa is some "dark" and deeply savage place, unlike any place else on earth. News reports about other regions refer to the inhabitants by their nationality, ethnicity, or political persuasion—as Germans or Japanese, Slavs or Arabs, nationalists or insurgents. News reports about Africa sometimes still call the people "natives." To some Western journalists a group of dark-skinned men in suits, meeting in an African parliament, is still a "native assembly" or a "tribal gathering." Journalists and academics alike lament the divisive "tribalism" peculiar to Africa, as if it were utterly unlike the intense in-group loyalties known by other names in Palestine or Northern Ireland or the former Yugoslavia. We're not much different from or more sophisticated than those Europeans who first probed the sometimes daunting coasts of "The Dark Continent" by ship, knowing nothing of the farming communities, the pastoral settlements, the thriving and peaceable cities without citadels, the great confederations and empires that lay inland along busy trade routes all across the great central African plateau.

It was in Africa that what we call human life—*Homo sapiens sapiens*—first appeared not less than 150,000 years ago. It was out of Africa that "wise wise man" hiked into Eurasia and later—between 30,000 and 15,000 years ago—over the Bering land bridge into the

Americas. Which means that African cultures are the oldest on earth and therefore more advanced, more "developed" than any other—at least in chronological terms. Nowadays, of course, "development" is a measure of industrialization, not the mere accretion of elapsed time, and it is commonly believed in the West to be the correct path, the *only acceptable* path, to the future. Other nations of both West and East have hurried along that trail, leaving the nations of the African cradle in the dust. But in prehistoric times, the inhabitants of Africa actually were further along the path of "development" than Native North Americans. The first stone tools—found at various sites in Africa—were made about two million years ago.

Historians say that African history properly begins with the spread of farming across the continent after about 6,000 B.C. Some date the Iron Age from as early as 500 B.C., when Africans of the Sudan and the upper Nile Valley learned to mine, smelt, and forge metals. By the end of the fifth century of the Christian era, nearly all of Africa was occupied by Iron Age farmers. Farming made villages possible; settlement in villages made the accumulation of goods possible and stimulated trade. During the period Europeans still know as the Dark Ages, Africa's Sudanic states carried on a vigorous trade—in gold, ivory, ostrich feathers, and slaves derived from the hinterland to the south—while the prosperous East African coast developed commercial connections with Arabia and India. The old state of Benin sent ambassadors to Portugal years before Columbus sailed for the New World.

Eventually, many African cultures below the Sahara developed systems of self-government based on participatory democracy. The kings or chiefs who headed such cultures were not rulers but symbolic leaders, charged like Queen Modjadji with maintaining harmony and balance among the ancestors, the people, and the elements of the natural and spiritual worlds, and above all with doing the will of the people. A privy council and a council of elders advised the leader, and the voice of the people was heard in the village assembly, where everyone could speak until consensus was achieved. The chief was kept in hand by various institutional checks and balances, and for such grievous offenses as greediness and refusal to heed good advice, he could be removed from office, or "destooled": lifted bodily from his stool of office and deposited on his rump on the ground. So devoted were Africans to freedom, and so distrustful of executive power, that many sub-Saharan peoples had no chiefs at all. Instead, the people of these stateless societies—people such as the Igbo and Fulani of Nigeria, the Mbeere of Kenya, the Konkomba of Togoland—ruled themselves through the council of elders and the village assembly, seeking, like the Lovedu, to resolve conflicts through compromise. Powerful states like Asante (Ashanti) that conquered their neighbors typically left them considerable autonomy, so that even an African empire might resemble a confederation of self-governing democratic states.

It's not that the continent was some idyllic Eden—some carefree "merrie Africa" without despotism, warfare, slavery, or treachery—before the white man came along. It was inhabited by human beings, after all, and customs varied from place to place. But sub-Saharan Africans generally seem to have come down on the side of participatory democracy, free speech, and the rule of law. And although wars were fought and people subjugated or forced to move, Africans on the whole must have been good at finding peaceable accommodation. How else could more than two thousand different ethnic groups speaking more than two thousand languages and dialects have survived as neighbors to the present day? Scholars say that the civilized art of living peaceably in small societies without establishing states is a distinctly African contribution to human history. Nevertheless, when Europeans arrived, it suited them to say that Africa had no history and no "civilization."

In the second half of the fifteenth century, Portuguese navigators made their way along the African coast, followed by the English, the Dutch, the French. So began centuries of trade relations that came to focus on the single product for which Europeans and later North Americans raised the greatest demand: slaves. At the end of the eighteenth century, European explorers first braved the interior of Africa, and in the nineteenth, European military men, merchants, missionaries, and settlers ventured after them to conquer, kill, trade, Christianize, colonize, and exploit. But Africa is an immense continent, the second largest after Asia. It's 8,000 kilometers long and 7,400 kilometers wide—about three times the size of the United States. Covering twenty percent of the earth's land surface, it is so vast and so daunting to outsiders that until late in the nineteenth century—little more than one hundred years ago—the European presence in Africa consisted merely of a few tenuous handholds around the edges, and Western influence was slight.

Then Leopold II, king of the Belgians, claimed as his personal property an enormous chunk of Central Africa, bigger than England, France, Germany, Spain, and Italy combined, and more than seventy-six times the size of his own kingdom. Other European heads of state, worried that Leopold had skewed the delicate balance of power among them, gathered in Berlin in 1884 to discuss the matter. There the eminent white men, seated around a table at Bismarck's house in the Wilhelmstrasse, resolved some conflicting claims to the African continent and affably began to parcel it out among themselves. What they wanted was natural resources. Leopold thought of Africa as a rich "unpeopled" treat—a "cake." Everyone wanted a piece. Less than twenty-five years later, when the European scramble for Africa ended, only two pieces of Africa remained independent: Liberia, a small impoverished West African settlement of repatriated American slaves, and the empire of Ethiopia. The rest of the African cake had been sliced into more than thirty pieces, snatched by chicanery and force, and packaged in the flags of England, France, Germany, Italy, Portugal, and Spain. Germany and Italy were to lose their colonies to England and France in the First World War, and Spain claimed only a small portion; so it was England, France, and Portugal that came to hold the continent. They clutched it tight until the middle of the twentieth century, when it began to blow up in their hands.

As things played out, perhaps this history is not so very different from that of many other parts of the world: successive waves of invasion ("exploration"), conquest and genocide ("pacification"), theft of land ("settlement"), theft of resources ("trade"), economic exploitation ("development"), and obliteration of culture ("civilization" and "Christian conversion"). The history of the American West is another, more familiar case. What makes Africa "dark" is our own ignorance of the place. We don't know its history or much about its present condition either. We've forgotten that it is the homeland of us all.

Lions flashed across the tiny video screen before me and rifle shots rang out. What a stupid film it was, and made too late. Who cheers for the Great White Hunter anymore? Who wants to see lions gunned down, no matter how many human intruders they've devoured? Kirk Douglas could have pulled it off in *his* day, before the World Wildlife Fund went to work and thousands of tourists set off for East Africa on holiday. But times have changed. Now we've been taught to save darkest Africa—or some big parts of it at least—as a kind of international theme park. But there's more to Africa than posh game preserves and European monuments and the superhighways of modern South Africa. The continent is not all of a piece, one entity with no other history than that imposed by its colonizers. It's a great jumble of individual countries, tiny and immense, poor and rich, agrarian and industrialized, home to countless colors, ethnicities, religions, languages, cultures. The African scholar Kwame Anthony Appiah, who grew up in Asante, notes great differences across Africa: "in religious ontology and ritual, in the organization of politics and the family, in relations between the sexes and in art, in styles of warfare and cuisine, in language." Nothing is more striking, he writes in *In My Father's House,* than "the extraordinary diversity of Africa's peoples and its cultures." Indeed, one of the great discussions among African intellectuals today concerns what it means to be *African.*

When most of the European colonizers were overthrown or bailed out (in the 1960s and after), they took with them their expertise and left behind whole nations of people who had never seen a school or a hospital. Nevertheless, hope hung in the African air like promised rain and fell on the shoulders of new nationalists and patriots: Ghana's Kwame Nkrumah, Tanzania's Julius Nyerere, Kenya's Jomo Kenyatta, Congo's Patrice Lumumba, Mozambique's Samora Machel, Angola's Agostinho Neto. But it was a bad time to be an African nationalist, or worse, a pan-Africanist; the Cold War powers demanded allegiance, and "nonaligned" leaders were subject to pressure and sudden accident. The World Bank and the International Monetary Fund (both established in 1945) also went to work to ensure—though this was not their stated intention—that in most African countries economic colonialism would replace the old-fashioned political kind. Other African "leaders" came to power as well who aped the arrogant authoritarianism of colonial rulers: Mohamed Siad Barre in Somalia, Mengistu Haile-Mariam in Ethiopia, Jean-Bedel Bokassa in the Central African Republic, Idi Amin in Uganda, and Mobutu Sese Seko in Congo, which he renamed

Zaire. They made themselves presidents for life (or, in Bokassa's case, emperor); they hired private armies; they slaughtered opponents; and they mortgaged their countries to the World Bank and other Western lenders, amassing immense personal fortunes in Swiss banks and saddling their people with debts so astronomical that merely servicing the interest is sure to keep them in poverty forever.

Since independence, then, some parts of the continent have done fairly well while others have fallen upon hard times—still trapped in the colonial enclosure with boundaries once drawn deliberately or in ignorance to pit one group against another, freighted with the secondhand machinery of the modern nation-state, stripped of natural resources, gutted by ill-conceived "development" projects that leave the natural environment a shambles and displaced citizens on the move, deprived of basic education and health services, ruled by military thugs or tyrannical kleptocrats, and sunk in irredeemable debt.

It's the hard-times Africa you read about: one vast undifferentiated lump of dismal news reports dispatched from dreary expat bars by disaffected Western journalists whose secret woe is that the AIDS epidemic makes it too risky to get laid. I wanted to see the rest of Africa, whatever that might be. Of course my friend Nell was right. We *could* simply fly into Jan Smuts International Airport in Johannesburg, rent a big air-conditioned sedan, and drive up the expressway to the Transvaal to call upon the Queen. I worried that perhaps I was one of those "Western journalists" myself—ignoring such conveniences of modern Africa for the sake of embellishing my own adventure. Yet I wanted to meet the common people, who, I imagined, must be very different from the governments that sell them out. I wanted to see the bits and pieces of the continent, so many, so varied, and so complex that they might include even a rainmaking queen. Ours would be no great expedition of discovery. But it wouldn't be a Hertz rent-a-weekend either.

Muggleton met me at Heathrow with the Land Rover. He was half an hour late and reeking of gin—straight from his duties as best man at his best friend's wedding—but he was there.

"What are you doing with all this stuff?" he said when he spotted me behind the luggage cart.

"You told me to be prepared for anything," I said, trying to shave the defensive edge from my voice. Wasn't that just like a wife, I thought, to feel unappreciated.

We pushed the overloaded luggage cart out to the parking lot, where, amid sleek Bentleys and Vauxhalls, the bright blue and yellow Land Rover stood.

"Great news, eh?" Muggleton said, beaming. "Go on. Get in."

I hoisted myself up into the cab and slid behind the wheel. My bottom sank into a deep hole in the seat cushion, and I found myself staring through the space between the horn and the top of the steering wheel. My gaze traveled out to the spare tire mounted on the hood of the Land Rover, and there it stopped.

"I can't see over the steering wheel," I said. "I can't see over the spare tire."

"You're a dwarf," Muggleton said accusingly. "It was a great buy." So he felt unappreciated too.

Together we hoisted some of the duffel bags to the roof and crammed the others inside. Muggleton was not a drinking man, and he was moving gingerly under the weight of his hangover.

"You'll have to come down by train," he said when we finished and saw there was no room for me.

"Fine," I said. "I'll pick up a seat cushion on the way." He laughed and raised a hand to his head. We were both trying hard, I thought. Like newlyweds determined to make a go of it, we became excruciatingly polite.

That night we stood in the living room of Muggleton's flat in Wiltshire—there was no place to sit—and visualized the size of the Land Rover parked just outside. Around us spread the contents of the duffel bags I'd brought with me from the States. "We've got too much kit," Muggleton said. "We'll never get it all in the vehicle." After all his work on the Land Rover, he'd taken to speaking of it reverentially, in tones that suggested his profound proprietary interest. He didn't want me to overburden *his* Land Rover, he said, with *my* superfluous gear. "We've simply got too much kit," he said again. He looked weary, verging on hopeless, but I could see that it wasn't just the gear that worried him. This expedition wasn't to be merely the lark we'd dreamed up during those fine days in Zimbabwe, drifting down the Zambezi, cruising through Gonerazhou National Park in somebody else's Land Rover, with somebody else as mechanic and guide. It promised to be hard. It would require—as Muggleton kept reminding me—a considerable amount of wit-pitting. Months earlier we'd tried to persuade auto-makers to lend us a four-wheel-drive vehicle, but when we sent them a prospectus of our proposed thirty-thousand-kilometer journey, they turned us down. Land Rover thought it over and backed out. "Too risky," they said. Toyota replied that our itinerary would destroy a Land Cruiser, and they didn't have the budget to write one off. Chrysler didn't bother to answer at all. So Muggleton's spur-of-the-moment army-surplus purchase was all we had to get us through. And the vehicle was Muggleton's baby.

Built in 1980. Strong. No nonsense. Meant to survive. But painted— for reasons about which I hesitated to inquire—that pale creamy yellow and that peculiar robin's-egg shade, like the sashes and doors of many an English cottage. The matching blue sand ladders edging the roof rack looked rather like window boxes from which geraniums might peep. Somehow Muggleton had transformed this army-surplus tank wannabe into a homey semblance of an English cottage on wheels. When he suggested that, as a security measure, we make some opaque curtains for the back windows, my first thought was floral chintz.

So I understood why he was flummoxed by the mountain of equip-ment I'd brought. Having been too successful at my job of garnering gadgets and gear, I imposed on Muggleton the job of helping to decide what could be left behind. His six-foot-three frame had slumped a foot to my level, and we stood eye to eye, buried to the knees in microfleece and politically correct recycled-fiber bags and bundles and bungee cords. I knew Muggleton was out to zap the stack of African novels I'd picked up in London.

"Okay," I said, only slightly testy, remembering the job it had been to gather all this stuff and move it to England. I felt I'd been packing for weeks. "Let's be ruthless. Do we really need the stove? Or the dishes? Or the mess kit?"

"We need all that," Muggleton said. He's crazy about eating. He himself had packed a garlic press and a pepper mill.

"Do you want to chuck your air mattress? Or your bivy bag?"

"Are you bonkers?" Muggleton said. He likes to sleep too.

"We could leave the shortwave radio," I said.

"And not get the BBC? Are you out of your mind?" He paused and I could see another worry cross his mind. "Don't forget Pamela," he said. "I've told her she can bring only one bag, but we've got to leave her some room." Pamela was a doctor, a friend of Muggleton's brother's girlfriend, who had offered to assemble a medical kit for the expedition. Muggleton had told me about that a few weeks earlier. What he hadn't told me, until a few days before I left to join him in England, was that on an impulse, he had invited her to come along to Africa for the ride, or part of it anyway. It had occurred to him in a flash that he could get Pamela to pay for his share of the gas. "It will be brilliant," he'd said on the transatlantic phone. "She can doctor sick villagers as we go along. It will give us entrée."

"We'll talk about it when I get there," I'd said and promptly forgotten all about it. Now Muggleton reminded me that the addition of Pamela to the expedition was a done deal.

"The doctor," I said. "I had forgotten about her. I hope she's short and tiny."

After a long worrisome pause, Muggleton said, "Actually she's a nurse." He paused again. "About five foot ten, I think."

"Anything else?"

"Rather overweight, I'm afraid."

"Well," I said, "you're right then, aren't you? We've got too much kit." Methodically I began to rip the little cardboard boxes off four hundred rolls of Kodak film. "This should save quite a bit of space."

When I finished, Muggleton suggested we take a drive. Both of us wanted nothing more than to be in the vehicle and on the road. Under the full moon, the land was transformed. The rolling fields of Wiltshire lay cloaked in silver. The tires of the big Land Rover sang on the pavement, a shrill keening that made conversation impossible. "I'll get the wheels aligned in the morning," Muggleton shouted over the whine. "And we'll take it out to the test-driving range so you can practice." Then he swung the vehicle off the motorway and just ahead of us dark shapes rose from the plain. Stonehenge.

We parked the Land Rover and walked down the fence line to see the shapes twist and bend and reconfigure themselves under the moon, like dark, full-bodied women slowly stepping through a dance. From the motorway beyond came the steady thrum of traffic, but the mysterious stones cast a stillness over the night and a restorative peace over my heart. Back at the house I slid into my sleeping bag. Lying in bed and thinking of the moonlit stones we'd seen, I tried to convince myself that the ancient mystical power of the people of Stonehenge would bear us on our journey. But I'm not the mystical type. And I couldn't sleep. Not on the hard, lumpy pillow Muggleton had given me. I crept back to the living room, and there, floating atop the wash of gear, I found a "Deluxe Camping Pillow." Soft. Sleek. The vibrant ultramarine color of the underwater print nicely matched the peacock blue of my satin pajamas, an outfit I never travel without. Perfect.

I carried the little pillow back to bed, hoping that tomorrow everything would come right. We'd find a space for all the gadgets—for the GPS and the solar battery recharger and the tripod, the shovels and the axe and the machete, and even Pamela the plump nurse. I closed my eyes, and there in the darkness I saw a fabulous queen, a large regal woman swathed in leopard skins moving slowly through the figures of a dance. I reminded myself that the Queen was really nothing to me but a good excuse for gallivanting. But there she was as I drifted into sleep, circling slowly under an English moon among women as large and grave as the stones of Stonehenge, circling slowly into the heart of my dreams. The next day we would pack up the vehicle and get under way. But that night our journey had already begun.

OFF THE EDGE

In the morning, at the military test-driving range, I tucked my pillow and a jacket under my butt and took the wheel. Pulling myself up to my full five foot three, I peered out over the top of the steering wheel, over the top of the spare tire mounted on the hood, into empty space. Muggleton had stopped the vehicle at the crest of a hill. The unseen road dropped away before us into oblivion.

"Put it in low gear and take your foot completely off the clutch," Muggleton said.

I did as he said. The Land Rover crept forward to the edge of the hill and suddenly plunged nose-down. Far below, at the base of the cliff, lay the earth, where we would crash and burn. How soft and dark it looked. How green. Automatically my left foot flew up to stab the brake pedal, and Muggleton yelled too late: "Don't hit the brakes!" But the sudden nosedive had lifted me out of my seat and thrown me forward over the steering wheel, raising my feet out of range of the brake pedal. I hung there, clutching the wheel, long enough to realize that we were not plunging to our death after all. We were scarcely moving. Slowly, steadily, the old Land Rover crept down the precipice like a fly walking down a windowpane.

"Good, eh?" Muggleton beamed.

"You might have told me how it works," I said, sinking back into my seat at the bottom of the hill.

"You'll get the hang of it," he said. "Turn around and go back up."

When the vehicle was well splattered with mud, we drove back to Muggleton's house and loaded our gear. First we stowed cameras, film, computer, printer, binoculars, radio, and other valuable and delicate equipment in the big strongbox behind the seat and fastened the lid with padlocks. Our duffels went on top: one for tents, mosquito nets, and bedrolls, and one small duffel apiece for clothing—one change of clothes—and personal equipment. Under my duffel I wedged my small, precious bag of African novels. In back, the tools and spare parts went into the boxes built into the wheel wells. Two metal boxes containing enough medical supplies to furnish a small hospital stood on top of the toolboxes, one on either side of the vehicle. On the floor in between went a big blue plastic crate—"the kitchen"—for stove, mess kit, lanterns, water-purifying pump, and food. A row of empty jerry cans, to be filled with drinking water and fuel when we reached Africa, was lashed to the roof rack. Behind them we lashed down the second spare tire and two shovels. Odds and ends went willy-nilly into the empty space just behind the seat: tire pump, guidebooks, maps, machete, axe, window squeegee, water bottles, rope, fire extinguisher, ponchos, flashlights, Cadbury's ginger-nut biscuits, licorice.

The neighbors stood in the road to watch the pile of bags and boxes disappear inside the Land Rover, and then, after we'd cleaned up the flat, Muggleton came out with the upright vacuum cleaner—the Hoover, as it's called in Britain. He put it in the back of the vehicle, explaining to the little knot of well-wishers: "I like to keep a tidy camp."

We waved goodbye and set off down the road to Andover to drop off the borrowed Hoover at Muggleton's brother's house and pick up Pamela, the nurse. She stood waiting in the hall—a large and formidable presence, wall to wall, encased in tight pink leggings and an oversize tunic emblazoned with sequins and assorted bits of glitter. Just the getup for a smart holiday. She had a pretty face enveloped in cascades of blond hair, and an eager, uncertain smile.

"I've only got the one bag," she said.

"Well done," Muggleton and I said in unison, adherents to the same high standards of minimal packing. (Hadn't I at the last moment jettisoned my shampoo—soap will do as well—and broken the handle off my hairbrush?)

"And my sleeping kit," Pamela said, indicating an oversize plastic Marks and Spencer shopping bag from which a solid-core foam mattress protruded. "And my binoculars and a few books." Another big shopping bag. "And my jacket." A big black fleecy one, like a small sheep. "And this." This was a full-sized bed pillow in a soft yellow pillowcase. "I have some trouble with my neck," she said.

"It matches the vehicle," I said.

"What's this?" Muggleton asked, pointing to a second bulging back-pack, the same color as the first and nearly as big.

"That's part of my bag," Pamela said. "It zips on."

"And that?" he asked, indicating a large leather pouch that stood open on the floor, revealing a jumble of hair rollers and a pair of bright yellow strappy high heels within.

"Oh, that's my purse," Pamela said. She climbed over the tailgate into the back of the Land Rover in place of the Hoover, shoved aside a box of medical supplies, and took a seat on one of the toolboxes, a perch just high enough to prevent her seeing anything out of the window. We piled her belongings around her and leaned against the back door until the latch caught.

Muggleton's brother rolled his eyes. "Are you sure about this?" he asked. "If she sits on one side of the Rover like that, you'll be doing wheelies in the desert."

Muggleton laughed. The two brothers scuffled a bit, shoulder to shoulder, throwing mock punches in some masculine equivalent of a loving and tender farewell. The stay-at-home brother presented the expeditioning brother with a regulation rugby ball for the road, then stood in the driveway to wave goodbye.

Scarcely an hour later we drove into Portsmouth and Muggleton parked the Land Rover out of sight in a cul-de-sac, then went around the corner to the office of the Automobile Association to pick up the ferry ticket he'd reserved. It was a special "Day Abroad" ticket, with a fare of only eighteen pounds, good for a twenty-four-hour excursion to France. He returned, smirking, and brought the jam-packed Land Rover out of hiding.

"How do we explain all this luggage if we're only going on an overnight trip?" Nurse Pamela asked.

"It's a fashion shoot," I said. "The Land Rover is a prop."

At the ticket taker's window, Muggleton leaped out to explain— smiling, charming, utterly convincing—and his words drifted back to us in the vehicle.

"Yes, we've even had that mud sprayed on the sides, if you can believe it," he was saying, pointing to the grimy remnants of the mud-driving lesson he'd given me that morning.

"The lengths these high-fashion people go to," the ticket taker said, working up a pretty pucker of disapproval. She waggled her fingers at Muggleton, waving him on. "See you tomorrow," she said.

It was dark when we rolled off the ferry in Cherbourg, and we pitched our tents at the first campsite we came upon. We crawled into our respective domes to contemplate the enormity of what we'd undertaken. I had sold my apartment in New York, Nurse Pamela had sublet her house in Middlesex, and Muggleton had turned the key on a Wiltshire flat that had never aspired to the status of "home." We were on the road.

The next morning we unfolded the Michelin map of southern Europe and spread it on the ground. It was the size of a large tablecloth. Our aim was to drive as quickly as possible to Algeciras, on the south coast of Spain, where we would get the ferry for Morocco. "We'll be there in a couple of days," Muggleton said. "Three maybe." No point in rushing. Normandy was charming on a sunny day—old stone houses and potted geraniums and dark bistros redolent of strong coffee and good bread. That afternoon we climbed to the highest terraces of Mont-Saint-Michel and gazed out over the sea and the broad tidal flats far below. Tourists in jogging shoes rushed past us in pursuit of their tour guides, but we lingered over the view and the eternal quiet of the place when the crowds had moved on. We were travelers now, pilgrims on a mission of our own.

That night we pitched our tents beside a lake in Brittany, having progressed only about three-quarters of an inch down the gigantic and increasingly intimidating Michelin map. The day had been one of diversions—literal diversions that carried us back and forth across the landscape, zigzagging on a course that ate up time but went nowhere. "France is very big," Muggleton said glumly, staring at the map. We drove on through rolling fields of wine grapes and corn and pink cattle and pine plantations to Biarritz, a froufrou confection of French and Basque and International Moderne styles decked in gingerbread and perched on rocks above the deep blue Gulf of Gascony. Three days on the road had brought us to the border of Spain. At San Sebastián we turned south again, skirting the Pyrenees, and climbed to the high plateau. It spread before us, tawny and bare, stretching as far as we could see to the towers of distant Pamplona. For days we pushed on across the plateau through immense barren fields of autumn where hay and grapes and sunflowers had grown. Every hundred kilometers or so there appeared against the sky the silhouette of Spain's most popular billboard: a gigantic black anatomically correct bull.

France had offered regulated campgrounds, with each site demarcated by some rudimentary wall of aspiring shrubbery. We'd use the whole of our assigned plot, pitching three tents around the Land Rover. But because Spain seemed to have no campgrounds, we pulled offroad each day, just before dark, to make camp in the woods. One evening, as we searched for a likely campsite, we came upon a wooded area designated in English on a signboard as a "Natural Park," but the entrance road was blocked by a massive pile of bricks and rubble meant to keep visitors out.

"Now you'll see what this vehicle can do!" Muggleton said proudly. He drove straight into the obstacle. The Land Rover easily mounted the barrier and came to rest there on its belly, its front wheels suspended in the air on one side, its back wheels on the other.

"Brilliant," Pamela muttered. "Now what?"

"Now," Muggleton said, cheery as ever, "we get to test our shovels."

Only an hour or two later, after we'd tested both shovels, the high lift jack, and one of our matched pair of blue sand ladders, the Land Rover slid off the rock pile into the Natural Park and lurched along the track. Although it had escaped the rock pile with only a few scrapes to the underside of the left gas tank, it began to sputter. Up went the hood, out came the tools and the maintenance handbook, a thick impressive hardcover document replete with complicated line drawings. I stood on the fender holding a light—for it had grown dark while we labored on the rock pile—as Muggleton pored over the manual, screwdriver in hand. Off came the distributor cap, out came some critical screws, on went a lead to the low-voltage terminal.

"In theory," Muggleton said, "as the gizmo turns, the juice should illumine the electric bulb at the other end of that voltage lead."

But in fact, it did not. Exasperated, Muggleton listened to the engine, made a guess, and slipped the screws back in the distributor, now canted at a rakish angle.

"That should do for it," he said.

When we pulled into a Spanish service station the next day, the attendant patted the vehicle admiringly on the fender, rubbed the toe of his shoe caressingly around the tires, and stroked the sand ladders. He had driven a Land Rover in the Spanish army in the Western Sahara, he told us, his round face radiant with nostalgia. He cocked a hip and flourished a few salsa steps, recalling his youthful days as a soldier at Smara. But attention and praise were not enough for our Land Rover. As we descended to the coast at Cádiz, it was still stuttering, and Muggleton decided to drive to Gibraltar for a professional tune-up.

Meanwhile, I had been trying to get off a dispatch to a webzine called *Global Network Navigator* on America Online. I'd signed a contract to send them weekly dispatches from the expedition, and for that purpose I was carrying thousands of dollars' worth of the very latest in electronic widgets, stowed in the strongbox. My computer had a built-in fax modem, but when I plugged an American phone connector into a Spanish phone line, nothing happened. I decided to print out hard copy to fax, but my super-tiny travel printer was equipped with a straight American 110-volt power cord. Spain runs on 220. So does France. And Africa. And most of the world, for that matter. The ever resourceful Muggleton cut the plug off the printer and connected the power cord to the engine of the Land Rover. Nothing. The Land Rover put out twelve volts. The printer needed thirteen.

"There must be a business center in Gibraltar," I said when Muggleton announced his intention to get the Land Rover tuned up. So we drove along the south coast of Spain, past Algeciras and the ferry that might have taken us to Africa—and on to Gibraltar. On the way, Muggleton told me about the last time he had arrived in the crown colony. He flew in, wearing a natty uniform, leading an elite British army diving team. A soldier fetched him and his men at the airstrip and delivered them, in silence, deep inside the Rock. That's as far as the story went, leaving the impression that Muggleton was engaged at the time in some deeply secret, highly dangerous mission. That, I realized, was the impression he wished to convey.

This time Muggleton drove a sputtering Land Rover onto the outer perimeter, with me as copilot and Nurse Pamela in the back. The Land Rover wasn't happy, and neither was Muggleton. The vehicle coughed habitually and rested at every stop sign like a tired horse. We wandered haltingly this way and that through the city center in search of the Land

Rover garage while glumness settled upon us like dust. Our journey in search of the Lovedu, the tribe where women rule, was supposed to bring us freedom, adventure, an inflating sense of our own weightlessness and intrepidity. But we'd been on the road a week now, and we felt in danger of sinking under the burden of the very gadgetry that was supposed to set us free—our Land Rover and our electronic wonderworks.

"Wearing a kinky black rubber dive suit gives one supreme confidence," Muggleton said, remembering.

"So does faxing," I said.

Two days later, after we'd accomplished our modest missions—the tune-up and the faxing—with time to spare for lunch at Burger King, we drove the revitalized Land Rover out of Gibraltar and back beyond Algeciras over a mountain studded with sci-fi windmills—perhaps the windiest mountain in the world—to a campground on the beach at Tarifa, the southernmost point of the Iberian Peninsula. There we rearranged our gear for the tenth time and did our laundry and leaped into the cold crystalline sea to clear our heads. We watched horsemen pass on the beach at dusk. We walked up the road for a last pizza, only to find that the Pizzeria Italiano had been converted to a curio shop selling sombreros and castanets and miniature renditions of the anatomically correct bull. Muggleton and I felt trapped on the edge of the continent, shuttling along the highway between Gibraltar and Tarifa, always with Nurse Pamela in the back, a too too solid presence, drinking Diet Coke, reading a fat romance novel, worrying about her tan, whittling our high adventure down to an ordinary excursion that might be undertaken by anyone with time on her hands and lots of luggage. Nurse Pamela had become our anchor. She was real.

Muggleton and I were in danger, both of us, of lapsing into depression, trapped on that treadmill of maintenance, until one morning, Wednesday, October 18, our eighth day on the road, when Muggleton replaced the dipstick, lowered the hood of the newly tuned Land Rover ever so gently, turned to me, and asked, "Should we go to Africa today?"

"Why not?" I said.

We boosted Nurse Pamela into the back, piled her bags around her, drove over the mountain to Algeciras, and aboard the *Ibn Battouta II* bound for Tangier, we leaped at last off the edge of the continent.

PARAMETERS

You used to be able to walk from one continent to the other—until plate tectonics remodeled the world. Or was it Hercules, who set one hand against the Rock of Gibraltar and the other against the adjacent Rock of Ceuta and pushed? The twin Pillars of Hercules, the rocks are called, though Ceuta now lies on the coast of Morocco, far away, and you have to take a ferry. This brief transit, this moment of suspension upon the sea, marks the clearest possible transition from one world to another, from where you've been to where you're going, from what you've known to what you can scarcely imagine. From the upper deck I watched the Rock of Gibraltar shrink into the continent and drift away under the deep blue skies of the European autumn. Ahead, could that be the Rock of Ceuta? There where that long dark line was materializing from the bright air? Africa. The light seemed to grow more intense, the sky pale, and from that effulgence the land emerged and drifted upward toward the ship. *Africa.* A swath of sand, the long shadow of the coastal plain, and there rising like clouds, the ragged mountains of the Rif.

"Passeport, s'il vous plaît." We motored off the ferry at Tangier straight into the arms of the law. Blue-uniformed police, green-uniformed customs officials, gray-uniformed gendarmes. All, of course, male. And all eager to peruse our documents. *"Passeport, s'il vous plaît. Carnet. Assurance. Carte verte. Permis international."*

Wasn't this Morocco? The land of dashing Berber chieftains? Of caliphs and amirs and sultans and pashas? A land once so rich that it devoted whole cities to the process of dying robes of royal purple? Once, powerful Berber merchant chiefs dominated the ancient trans-

Saharan trade. Then in the seventh century great armies swept out of Arabia, bringing Islam to Morocco: al-Maghreb al-Aqsa, the land of the setting sun. As the eighth century opened and Europe slumped into the Dark Ages, the Berber Tarik ibn Ziyad led a Muslim army from Morocco across the strait we had just crossed, crushed the Visigoths in Spain, and ushered in seven centuries of brilliant Islamic civilization in Andalusia. At the close of the eighth century, the Idrissids, descendants of the prophet Mohammed, founded the city of Fès, which quickly became the center of trade, politics, and cultural life for Islamic North Africa and Spain. Within its walls, a woman named Fatma built the Islamic Qaraouine (or Kairaouine) University—today the oldest university in the world.

In 1415 Ceuta fell to the Portuguese, led by Prince Henry, later "the Navigator." The year 1492, though, was the real turning point—a date remembered in Morocco, not because in that year Ferdinand and Isabella, the Catholic monarchs of Spain, dispatched an Italian navigator to the Indies, but because they dispatched an army to take Granada and oust the Muslims and Jews from Spain. Even after that, when Europeans cast covetous eyes on Africa, they saw in Morocco no easy pickings. They saw instead a Muslim nation with a thousand-year history of dynastic rule—the Idrissids, the Almoravids, the Almohads, the Merinids, the Saadians. They saw a vital culture, great and venerable cities, a militant religion inspired to *jihad* by the persecution of the Spanish Inquisition, and powerful armies capable not only of resisting invasion but of themselves invading Europe. Nevertheless, this nation lay within the northwest quadrant of Africa, the area designated by an Anglo-French agreement of 1890 as the French "sphere of influence" on the continent. France built its West African empire and exerted its "influence" on Morocco, waiting for the country's inevitable fall; but with only four other independent African states still standing, Morocco held out. (Two of those states, Tripoli and Cyrenaica, were soon combined as the Italian colony of Libya.) Stronger measures seemed necessary. France and England, always careful to conduct the African dance without collision, signed an *entente* in 1904: England would do as it pleased in Egypt, and France would have a free hand against Abdel Aziz, the twenty-five-year-old sultan of Morocco. By 1912 France had swallowed Morocco, placed it under French "protection," and conferred upon it the civilizing benefits of the French language, French forms, French epaulets, French braid, French brass, French bureaucracy. Even now, more than forty years after regaining independence, Morocco still maintained all these men in uniform, the outward manifestation of the modern nation-state. Like French bread, bureaucracy had gotten into the system.

The men in uniform washed over the vehicle, wave after wave. *"Passeport, s'il vous plaît. Carnet. Assurance. Carte verte. Permis international."* All of these documents we possessed. All in good order. All carefully arranged in one of those reddish-brown cardboard accordion files, bound by a little elastic band. Dutifully we opened our portfolio and produced our documents for this official and that. Ah, but we must visit this office, and that one over there, for the registration, the inspection, the stamp official. Muggleton seized the file and shuffled doggedly from one office to the next, documents in hand, patience mustered, while I climbed into the back of the vehicle and sat on top of the big lockbox filled with cameras and electronic gadgetry. I smiled and chatted up the officers, hoping they wouldn't notice that what I was sitting on wasn't exactly an ordinary seat. They didn't. Instead, after a couple of hours, they rummaged through our bags—not seriously searching but going through the motions—and waved us on.

"We should have smuggled some drugs," Muggleton said regretfully.

"Why risk it?" I said. "They grow Riffi kif right down the road." But I knew that wasn't the point. Muggleton didn't even like drugs; born too late, he thought there was something morally reprehensible in a recreational toke. What he liked was the heady rush of getting away with something. He eased the Land Rover through the last gate on the pier and turned toward the highway.

"Don't you want to see if there's a campground in Tangier?" I asked. "It's quite a town."

"No," Muggleton said. "We're way behind schedule. We should make tracks for Africa."

"This *is* Africa," I said. "Tangier, Morocco, Africa."

"No, no," he said. "I mean the *real* Africa." He had paused at an intersection and was staring blankly at a bank of road signs lettered in Arabic and French. "Help me read these signs," he said. "This isn't the *real* Africa."

"Tangier is pretty real," I said, remembering other visits. "Haven't you read Paul Bowles?"

Muggleton didn't answer. Instead he flashed me a winning smile and said, "Come on, Jones. We can't stop here. We just got off the boat." Laid-back Muggleton had become a man on the move.

Yet all around us, lying in ambush, were the diligent agents of the bureaucracy. Driving away from the city, we met the Securité de la Ville. *"Passeport, s'il vous plaît,"* the officer said, holding out his hand. *"Carnet. Assurance. Carte verte. Permis international."* A little farther down the road we met the gendarmerie. *"Passeport, s'il vous plaît. Carnet. Assurance. Carte verte. Permis international."* Trying to make up for lost time, Muggleton almost missed a checkpoint—speeding through signs commanding him to slow down for the police. *"Passeport, s'il vous plaît."*

The big officer wasn't pleased. He was young and full of himself, and after he commanded Muggleton to descend from the vehicle and stand in the road, we could see that he was exceedingly tall. And very angry. He would send Muggleton to jail, he said. He would confiscate his vehicle and throw his women into the street. And also he would fine him four hundred dirhams for his vicious conduct. Was he uncivilized? A pig perhaps?

Apologies flew from our side. And excuses. That we had only just arrived in Morocco. That we had failed to see the signs, having been blinded by the beauty of the country. That Muggleton is British and therefore naturally dull-witted and slow. The superior officer, a pudgy middle-aged man with bad teeth and a broad smile, received our apologies with genial aplomb. But in the end he took out his charge book and his ballpoint pen, and laying the book on the hood of the Land Rover, he prepared to write Muggleton up for "disrespect of the police," a serious charge but one that involved no jail time, no confiscation, no shame to his women. He was filled with sympathy for us, he said. His heart overflowed. But after all, he was an officer of the police. What could he do? The wind blew the pages of his charge book, and I extended a hand to hold the paper down for him. Muggleton, feigning a fit of weeping, handed over one hundred dirhams. "You are very kind, madame," the officer said, "and the performance of the gentleman—it is very good, don't you agree?"

We drove on until the light began to fail and then made camp, only forty kilometers down the road from Tangier, in a windswept field near

Asilah. Pamela fired up the Coleman stove and prepared a glutinous mass of overboiled pasta in which greasy tinned British pork sausages lurked like worms amid a slime of sodden tinned peas. (Pamela had taken over the cooking. Her tastes were large and patriotic.) I turned in and lay in my tent, battered by the stiff wind off the Atlantic, and thought of the steamy city of Tangier: the dark, deep-cushioned restaurants, the steep stone streets of the medina, the eager touts tugging at elbows, offering hotels and tours and, to the right clients, kif and young boys to smoke it with. I thought of Asilah—I could see the lights of the town just below us—where even now there would be laughter and music in the beachfront cafes. That was modern Africa—urbanized, sophisticated, lively, full of sex and petty crime and hot music. So what was this? This wind-cursed rocky plain. Centuries before, a mighty Portuguese army, bent on Christian conquest, had landed at Asilah and marched south to be annihilated. They must have scuffed at the same rocks, bent under the same sharp wind. Was this the *real* Africa?

The next morning we talked things over. Muggleton was determined to reach our first great obstacle of the road as quickly as possible. The Sahara. He argued that it was pointless to loiter along the way when that critical test lay before us. If we could meet that challenge and overcome it, then perhaps we could relax our pace, confident that in due time we would complete our journey. But if we were to come up against the Sahara and fail—well, better to face defeat at once.

He made a persuasive case, but it seemed to me that looming disaster was the best argument for present pleasure. If defeat lay ahead, why rush to meet it? Why not postpone the day of reckoning and enjoy ourselves while we still had time? *"Carpe diem,"* I said, or words to that effect, pleased to have the full weight of that philosophy on my side. But it counted for nothing against the burden of Muggleton's anxiety.

"Don't be irrational," he said. "You can't just have a good time."

"I don't see why not," I said.

It was a long discussion, and I fought valiantly, if I do say so myself, but in the end Muggleton did make me see why not. You can't just have a good time in the company of someone who is determined to be down the road overcoming a bad one. This first big quarrel originated in our first day in Africa and became the existential nub of our journey. The upshot of round one was this: we decided to drive on at once to Rabat, the capital, there to obtain as quickly as possible our visas for Mauritania, and then to set off with all due speed for the Sahara. You can see how, once you start hurrying, one thing leads to another.

Muggleton pushed the Land Rover to top speed—about eighty kilometers (fifty miles) per hour—and we chugged south over the fine modern highways of Morocco toward Rabat. To the right lay bright, white seaside villages strung at intervals along the long sweep of Atlantic beach like baubles on a golden chain. To the left, other highways swept off to Fès and Meknes and other exotic places unknown. As Muggleton drove I consulted our *Lonely Planet* guidebook and the map, so that when we reached the outskirts of Rabat I was able to direct him through the avenues of orderly suburbs to a small villa distinguished from its neighbors only by the flag hanging limply on the roof—the blue and white flag of Mauritania. Once inside, we filled out visa application forms, waited our turn, and at last were ushered into the tight, stuffy office of the consul general himself, emissary to the Kingdom of Morocco.

The consul was a small man in a big blue suit with a big Windsor knot in his tie. Before him on his desk lay the application papers upon which we had indicated our intention to drive our vehicle from the top of Mauritania to the bottom. Quickly, with an abrupt gesture of irritation, he picked up the papers and waved them under our noses. *"Non. Non. Non,"* he said. *"Absolument. Non."*

From his mouth poured swift, sinuous sentences of French, plentifully studded with the word *"Non."* Mentally I paddled through the tide to catch the drift of his declaration: our request to pass through his country was denied, our proposed sojourn in the happy and blessed nation of Mauritania would not take place, our application for visas was rejected. Stunned, I glanced quickly at Muggleton, who sat politely upright in his chair, smiling anxiously at the consul general. I remembered that Muggleton knew just about as much French as his average countryman, which is to say not a word.

"No visas," I said to him. "They've turned us down."

"What? What do you mean, 'turned us down'? He can't bloody well do that!"

"I think he can," I said, but my heart was sinking. The only other route south to Mali lay through Algeria, a disturbing and dangerous place given the political conditions of the time. We'd heard tales of

Algerian snipers along the roadside picking off passing Europeans just to show that the anticolonial spirit still ran high among Islamic revolutionaries. Even the Moroccan police had warned us not to get lost and wander over the border into Algeria.

"No, no, *non,*" Muggleton said, echoing the consul general. "Tell him I'm not driving through Algeria. Is he trying to kill us?"

With just a hint of impatience the consul general explained his position in exquisite French. The problem, it seemed, was that Mauritania did not wish to mislead international motorists by applying to any of its quaint country paths the elevated designation of "road," thereby encouraging overland ventures that must inevitably prove inconvenient to the international visitor and embarrassing to the government. Besides, there were mines—land mines left over from one conflict or another—and no one remembered exactly where they were. Mauritania was eager, however, to encourage visits to its lovely capital, Nouakchott. Therefore, travelers holding round-trip air tickets to Nouakchott would be granted a visa. Overland travelers would not. As for our request, he said, handing over our rejected forms in triplicate, the answer was *"Non. Catégoriquement, non."*

I protested as best I could, given that my French was only marginally better than Muggleton's. My conversation consisted largely of simple sentences constructed on an Anglo-Saxon model. "We are an expedition," I said to the consul general. "We *must* travel overland. We have a scientific purpose," I said, stretching it a bit. In that case, said the consul general, we must have the approval of the Ministry of Science and the faculty of science at the university. We must duly present our credentials. We duly produced some, but the consul waved aside our letters of introduction. He grasped only at a small plastic badge that Muggleton proffered, perhaps mistaking it for a Visa card. When he examined it and found that it merely identified Muggleton as a fellow of the Royal Geographical Society, he tossed it back, muttering *"Royale"* with considerable disdain.

"I suggest you purchase air tickets, madame," he continued in his precisely nuanced French.

"But we need our vehicle, our equipment," I persisted.

"Madame," he said in a sentence so heavily laden with conditionals I could scarcely follow it, "if you were to flourish an air ticket, you might find that a visa would devolve upon you, and in that case, should you subsequently depart from these premises, having completed your business here, it might happen that I would lamentably become unaware of where you might go or what you might do thereafter." He paused and cocked an eyebrow at me to suggest that now, at this precise moment, the fate of our expedition hung suspended like an acrobat in flight somewhere in the air between us. I blinked. "Ah, madame," he said, truly disappointed and scornful, "I observe that your French is insufficient for the occasion."

"Mais dit la visa pour la aéroport seulement?" I persisted in my blunt Franglais. "Does the visa say it is for the airport only?"

"Madame, yes," he said sadly. "There is that small detail." He rose to end the interview, and Muggleton and I found ourselves outside the door.

"Now what?" Muggleton asked, pocketing his royal identity card. We sped along the boulevards to the American Embassy, but the consul was nowhere to be found. "Bloody worthless," Muggleton said, and drove on to the British Embassy, where an underling handed us two printed advisories: one saying that British nationals could not travel to Mauritania overland, the other saying that they should exercise caution when they did. Then the day was over, and there was nothing to do but sleep on the problem. We crossed over the river from modern Rabat to the old town of Salé, in search of a lovely campground designated on our map by the outline of a tiny tent right on the beach. "No worries," Muggleton said. "We'll think of something in the morning."

The campground turned out to be a bare, sandy plot surrounded by a concrete wall topped with broken glass and barbed wire. When we pulled in, it held a couple of caravans, two motorbikes, a heavily laden Land Rover, and two monstrous trucks carrying parties of twenty young European tourists—students mostly—on overland journeys of many months. Most of the travelers were British, and all of them were headed south through Mauritania and the Sahara. Chris, the British driver of the Land Rover, showed us the currently preferred route: due south through the Western Sahara, then due east along a railroad track on the northern border of Mauritania. There was an overland pipeline, it seemed, flowing south, and we had only to drop into it. "But what about visas?" we asked. And that's when we learned from our fellow overlanders how to work the scam.

The next morning I crossed the bridge again to Rabat and made my

way along the broad palm-fringed Avenue Mohamed V in the heart of
the *ville nouvelle,* the modern city the French built to separate themselves from the unknown sounds and smells and secret luxuries of the
old walled Arab town. I was looking for a travel agency where I could
buy air tickets for Muggleton and Nurse Pamela and me: round-trip
flights from Casablanca to Nouakchott. Our new acquaintance Chris
had told us that any travel agent would sell us the air tickets, put the
charges on a credit-card form, then tear up the form when we returned
the unused tickets (after first obtaining our visas at the Mauritanian
consulate) and paid a "cancellation" fee of about sixty dollars. But
purely by chance, I found an enterprising young woman working her
own version of the standard shuffle. Her boss wasn't in yet, so she gave
me the plane tickets on the spot at no charge in exchange for the cancellation fee up front in cash. She opened her desk drawer and slipped
the sizable pile of dirhams into her pocketbook. Women in Morocco, I
remembered, have had access to education and real jobs only since
independence in 1956. How quickly we learn to do business, I thought.

"I help you," she said. "I do this only for you—*parce que votre visage
me plaît.*"

"*Merci, madame,*" I said, clinging to her hand as I accepted the tickets. "I like your face too."

We filed our applications again at the Mauritanian Embassy and
returned to camp to wait out the weekend, observing the steady flow of
southbound travelers. Nurse Pamela hurried about the campground
like an eager hostess, delighted at the prospect of chatting with British-
ers like herself. But waiting was not easy for Muggleton. To pass the
time he rotated the tires of the Land Rover and fine-tuned the engine
again. He set himself problems on the Magellan Global Positioning
System unit, and guided solely by that instrument, he successfully
returned to his tent again and again from the shower block at the far
side of the campground until he wore out the batteries. Then he set out
to master the Trimble Navigation System, having first thrown away the
instruction manual to make the task more challenging. He busied himself fiddling with buttons and antennas, drawing down fixes on tran-
sient satellites.

On Monday, Muggleton and Pamela and I claimed our visas at the
Mauritanian Embassy, turned in our air tickets at the travel agency, and
headed south to the red walls of Marrakesh and beyond. Soon the

bright cities and broad highways were behind us, and we began to climb on a narrow track of pitted asphalt and gravel among the barren brown peaks of the High Atlas. By the time we reached the tortuous curves of the Tizni Test—a pass under the shadow of Toubkal, the highest peak—Muggleton was announcing our position at every stop. As we ascended the pass, elevation became more significant than latitude or longitude. Three thousand six hundred forty feet at the cafe where we stopped for a *tajine*. Three thousand one hundred fifty feet at the stream where we stripped down for a bath. Six thousand eight hundred sixty-five feet at the pass itself, where we met a black-turbaned Berber trader carrying silver jewelry from women of the Sahara to Marrakesh for sale. His father, he said, traded along the trans-Sahara caravan route—fifty-two days from Zagora to Timbuktu by camel—as his father and his father's father had done for more than a thousand years. He himself was walking in his simple leather slippers over the High Atlas to Marrakesh, carrying the heavy basket of silver.

As we drove deeper into Africa we drove backward in time, or so it seemed as the distance widened between the lives around us and our own. We pulled offroad at night to camp and came upon a salt mine, where five men in cutoffs and brine-encrusted tee shirts were spreading and raking the pools, harvesting white crystals. They greeted us with hands outstretched, offering salt. In return we offered Polaroid photos of the group, which caused them literally to fall out laughing. They howled with delight, clutched their sides, fell to their knees, and tumbled over, rolling in the dust, gasping for breath, all the while holding the little Polaroid images aloft, safely out of harm's way. It was as if they could see in the photographs, as they could not in real life, how comical an appearance they made with their raggedy clothes and their dark faces painted white like clowns. Akhmed, the foreman, brought forth his mule for me to ride, a thin but willing creature with a fine homemade saddle of yellow leather. I set off, whistling, uphill along a dry wash, and soon I was high above the little knot of men who still howled and howled beside the field of salt.

There weren't many men to be seen in this lonely countryside, so many having gone to the big northern cities or to other countries in search of work. The mountain villages were occupied instead by women and old men, who managed the cows and goats and harvested olives, walnuts, and vegetables on the steep hillsides. And by many young children—for men do pay visits home. One day, as I slowed the Land Rover to let a young girl pass, driving a passel of goats ahead of her with a long stick, I was struck by the trite but inescapable thought that her life and mine were about a century apart. The difference seemed so great that it did not bear thinking about. It was easier by far to consult Muggleton and the Trimble Navigation System to find out where we stood in space than to dwell on other parameters.

At night I climbed atop the vehicle with my bedroll and settled myself against the second spare tire. Overhead, in a black sky brilliant with stars, passed the satellites that told Trimble and Muggleton where we were. The breeze was cold as the night deepened, the silence of the mountains unbroken, and the faint odor of the worn rubber tire oddly comforting. Three thousand kilometers and still rolling, with our Mauritanian visas in our pockets. So what if the designated port of entry was Nouakchott Airport? We would descend from the High Atlas and thread the barren undulations of the Anti-Atlas to the Sahara.

CONVOY

"*Bonjour, monsieur le gendarme. Bonjour. Ça va? Ça va? Oui. Oui. Oui.* I speak Fraaanch.*" Muggleton was practicing exuberantly for the road ahead. *"Le prénom de mon père est Graham, monsieur le gendarme. Le prénom de ma mère est Julie."* He was sprawled on his back in the sand under the Land Rover, wrench in hand. Black oil ran down his arm into his tee shirt. Maintenance.

The descent from the Tizni Test had been abrupt. One evening we'd camped near a stream that was scarcely a trickle among terraced plots of carefully irrigated corn. We'd been welcomed to the land warmly by the farmer, a young man in a pale djellaba who stood in the field waiting for his wife to finish loading dried cornstalks onto a donkey. Around us towered the Anti-Atlas Mountains—all red rock, the granite swirling in graceful waves, as though the mountains had drifted inland on the tide. This was a country of stones that farmers and farmers' wives had gathered and stacked into terraces and fences and cairns, a country that exuded always more red stones, bleached under the white sun of midday to the color of dull rust. The next day we were over the pass and spilling headlong down the hairpin road to the great flat stretch of *hammada*—the stony desert—that marks the edge of the Sahara and plunges precipitously into the Atlantic.

The villages changed as suddenly as the landscape. In the mountains behind us many-storied houses of brown adobe clung to the hillsides. Goats and donkeys lived in the stables at the bottom, with the family in quarters above and the women upstairs, cooking in dark smoky kitchens, spreading laundry to dry on rooftop terraces. One house in almost every village was painted pink and equipped with a white satellite dish. (What did that man do, I always wondered, to become so much more prosperous than his neighbors and so keen to rub it in?) But here in the *hammada* the low flat-roofed houses seemed to rise out of the level earth, like extrusions of red mud thrown up haphazardly without intent. We passed through Guelmim, a big sprawling town of deep-red houses and drifting sands, to camp nearby at Abaynou. From here a single red line on the Michelin map led south—a long relentless runway on the verge between sea and sand, 1,381 kilometers through the disputed "Spanish Sahara" to the border of Mauritania.

Guelmim was the supply station for the first leg of the journey south—gas, oil, water, bread, oranges—but Abaynou had the advantage of being a genuine oasis with medicinal thermal springs. Amid the palms stood separate bathhouses for men and women, and within them comforting pools of murky warm water redolent of minerals said to cure arthritis while getting you clean. I sat in the bath until I felt well done and then moved to the village's one small cafe to drink *nous nous* (Morocco's version of cappuccino) while Muggleton crawled under the Land Rover with his illustrated repair book and the French dictionary. The adoring Pamela hunkered down by his side, dutifully handing him tools and marveling at his rapid foreign-language acquisition. In this way we readied ourselves for the push south.

The king was going too. Not with us, of course, but with his own entourage to celebrate the twentieth anniversary of the Green March—November 6, 1975—when 350,000 Moroccan women and men, armed only with copies of the Koran and pictures of the king, walked into the Western Sahara under the guns of the Spanish Foreign Legion to reassert Morocco's historical claim to the land. It had been part of Morocco until Spain claimed it as a protectorate in 1884; and even after France seized Morocco in 1912, it remained in Spain's hands, a useless scrap of desert that France was content to let go. But by 1975 the Spanish had tired of the place they called Spanish West Africa and announced plans to pull out, leaving the former colony to govern itself. That's when the Green Marchers poured into the desert to remind the world of their ancient claim. To avoid a nasty colonial war, Spain signed most of the territory over to Morocco and a smaller part to Mauritania.

In the meantime, however, the folks who actually *lived* in the Western Sahara had developed a mind and a voice of their own: the Polisario—Popular Front for the Liberation of Saguia el Hamra and

Río de Oro (the northern and southern districts of the territory). The left-wing force, bent on independence, proclaimed the sovereignty of the Saharan Arab Democratic Republic (SADR). Neighboring Algeria, which had long backed the land claims of Morocco and Mauritania, chose this moment to switch sides and support the Polisario. So began a war that lasted for more than a decade between Morocco and the Algerian-backed Polisario guerrillas. The SADR became another African token in the Cold War, backed by North Korea and Cuba, armed by the Soviet Union, financed by Algeria, with the United States and France on the other side backing Morocco. Stalemated, Morocco and Algeria made a peace of sorts in 1988 and agreed that the little bands of nomads who actually made their home in the Western Sahara should decide their own fate in a referendum. But as we and the king prepared to enter the Western Sahara, the referendum was still a dream and the Polisario was still angry and agitating for self-determination. Security was tight in the best of times. With Hassan II on the way, it would be tighter than ever.

So Muggleton kept practicing. "*Voilà, monsieur le gendarme. Mon passeport.* I am *Anglais. Grande* Britannia. U.K. Brit. I speak Fraaanch." We met the first police post on our way into Guelmim, the next on our way out. There was a checkpoint before and after every town along the road, sometimes within sight of each other. At each we were required to "descend" and provide to the uniformed officials our passports and certain additional facts: profession, names of mother and father, and marital status. All this information the officials dutifully transcribed onto tattered forms.

"*Situation familiale?*" the gendarme would ask politely, doffing his red-ribboned hat.

"*Célibataire,*" I would reply and see his pen hesitate over the scrap of paper to which he was committing my vital statistics.

"*Célibataire, madame? Pourquoi?*" They always wanted to know why. "*Pourquoi vous n'êtes pas mariée? Pourquoi?*"

At checkpoint one I tried to explain. "I like to travel," I said. "I make many long journeys. My husband would not be happy."

"You must stay at home, madame," the gendarme said, stamping my passport with greater force than was strictly necessary.

At checkpoint two I tried another approach. "I must work," I said when the gendarme demanded to know why I was not married. "I must do my job. At this very moment, *monsieur le gendarme,* I am working. I am inspecting the world. *Je suis un inspecteur du monde.*"

A sneer of incredulity passed across his face. "Madame," he said, "you must work at home."

We entered Laayoune, a city of one hundred thousand Moroccans and mountains of consumer goods that had bloomed overnight in the Western Sahara, peopling the desert in the interests of God, king, and country. The handsome young gendarme shook his pen at me. "I believe," he said, "that women in America are very hard, and that they cause many, many problems." He was pleased to inform me that Moroccan women, on the other hand, *"ne pensent qu'a se marier."* Unlike those steely, trouble-making American women—of whom I seemed to be a particularly noxious specimen—well-bred Moroccan ladies thought of nothing but getting married. American women would do well to follow their happy example.

This was too much. These know-it-all guards never asked Muggleton why he wasn't married. They never told *him* to stay at home. What gave them the right to tell me how to live my life? I knew the answer, of course. They were guys. I was not. Besides, they wore uniforms. They had all the weight of the Islamic nation-state—not to mention ancient prejudice—on their side. My very presence on the road repudiated everything they'd been taught to believe about this "man's world." To them, I was a walking insult unfortunately licensed by an infidel foreign power to walk on their soil. So they spouted off just like any right-wing American fundamentalist preacher. It made me mad. And devious.

"Malheureusement, monsieur le gendarme," I said to the handsome and opinionated gendarme—I allowed a little quaver to creep into my voice and lowered my eyes in what I hoped would be a suitable approximation of bravely controlled grief—*"je suis veuve."* I wiped an imaginary tear from my eye, and repeated with just the hint of a sob, "Unhappily, sir, I am widowed." I watched a gratifying look of genuine mortification pass over the gendarme's handsome face.

"Please pardon me, madame," he said, throwing down his pen and clasping my hands. "To have spoken so thoughtlessly when you have suffered such a loss! A thousand apologies, madame. I beg your forgiveness." He seemed genuinely aggrieved, but still curious. "Please permit me to ask, madame: When did you become a widow?"

Dabbing at my eyes, I paused to let him suffer, and then I replied, *"Récemment.* Very *récemment."*

My invention and the obvious effect it had upon the gendarme proved an inspiration to Muggleton. Recognizing how slavish and boring it is to deliver the same answers at one interrogation after another, he determined to change his career. Muggleton had always acted upon his theory that travelers receive the treatment they appear to deserve. When confronting officials, he was careful to present himself attired in modest long trousers and a clean, long-sleeved, collared shirt—the nattiest overlander on the road. Now he reasoned that a change of profession—from *photographe*—might win him more respect. Rocket scientist was his aspiration, but he couldn't find it in the French dictionary. He mulled over other possibilities. Professor? Poet? Philosopher? *"Je suis philosophe,"* he said in the tone one uses to test a microphone. "I think I'll have a good think about it. Ah ha, yes. It does make you think, doesn't it? I mean, just think about it. If I say *'philosophe,'* you simply can't help thinking, can you? About me, I mean." Philosopher it was.

On Tuesday just at sunset we drove onto the Dakhla Peninsula, a long skinny finger of land pointing south into the Atlantic. To one side lay the ocean, to the other the great blue basin of the bay. Ahead lay a dead end: the military town of Dakhla, where all overland travelers were required to register with the local authorities and the army. From Dakhla we would be allowed to depart for the south only as part of a convoy with a military escort. The king couldn't afford to have European tourists larking about his desert, colliding with long-forgotten land mines that laced the Western Sahara, mementos of decades of war. Nor could he afford to have sneaky communists creeping off into the dunes to join the Polisario guerrillas. Hence the registration and the convoys, which left twice a week—every Tuesday and Friday—for the border of Mauritania. We knew we must have missed that day's convoy, so we drove slowly, admiring the sea views, along the rocky road to the outskirts of Dakhla town, where we came upon "Camping Moussafir." It was another barren field, equipped with two recalcitrant toilets and running water, enclosed behind stone walls like the exercise yard of a maximum-security prison. There we pitched our tents.

The next morning we presented ourselves and our passports at the office of the Sécurité in the town. Data were transcribed, papers were stamped, and we were dispatched to the Customs Office, where a young woman in a red veil copied out our data onto another scrap of paper and pointed the way to Army Headquarters on the other side of town, where we did it all again with an officer who typed our data on an ancient machine. In less than an hour we'd officially registered to be part of the Friday convoy from Dakhla to Mauritania.

We bought mandarins and tomatoes and tinned sardines for the journey and filled the vehicle's tanks and nine jerry cans with Super Petrol—to the tune of two hundred American dollars. We took long lazy swims in the warm salty waters of the bay. In the evenings I visited the ladies of the family of Mr. Moussafir, the owner of the campground. He was not present, for women and men don't socialize together, but his wife and daughters and their girlfriends lounged on the divans of the sitting room, talking and laughing and painting one another's hands and feet—and mine—with intricate designs of henna. On Thursday evening, our last night in town, we went to a fragrant restaurant to have for the last time in what would be many days what Muggleton called "a proper meal": meat, potatoes, two veg, and a Coke.

Early the next morning, Muggleton and I drove an unhappy Nurse Pamela back into Dakhla town to the office of Royal Air Maroc. She had joined us in London wanting a holiday, but when the road narrowed and the dunes began to rise, it became clear that she was in the wrong vehicle. There is a difference between a tourist and a traveler after all, and the desert is no place for high heels. Muggleton helped her check in for her flight and gave her a hug. She slumped onto a bench to wait, and for the last time we piled her bags and boxes around her. We left her drifting there aimlessly amid the flotsam of her luggage, doing her nails, and ruthlessly we waved goodbye.

Soldiers appeared at the campground just after nine-thirty, hustling us into action. *"Vite! Vite! Vite! Attendez!"* It would be the motto of the day: hurry up and wait. We fell into line at the security post to be checked again by Sécurité, Customs, and the army, and relieved of our passports. It was a big convoy. Travelers we'd met at the campground in Salé had been drifting into Dakhla all week: Chris and his friends in the Land Rover, the three British bikers traveling on two bikes, New Zealanders Colin and Jane, two disreputable Germans (Manfred and Heinz) in a Datsun they meant to sell in Algeria, plus a score of other Land Rovers and Range Rovers, a Toyota Land Cruiser, and a Nissan

Patrol—all packed mostly with Brits except for a token Swiss-owned vehicle (a Land Rover with built-in library) and a Spanish-owned Land Rover chauffeured by a grimy frazzled man who never doffed his oily coverall. There were two Peugeot 504 diesels manned by squads of shaggy Frenchmen gone native. Three powerful trucks—two Bedfords and a Mercedes—hauled squads of student tourists, each twenty strong. There were thirty-five vehicles and more than a hundred people, and all of us had to be checked and stamped and checked again. Time enough for chairs to be set out and lukewarm drinks produced from coolers. Then tables appeared, then lunch, and after a suitable interval a British truck produced a rugby ball and the guys got up a game. Time passed in silence but for the grunts and shouts of the men and the *thwonk* of the leather ball.

"*Vite! Vite!*" the cry went up from the soldiers at the head of the convoy line. It was nearly two-thirty. "*Avancez! Vite! Vite!*"

Voices all along the line called out, "Come on! We're leaving!" And an Aussie voice rang out from the field: "Tell 'em to get stuffed, mate. We're playing rugby!"

All afternoon we drove south at a steady sixty kilometers per hour along a skinny paved road that lay like a flimsy bit of tape across the bleached and stony ground. At seven o'clock, when the desert night suddenly fell upon us, the soldiers ushered us off the road to make camp under the walls of a fort that stood against the starry sky like the set of an old black-and-white movie about the Foreign Legion. We ate in silence, worn out by heat and dust and the unrelenting pace of the march, and slid into our bivy bags.

At dawn the Moroccan soldiers guided us back onto the road and returned our passports. They'd been efficient, helpful, good-spirited, even kind. We waved and called out to them—"*Shokran! Shokran!* Thank you!"—and they called back, wishing us a good journey, God willing. *Inshallah.* Then we drove up a hill to the end of the asphalt and fell into the sand of Mauritania. The Peugeots bottomed out at once, useless in the deep sand. Doors flew open and half-clad Frenchmen spilled out and scrabbled with their hands to find their buried tires. They pushed and hauled and raced the engines and bounced on the back bumper, gaining ground by inches. The bikers sank too. We watched them go down behind like tired swimmers.

Despite our dodgy visas that listed "place of arrival" as Nouakchott

Airport, the Mauritanian army stood waiting to meet us. They wore combat uniforms of desert camouflage and carried Russian-made semi-automatics. They took away our driving permits and indicated that some small gift to the armed forces of our host country would be in order—cigarettes, pens, clothes, watches, dirhams. We coughed up our small Moroccan change, useless to us now, and they asked for more. We turned out our empty pockets and they shrugged in weary resignation.

We pushed on through miles of deep sand that lay between the border and the Mauritanian highway. At last we reached it—a strip of broken tarmac half buried in sand. It wasn't so much a road as an ancient marker indicating the general direction of travel. You couldn't drive on it without risking a broken axle, so we crept along beside it slowly all afternoon to Nouadhibou. The city lay out of our way, some fifty kilometers down another dead-end peninsula, but if we wished to retrieve our confiscated driving permits, our presence there was required. We would be obliged to make the rounds once again the following morning—Sécurité, Customs, Bureau d'Assurance, Gendarmerie.

Late in the afternoon we reached the shantytown that marked the outskirts of Nouadhibou. The bleak wooden shacks, little more than boxes really, stood wide apart, as if isolated even from one another in their poverty. Boys ran into the dusty street to throw stones at the passing vehicles. Welcome to Mauritania. The convoy split up into smaller groups, and we drove on through town with a few of our cronies of the road to camp on the beach at Cap Blanc. Abandoned houses of a ghostly village climbed the dune behind us, and before us the hulks of wrecked ships lay in the water. We circled the vehicles, finding comfort in numbers, and there on the sand between the ruins of sea and shore we passed our first uneasy night in Mauritania.

In the morning, we drove into town and trudged from one office to another to complete the necessary round of formalities. With our passports in our pockets, our hard-won Mauritanian visas duly verified and stamped, we waved goodbye to our friends from the convoy. Then Muggleton and I drove off again—on our own at last—into the sand.

SAHARA

I lied to the policeman who checked our passports on the way out of Nouadhibou. Did we have a guide? *"Non."* That was the truth. Did we know well the route? *"Oui."* That was the lie. He handed back the passports and wished me a good journey. A soldier tugged aside the spiked barrier, and Muggleton drove through the gate. We stopped at a well nearby to fill our jerry cans with fresh water. Then we got back into the Land Rover and sat perfectly still. Before us lay the Sahara—not the rolling red dunes of travel posters but the real thing: a vast gray stony plain that seemed to reach to the ends of the earth, an anonymous landscape devoid of mark or sign, a great empty space over which the wind blew so fiercely that it set the straps on the roof rack vibrating until the whole Land Rover seemed to resonate with the terrain that lay before us.

Once we'd had a plan: we planned to put the vehicle on a flatcar on the train. I say *the* train because it's the only train in Mauritania. It runs due east to Choum, some twenty hours away, and from there we planned to drive to Atar and on to the "picturesque and colorful" Adrar region of the Sahara, still supposedly peopled by nomadic camel drivers. Some second-rate guidebook suggested we do this. But as we tried to put our plan into effect, it became obvious that the author of the guidebook had not done this himself. It seemed likely, in fact, that the author of the guidebook had not visited the country at all. He probably wrote the whole thing in some airy hotel in Marrakesh, questioning passing travelers for rumors of Mauritania.

You couldn't blame him. Mauritania is a big country—more than a million square kilometers. About eighty percent of it is desert, and the percentage of desert steadily rises like the dunes that pile up even in the streets of the capital. It's one of Africa's forgotten countries—impoverished, almost devoid of natural resources, almost uninhabitable. The climate is so harsh, the drought and desertification so intense, that even the centuries-old trans-Saharan trade collapses as camels die of starvation. Mauritanian society is as harsh as the desert, organized in a rigid hierarchy based on race. The ruling Moorish Arab class dominates a black minority of slaves and former slaves. Islam forbids enslavement of Muslims, but enslavement of blacks was practiced legally in Mauritania until 1980, and is practiced illegally today. People say that some black Mauritanians prefer slavery to freedom because so many free people starve. But from time to time the ruling regime undertakes to rid the country of its independent-minded black population. It expels black Mauritanians or forces them to flee across the river to Senegal, and Senegal retaliates by expelling Moorish traders. Between 1989 and 1991, the regime of Mauritanian President Maaouya Sid'Ahmed Ould Taya deported seventy thousand blacks, detained two or three thousand others without charge, and massacred at least five hundred.

Riven by racism, Mauritania is easily bullied by its neighbors. It was drawn into an insupportable war against the Polisario in 1975 after Spain signed over part of the disputed Western Sahara. It pacified the Polisario by giving up the land, only to have Morocco furiously break off diplomatic relations. It's such a hard-luck, hardscrabble country that even the normally intrepid and inspirational *Lonely Planet* guide says, "One could almost suggest that Mauritania was *the* place to avoid." So we could understand why a person dispatched to Mauritania to write a guidebook might prefer to hang out in Marrakesh, sipping fresh orange juice in the souk. But there we were in Mauritania.

What happened to the train plan was this: We met Abdullah. He sauntered into our camp on the beach at Cap Blanc, smartly clad in stylish Western leisure wear and a blue baseball cap. He displayed a tattered notebook full of letters from satisfied clients. Abdullah was an *agent du tourisme*. Abdullah would help us—indeed he would help everyone in our encampment—to complete our "formalities" in Nouadhibou. After that, he said, he would put us on the train that very day. He himself, Abdullah, had reserved already one flatcar for his clients, and he could guarantee us a place no problem.

So we trotted after Abdullah to the police and customs and the insurance office—we were required to buy insurance for the vehicle, which was, of course, already insured—and then to the bank, where we exchanged a modest number of French francs for thousands upon thousands of bright blue paper *ouguiyas*. As to the train. "One minute," Abdullah said. "Sit down please." One minute became several. The periods of sitting became several. The periods of sitting grew longer. But at last, true to his word, Abdullah led us to the railroad office, a shabby shack on the outskirts of town. This was not a real railroad station, for the train from Nouadhibou to Choum was not a real passenger train. It was merely the goods train that intermittently ran down from Zouérat carrying iron ore—practically the sole resource of Mauritania—and ran back empty. Abdullah addressed the station agent, a somnolent fellow behind a big desk, who seemed not to hear him. Meanwhile Muggleton parleyed with a group of gaunt overlanders who sat beside half a dozen Land Rovers and as many cars lined up next to the railroad track. The overlanders had arrived in convoy in Nouadhibou last Tuesday, or last Friday, or a week ago Tuesday, and they had waited at this spot for three days or seven or ten for the place on the train promised for sure no doubt without fail no problem tomorrow by Abdullah.

That's when we drove back into town, and—just as we were sitting now in the Land Rover on the edge of the sandy void—we sat in the Land Rover in the inhospitable streets of Nouadhibou, surrounded by persistent vendors and guides and beggars tapping at the windows, and discussed what to do. There was rumored to be a road to Choum and beyond to Atar, connecting to the main road—an actual red highway on the Michelin map—to Nouakchott. But the alleged road to Choum lay east across the Sahara through shifting dunes, its existence unconfirmed by any map. Local guides warned us against it. One of their friends and the group of French travelers he was guiding had been killed not long before when they'd driven off the inner knife edge of a big barchan, a crescent-shaped dune on the move. The other route, the direct route to Nouakchott, lay to the south along the coast, about three days' drive. But in that direction there definitely was no road at all, only miles and miles of flat, rocky desert over which the wind blew ceaselessly and treacherous sand dunes slumped. This was the route the guides preferred, presumably because none of their friends had perished there in recent weeks. They'd attached themselves to us in Nouadhibou, self-important in their flowing blue robes and white turbans, their dog-eared portfolios crammed with the testimonials of desperate travelers. " 'Mohammed is a splendid fellow.' Desmond Hobbit, Manchester." " 'Ahmed is good guide and English speak.' Kurt Futter, Mannheim." The guides warned us of the dangers that lay before us in the Sahara, and one by one our cronies from the convoy succumbed. They paid forty American dollars per vehicle to travel south in groups of five or six vehicles, each group under the leadership of one of these genuine portfolioed guides. But Muggleton, being an independent fellow, was reluctant to be guided anywhere by anyone. And being by nature frugal, he certainly didn't want to pay for the indignity. He reasoned like this: "All you do is drive south along the coast, and after a few days you muddle in to Nouakchott. How hard can it be?" Muggleton wanted to go it alone.

We had no bearings for Nouakchott, no proper map. There was no road, perhaps not even a track, across the 535 kilometers of hardscrabble and sand that lay between us and the southern edge of the Sahara. Across the plain, we had been told, enormous sand dunes the color of apricots crept relentlessly toward the sea. And there were land mines lurking who knew where to blow up the occasional mad traveler. All the books said things like "Do not venture into the desert alone" and "In no case travel without a guide." Yet there was Muggleton, my colleague, brash and confident as only the privileged or the truly lucky can be, draining a Coke that miraculously was actually cold, and saying, "We can do this on our own."

He was a formidable driver, massaging the Land Rover—his baby—like a second skin, while I still tried to drive it like a car. He was a wizard with the engine. He was big. He was strong. We had sand ladders and jacks and shovels and spare parts. We had gas and more than enough water to last us a week if we used it sparingly. Would I bet my life on Muggleton's ability to cross the desert? The answer was yes.

That's how we came to be sitting there now, outside the spiked gates of Nouadhibou, rudderless, without a guide, with the Western Sahara spread before us. Muggleton turned the key, and the Land Rover moved out across the sand. We drove only a few miles from town and pulled in behind a rocky outcrop for the night. We slept on the roof under a brilliant sky, but the wind blew cold and strong. In the morning our tracks had been erased. The peace of the dunes was perfect. The silence. The fresh-blown sand making the landscape new. "I could stay here for days," I said to Muggleton.

"No, you couldn't," he said.

We searched out the trail of a pickup truck that had passed nearby and followed its tracks. We were still heading north on the Nouadhibou peninsula, and our first navigational problem was to get around the top of the bay and onto our proper course, due south along the mainland coast. All at once the truck tracks dropped off the edge of the rocky flats onto the broad tidal beach, and Muggleton followed.

"These locals know a shortcut around the bay," he said confidently.

"These locals are going fishing," I said, uneasy. But he had made up his mind.

"They're not fishermen," he said.

"You don't know," I said. "How can you possibly say that?"

"They didn't bloody well look like bloody fishermen."

"Have you ever actually seen a Mauritanian fisherman?" I said. Muggleton was forever making decisions on the basis of information he had manufactured himself. "Have you ever actually seen the people we're following?"

Muggleton swung wide to avoid one of the deep pools of water lacing the tidal beach, and all at once the vehicle lurched left and died. I scrambled out to take a look. The front wheels were submerged to the hubs in a slough of sucking clay; the back left wheel was buried. Water oozed from the wet sand, and tiny bubbles rose from somewhere far below to break at the surface with a flat pocking sound. The Land Rover began to sink.

Muggleton emptied weight from the vehicle, rushing back and forth to firmer ground with loads of jerry cans and duffel bags. I dug out the jack and the shovels, and while he unbolted the reluctant sand ladders from the roof rack, I scraped sand out of the exhaust pipe with my hand. We shoveled. We placed sand ladders. We got one wheel free while another dug in deeper. Muggleton was confident. Getting out was just a matter of planning and time, he said. But just beyond us, at the edge of the tidal flat, the sea was rising. A wall of water hung on the horizon, threatening at any moment to wash us away. Silently I put in one of my infrequent, always urgent, requests to the Great Goddess, and she answered with a miracle: seven Moors in a pickup truck. They got out, wrapping their robes about them in the wind. They clucked and *ahem*med, wagging their fingers at us to show that the track lay through the pool Muggleton had tried to avoid, and not around it. Then they pitched in, placed the sand ladders under the front wheels, and pushed as Muggleton reversed out of the hole. The vehicle rose again from the slough. We thanked our helpers and explained to them sadly, when pressed, that despite the profound and everlasting debt their generous humanitarian services had placed upon us, we could not possibly give them our tires. No, not even one. Then we loaded up our jerry cans and headed for higher ground.

Muggleton was chagrined, not because he'd made a mistake, but because he'd been rescued by a bunch of guys in long dresses. "I could have freed the vehicle myself in a minute or two," he said. I could see him fretting inwardly, but after that we took the overland route. There were plenty of tracks across the sand, all heading in roughly the same direction. We drove north, circled the bay, and turned south, hoping to stumble upon a well-traveled route. Instead we stumbled upon a group of six vehicles from the convoy, led by a Moorish guide. The vehicles were standing together, the drivers taking the lay of the land. We stopped to exchange a few words, but the guide drew himself up and ordered us to drive on immediately. He himself would not go forward, he announced to his clients, until we had departed. "They do not pay," he said tersely. "They do not follow Ahmed, *guide du Sahara*." We laughed, but he was deadly serious. "Today they are getting lost in trackless desert," Ahmed went on, rumbling like an oracle.

"Trackless?" Muggleton puzzled. "There are tracks everywhere."

Ahmed shook his fist. "Today you die!" he said. I was prepared to be impressed by this prediction, but not Muggleton.

"Cheerio!" he sang out to our friends. "See you in Nouakchott."

"Cheerio?" I said to Muggleton. *"Cheerio?"*

We set a course to the southeast, but after a few miles we bottomed out in heavy sand. "Sand ladders!" Muggleton snapped, automatically giving orders, but neither of us moved. No doubt he was thinking, as I was, of our pretty blue sand ladders: of how much we needed them and how frequently, of how very much they weighed and how murderous they were to move. In front of us stood a ridge, and beyond it the vast expanse of vehicle-eating sand, but as we gazed in silence at this appalling landscape there suddenly appeared before us, topping the ridge from the other side, two German men from the convoy. They were carrying a sand ladder—a sensible modern sand ladder of the lightweight aluminum perfectly manageable kind.

"Right here, mates!" Muggleton called. "Good man!" The two men pushed and hauled, and soon we were out of the sand and rolling again without ever having stepped out of our vehicle. Muggleton was beside himself with glee. "Am I lucky or what?" he crowed. We dropped over the ridge and came upon the rest of the German group from the convoy digging themselves out of heavy sand. "You go," one of the Germans said when we stopped to help. "The guide," he said, indicating a Moor who stood apart, glowering at us. "He will not go because you not paid. First you must go. He say very big sand mountains ahead. He say you will get lost."

Muggleton sailed off again, delighted at the prospect. "Cheerio, Manfred. Good man. Cheerio, Heinz." For the next three days, Muggleton worked with the vehicle against the sand. I could see him calculating his line, the lay of the land, the slant of the sun, the distance from one patch of firm ground to the next, the precise moment to shift and grind and slam the gears home. The Land Rover pounded over the rocks and strained through deep seas of sand, the engine churning, the temperature gauges ratcheting into the red. Around us, in the heat of the white sun, pink dunes shimmered like clouds just above the horizon. Inside the Land Rover, the heat of the engine slowly cooked the oranges we'd brought to quench our thirst.

We'd taken GPS readings as we left Nouadhibou and periodically along the way, just in case we had to turn back. But we had no coordinates for our destination: Nouakchott. So we followed the sun and fresh vehicle tracks where we could find them. We charted a compass course to the southeast and stopped from time to time to take a reading in case the tracks disappeared. But they didn't disappear. Instead they merged to form a track so well worn in places that it seemed paved. Tracks swung off to the left or off to the right for short distances and then converged again upon the main route. We imagined we could hear the sharp voices of the guides behind us, barking orders to drivers who fancied they'd be lost without them: *"À droite! À gauche ici! Faites attention! À droite!"* But we kept as best we could to the straight and narrow, and when the tracks disappeared altogether we drove on into the sun. On our right hand, we knew, lay the ocean, and we came to it at last, to make a highway of sorts of the white sand beach between the slouching dunes and a sea that glinted like silver foil. For a hundred kilometers great schools of dolphins and the long graceful boats of black fishermen ran beside us as Muggleton rode the fine hard line at the edge of the rising tide, always looking ahead for the moment when the beach might go under.

All the while I sat beside him, peeling hot oranges, passing the Sidi Ali bottle of hot water that tasted of chemicals. I assumed these simple supportive tasks because Muggleton had claimed the challenge of driving as entirely his own—his masculine duty and privilege. Hadn't we seen in convoy camp that driving is a guy thing? Men traveling in pairs or groups shared the driving and the camp chores as well, but a man traveling with his girlfriend did all the driving himself and then lounged about camp with other men, talking about tire pressures and bushings, while his girlfriend set up tents, did laundry, cooked meals. There were only a handful of these girlfriends and wives among the overlanders, all working hard to earn their keep. Muggleton was the oddity in camp: a man traveling with a woman who nevertheless set up his own tent, did his own laundry, and often cooked. What kind of a wuss was he? You could see the men wondering about him, feeling sorry for him, poor bastard. But the thing that distinguished real men was this: they drove. So when we set off into the sand, waving cheerio, it was Muggleton behind the wheel. Alone in the middle of the Sahara, where nobody else in the world could see, it was Muggleton who drove. I leaned out the window for a glimpse of the tires. Did they need more air for this rocky stretch? Should they be let down for the sand wallow ahead? I watched Muggleton's hand on the steering wheel and on the gearshift, the clench and release, the tension again. I watched the dunes rise, casting us adrift in a sea of sand, and then ebb away until nothing lay around us but the great flat bleached emptiness of rock. I searched the horizon for animals and people that were not there. Once, when we came upon a few black fishermen and their families huddling in makeshift lean-tos on the shore, a skinny young girl offered to give me her baby sister. The child's head was scabrous, her gaze filled with confusion. After that I looked out on the bare land with some feeling akin to grief.

At day's end we'd draw the Land Rover behind a dune for shelter and prepare some slim waterless meal—tomatoes and tinned sardines and bread as dry as dust. Muggleton sheltered in the vehicle or under it, and I lay on the roof while the persistent wind slowly covered us in sand as fine as the air. It crept into our sleeping bags and worked its way between our toes. It silted up our ears. It seeped into our mouths when we spoke and grated between our teeth. It gathered in our eyes and made us weep. From behind the long slope of the dune the full moon rose like a coppery bangle, a bit of juju that a proud woman might wear in the middle of her forehead. It lit the desert and drew on the tide.

On the third day, as Muggleton coaxed the Land Rover along the shore, the sea swept in to stop us. We turned inland and waited for hours amid the dunes until the tide turned. Then we sped along a broadening beach to the capital. The dangerous verge between land and water was marked by skeletal vehicles trapped by the tide and sailing ships cast inland by the waves. But flights of seabirds—terns and gulls and cormorants and great white pelicans—whirled before us like celebratory confetti.

"How will we know when we get to Nouakchott?" I wondered aloud. The city, we knew, lay several kilometers inland from the endless beach.

"If we cross a river we're in Senegal," Muggleton said, racing over the sand.

But just then we were given a sign—a European jogger on the beach. We pulled up, stripped off our grimy clothes, and plunged, *yahoo*ing, into the surf. We hung the solar shower from the top of the Land Rover and used the last of our fresh water for a shower and shampoo. We donned our other clothes—the clean ones—and then, all fresh and tidy, we turned inland to the capital, some 535 seat-of-the-pants kilometers from Nouadhibou. We found a place in the public campground, where our companions from the convoy would appear in the following days, gaunt and exhausted. Hastily, before falling into their tents, they would pen testimonials for their proud desert guides.

After we put up our tents, we went into Nouakchott in search of a proper meal. The capital of Mauritania is a new one, specially built in the 1960s with the spaciousness befitting a national capital. It seems an ordinary Arab town that giants have laid hold of at the edges and stretched in all directions. The streets are broad, the buildings newish-looking and white, the lights fluorescent and colorful. There are handsome walled villas awash in bougainvillea for the diplomatic contingent, and tidy shops; but it has the look and feel of a city abandoned, or about to be. What gives the place that eerie feeling is the sand. Nouakchott was built far, far away from the desert. Now the desert laps at the city's doorsteps. The sand piles up against the houses and spills in at the windows. It blocks alleyways and raises roadblocks in the middle of boulevards. It moves about town, whisked by the wind, like a messenger hurrying from the Avenue du Général de Gaulle to the Avenue Abdel Nasser, from the Avenue Boubacar Ben Amer to the Avenue Bourguiba. It announces: the desert is coming.

Muggleton ordered up a whole roast chicken at El Frisco Snack on Avenue Kennedy and washed it down with a gallon of lukewarm Coke, feeling well pleased with himself and the vehicle and our passage through the Sahara. He'd planned the journey well. He'd driven it well. In the next few days he would joke with other overland drivers, as they drifted into the campground, about the guides who had *followed* him. It's true that he'd had a sleepless night in the desert when our starter motor failed one evening, but he'd pulled out his maintenance book and fixed it good as new in the morning. We hadn't gotten lost or broken down irretrievably or been hopelessly mired in sand. We hadn't been blown to bits, though we had inadvertently passed through a minefield. We hadn't perished of heat or sunstroke or been eaten by the wild dogs and jackals that circled our camp at night. We'd had gas and food to spare and enough water to take a shower. Muggleton had brought himself and me across the Sahara by using his wits, his strength, and his skill.

I, on the other hand, had been merely a passenger, buffeted from there to here across an emptiness that left me aching—smaller than I'd been at the start, and insignificant. I had crossed the western Sahara chiefly by an act of faith in my friend. The desert crossing might have been a spiritual experience, a shared passage to bring us closer, to seal our friendship and respect. We might have thrown our money belts to the wind and run hand in hand naked through the sand. We might have made passionate love under the desert moon and sworn fidelity to the ends of the earth, or at least as far as Nairobi. But in fact we had fought bitterly, perhaps because of the anxiety, the fear of everything that might go wrong, and our common discovery that in Muggleton's macho adventure I was inessential. Left to my own devices, I might have made an easier journey, in company with friends, in company with a genuine portfolioed Mauritanian *guide du Sahara,* who might have taught me things about his country. Left to himself, Muggleton would have fallen into more holes, climbed more dunes, overcome more nearly insurmountable difficulties, brushed more closely the sleeve of death, and survived just barely, alone, to tell the tale.

As it was, we sat on the terrace at El Frisco Snack and chatted amiably, restoring an equilibrium of sorts, celebrating what Muggleton generously referred to as what "we" had accomplished. Earlier, playing with the computer, he'd discovered that we'd had a GPS reading— longitude and latitude—for Nouakchott all along. Trimble and Magellan could have guided us exactly to our destination. "Isn't that the way of things," Muggleton said. He shrugged. He'd taken to making such observations about the way of things ever since he'd changed his profession to *philosophe.* "It's just as well," he said. "It might have taken the fun out of it to know where we were going. And things have turned out rather nicely after all."

"Yes," I said. "I suppose they have."

I looked out over the broad avenue where men in blue robes were strolling arm in arm, slowly, going nowhere in particular. Among them passed a few women wrapped to the eyebrows in black cloth. Invisible as shadows, they scurried on necessary errands. Soon it would be dark, and then the streets and public spaces would belong fully to men. Among educated urban classes in the great cities of Morocco— Rabat, Casablanca, Marrakesh—I had seen the changing lives of men and women in their clothes, their occupations, their presence. But here in the new streets of Nouakchott I could see only an old, old way of life. And no African queens. *Plus ça change, plus c'est la même chose.* Muggleton was talking and laughing, reliving some triumphant moment behind the wheel. A tiny black woman approached our table, bent double with a baby wrapped in rags upon her back. She smiled at me and held up a basket half full of peanuts, some of them already wrapped in little paper cones. I took her hand and pressed into it all the pretty blue money I had.

THE ROAD TO BAMAKO

Our expedition was proceeding like hopscotch, by a series of leaps: from England to the Continent, from Europe to Africa, from one edge of the Sahara to another. Our next leap, over the Senegal River, would carry us into sub-Saharan Africa—black Africa. There the rhythms would change, and the spirit, though beyond the simple appearance of things, it would be hard to say just how. Still, all travelers feel it—that great divide between Africa above the Sahara and Africa below. The rhythm of our expedition would change too, I thought, now that we had hurdled the Sahara. We'd take things easy. Take things in.

But first we had to escape from Mauritania, land of the *cadeaux* cops. We drove south from Nouakchott toward the border, stopped sixteen times along the way by policemen seeking some small tribute to their fine public service. Muggleton's classy shades, perhaps? Or his watch? You could hardly blame these petty officers of the state for their free-lance hustling. Who knew when they'd last been paid? Or how much? But by the time we'd run the gauntlet and reached the ferry landing at the river, the sun was sinking and the gate was closed. *"Fermé!* Finished. Gone today. Come back *demain. Mañana."* The uniformed guard was adamant. Talking our way through police posts, we'd missed the last ferry to Senegal. I pleaded, but *demain* it must be. Unless, of course, madame would pay six hundred French francs, in which case a special ferry could with some difficulty be arranged. I laughed. Madame would do no such thing. I got back in the vehicle, and Muggleton slammed it into reverse. He'd drive to the bridge, he said. Suddenly the guard threw open the iron gate and waved us on. A small mistake. There was indeed a ferry leaving in five minutes. Even now it was loading. Hurry! Hurry!

The guard rushed me to a tiny office in a long tumbledown building on the wharf. Passports were examined and stamped. He rushed me to a second office. The vehicle carnet was examined and stamped. He seized my arm and hurried me to a third office, tinier and dingier than the others. The door closed behind me. I was surrounded by uniforms. Mauritania's finest.

"Two hundred French francs, madame, if you please," the guard said. That was more than $40.

"Two hundred francs!" I said. "It's only a hundred yards across the river. I could swim."

"Two hundred francs," the guard said. The ticket agent, a lean toothless fellow in blue robes, fingered two slips of pink paper, then started to replace them in his desk. The real price was plainly written on the tickets: twelve hundred *ouguiyas*—$8. "The boat, madame. The boat is go."

I handed over the money, snatched the tickets, and sprinted to the Land Rover. Muggleton drove onboard just as the lines were cast off. He stared when I told him what I'd paid for our liberation from Mauritania. "Cheer up," I said. "You've still got your shades and your watch. It's only money."

Across the river everything changed. In Mauritania red dunes drifted over the road and the air was filled with dust. In Senegal, plots of vegetables grew beside the river, tended by women, and the air was resplendent with birds. In Mauritania, among the dunes, the tattered white tents of nomads leaned into the wind. In Senegal, square mud-brick huts with elaborately thatched and tasseled roofs stood shoulder to shoulder in compounds neatly fenced by reeds. In Mauritania the men were glorious—brown-faced Moors cloaked in voluminous boubous the color of morning glories—while the tiny women, muffled to the eyebrows in black, were scarcely visible. In Senegal, tall lean black men, who once must have worn exotic garb, had repackaged themselves in nondescript Western tee shirts and trousers while women wore the plumage: layers of bright cotton prints with matching cloths fancily wrapped and knotted about their heads. As we drove south, there were horse-drawn calèches in the road, loaded with fresh watermelons, and files of gentle white long-horned cattle in the dun-colored grass.

Muggleton drove on apace. He burned up the road. Gradually it came to me that during his macho conquest of the desert, he'd become something of what the British call a petrol head. Perhaps he'd inhaled too many fumes. Perhaps he'd spent too much time comparing fuel-consumption records and tire pressures with other overlanders. Perhaps during all that time flat on his back under the vehicle—tuning, prodding, adjusting, testing—perhaps small bits of petrochemical grit had worked their way into his central nervous system. Whatever the explanation, no sooner had we crossed the Senegal River than Muggleton's attention focused on the next great motoring obstacle in our path: the rain forests of Congo—still known at the time as Zaire and still thousands of kilometers ahead. To get there, we needed more parts and supplies, he figured, so we headed southwest from the river toward the sea and the capital, Dakar.

As daylight waned we made camp under some trees in a field of golden grass near the edge of the Parc National des Oiseaux du Djoudj, in the delta of the Senegal River. The famous park is the largest sanctuary for migratory birds in West Africa, and one of the most important bird sanctuaries in the world. That made it, for me, something to see. As I assembled dinner Muggleton pored over the map. He studied routes and distances and rainfall charts. He announced selected relevant statistics in the voice of the BBC presenter who reads out the world soccer scores. And he began to speak of Zaire as if it lay just ahead when in fact whole countries stood in between: Mali, Côte d'Ivoire, Ghana, Togo, Benin, Nigeria, Cameroon, the Central African Republic. All these countries, as well as Senegal—where, in the gathering dusk, great white pelicans were settling into the marsh and frogs were commencing a rhythmic chant—seemed to Muggleton mere obstacles to be got through as swiftly as potholes and police checkpoints would permit. In the morning I took the wheel and drove deeper into the Djoudj to gape at lagoons aglow with the pink plumage of flamingos and white flights of pelicans. Muggleton grumbled. A captive bird-watcher, he studied the pelicans' dazzling capacity for acrobatic flight, which reminded him of certain British fighter planes that routinely performed far beyond the capabilities of any airplane ever produced by the bloody Yanks. Then Muggleton seized the wheel again and drove on, pushing for Zaire.

The road lay along the south bank of the river, and as it curved southward a bridge came into view—an immense iron structure spanning the Senegal and leading to what appeared to be an old French provincial town on an island in midstream. For a moment it seemed that the Île de la Cité had drifted down the Seine and come to rest in another river. Even Muggleton was enthralled by the prospect, as so many European adventurers of the past were when, in search of the real Africa, they came upon a little trumped-up replica of Europe. "Bloody marvelous," he said, and swung the Land Rover onto the bridge.

It was the Pont de Faidherbe, a venerable cast-iron fabrication that spanned the Danube until the French bought it and reassembled it here to attach to the mainland what they called the Île de Saint-Louis. On this strategic island, protected from the sea by a coastal sandbar, the French established their first headquarters in West Africa. They built a fort at Saint-Louis in 1659 and began to trade in valuable local commodities, such as gum arabic—once essential to the textile and printing industries—and slaves. The ready marketplace there at the mouth of the river must have energized the assault upon the people and the *Acacia senegalensis* trees upstream. Trade flourished. By 1854, when the French dispatched the first governor of Senegal to Saint-Louis, the trading post had become a settlement of several thousand people, many of mixed race. The new governor was General Louis Faidherbe, a veteran of French military campaigns against Islamic leaders in Algeria. At the end of the century, when the French erected their secondhand bridge, they named it in his honor, for Faidherbe is the man historians generally credit with transforming a few trading posts and a military base into a powerful French colony, the showpiece of a great swath of West Africa that came to be known, by the time the bridge went up, as Afrique Occidentale Française—French West Africa. It was Faidherbe who dreamed of plundering the riches of a new India, or a *"Californie africaine,"* on the banks of the Niger River, to the east. Preparing for empire, he founded the modern city of Dakar and the Bank of Senegal and launched in the interior a half century of military conquest and destruction aimed not just at subjugating Africans but at transforming them into little Frenchmen, loyal to the *tricolore*. Having lost their land and their freedom and been impressed into what the French called "compulsory labor," African residents of the commune of Saint-Louis had the honor of being considered citizens of France.

We parked at the end of the bridge and wandered back into the nineteenth century—past the Cathédrale and the Palais de Justice, past the

Hôtel de la Poste and the Hôtel Palais, along the Rue du Général de Gaulle and the Rue de France to the Place Faidherbe, where the great man himself fixed a bronze gaze on the vacant square. In the midday heat the streets were nearly deserted, and the crumbling old buildings were shuttered against the sun. At a sidewalk cafe just off the Rue de l'Église, two young men in flashy shirts and Rasta locks sat under an umbrella, drinking coffee and making music. One sang while the other drummed with his hands on the table. "Hey, mon," one of them called to us in Jamaican-inflected English. "You dig the music, mon?" We joined them and soon we were all singing, drumming, beating out counter-rhythms on the china cups with coffee spoons, winging riffs on imaginary horns. The drumming was African. The tunes were Bob Marley, Baaba Maal, Salif Keïta, Youssou N'Dour.

Louis Faidherbe and the military governors who followed him established schools to teach the sons of chiefs and other African notables about their motherland, France, and offered them the privilege of serving in the Tirailleurs Sénégalais, an elite corps of "native infantry" who donned fancy white turbans, baggy blue pants, and red belts and sallied forth under the French flag to kill other Africans whose homes lay farther east. The Tirailleurs—"Sharpshooters"—provided the firepower for the conquest of the West African interior. Other European colonizers were afraid to put guns into the hands of Africans who might so easily turn them on their oppressors, but the French recognized the value of manpower. Especially after 1870–71, when they were outnumbered and humiliated in the Franco-Prussian War, the French extended military "privileges" to all their male African "citizens" and subjects. They flattered, persuaded, coerced, pressed, and enslaved Africans, and filled their minds with dreams of Paris. The payoff came in the First World War, when more than a hundred thousand Senegalese soldiers served in the trenches of the wintry motherland, and tens of thousands died there, fighting for the freedom of Europeans. They fought in even greater numbers in the Second World War, and when some protested on their return to Senegal that they hadn't been paid, their French comrades opened fire on them. Many were killed. In ages past, young Senegalese like our new Rasta friends died in battle, or under the guns of their French comrades, on the Upper Niger or the Somme, but now their heads were filled with other cultures, other dreams, and with music of their own. These guys wanted to get a gig in Dakar. They had no time for Louis Faidherbe. Their hero was Youssou N'Dour.

Soon we raced on to Dakar, ourselves. It's one of the great cities of the world and West Africa's most cosmopolitan capital, an elegant place of broad boulevards and public squares and grand corniches fronting the sea, all the more alluring for having aged and frayed and grown a bit seedy and dangerous. It's famous for its nightlife, its French-influenced cuisine, its hot clubs where some of the best musicians on the continent play some of the best pop music in the world. It's a place to linger and enjoy. But we raced out again, once we'd acquired a few essential auto parts, for Muggleton was in a hurry now, propelled by his own dreams of conquest. We raced along rural highways and sped through villages, tooting rudely at resplendent Senegalese women who walked in the road. Sometimes we saw markets crowded with vendors and customers who'd come from miles away, but we couldn't stop. No. We were racing for Zaire.

It dawned on me as I saw in the rearview mirror yet another beautiful watermelon vendor swallowed in the dust behind us that our expedition was split down the middle as surely as if the Senegal River ran straight through the center of the Land Rover, separating Muggleton from Jones just as it separated north from south, pastoralist from farmer, Moor from Wolof. For me the journey had ceased to be a foolhardy adventure and become a sort of quest—not merely for Loveduland, but for Africa. I yearned for the slow pace of African village life, not the forced march of the European barging through the land with conquest in mind. Of course, I wanted to reach Loveduland and see the Queen. Being an aging female, how could I help but be drawn to a community that values aging females, submits to the power of an aging female ruler, recognizes her experience and wisdom, and chooses to be guided by her? What could be more natural? But more than that, I wanted to learn from the Africa we were passing through. Today. Now. That would have meant wandering in the streets, lingering in the markets, falling into conversations, and for that Muggleton had no time. Being a young man, he hoped to find himself in adventures that could not come fast enough. He was always throwing his heart before him, someplace down the road.

Ruefully I stared out the window at the people around me, imagining lives lived. It was fine to see that despite the legacy of Louis Faidherbe, Africa was Africa still. At early light women filled the roadsides, flagging bush taxis or going on foot. They carried baskets or snazzy new plastic buckets or basins of purple, green, blue. The women stood in fine bright clusters, talking together in the villages and along the road. By midmorning they'd taken their posts in the market. They sat on bits of matting or paper in the dust, legs thrust out before them, and arranged their merchandise in tidy piles: a stack of green mandarins, a mound of red and green chilies, a spray of yellow bananas. Patiently they stuffed groundnuts into tiny plastic bags to be sold for a few cents. Whenever we stopped in a village, just long enough for me to shop for food, I was surrounded by beautiful women, many of them mere girls, each with a basket or basin of items for sale: kola nuts, bananas, mandarins, yellow apples, tiny bags of groundnuts, perfectly hard-boiled eggs, crusty baguettes fetched from a bakery in a larger town. Always one woman took charge. She was somehow distinguished from the others—taller, more beautiful, stronger, more carefully turned out in a yellow scarf or a head cloth of bright magenta. She let me know that her eggs were best, and by dragging her friends forward, she told me whose bread I must buy and whose tomatoes. The others muttered protests and shyly pushed their baskets toward me, but they knew it was no good. This woman had caught madame's eye and would sell madame more than madame wanted for more than madame meant to pay, and she'd see to it that there was a little money in it for each of her friends. It wouldn't do to quarrel. Besides, they were proud of her.

At midday, when the heat was most intense and the light enervating, the villages were quiet. Pans and basins from the market and from the midday meal of dried fish and rice had been washed and upended to dry in the sunshine. A woman swathed in a purple cloth emerged from a dooryard to cast away one more basin of water. Perhaps she'd had a wash. In each hut, I imagined, people lay about in sleep or desultory conversation, the arm of a dozing child flung across her mother's legs. Midday was a moment of perfect stillness, broken only by the steady whine of our sleepless vehicle.

By late afternoon, when it was my turn to drive, the roads were alive again with women selling things, and men too, returning by bush taxi from work or visiting, or driving their horse carts toward the village, loaded with big red drums of water or piles of straw or groundnuts or watermelons. They beat their bony horses into a trot and clattered along. Tall men in robes of white and brilliant turquoise drove cattle across the road to new pasture, calling out thanks when I stopped the vehicle to let them pass and to watch the slow-moving placid creatures on their way. In every village, men sat together talking, watching the passersby. They smiled and waved at us. A flash of white teeth in a black face, an offer of friendliness, an invitation, a welcome. But Muggleton took the wheel again and we sped away, bound for Zaire. I looked back at villages where melons grew over the roof thatch and at golden fields where pale cattle were grazing, and I thought I could see the beauty of life lived. There are those who are living, I thought, and those who are rushing on.

Muggleton made tracks. He revved the engine and flew over the corrugations in the road, utterly focused on impending potholes and the way around them. I, on the other hand, whenever my turn came to take the wheel, found myself distracted by the moment—by the sight of a lovely woman in a yellow robe, a brilliant turquoise bird overhead, or fuchsia flowers blooming beside the road. Without a thought I arrived at precisely the right speed to hit every fold in the roadbed and set the Land Rover shaking. I dove with the unerring accuracy of a kamikaze pilot into every deep pothole. Trying to remain calm, Muggleton chewed the ends off his fingers, one by one. It wasn't that he never hit potholes himself, but as he so often explained to me, he hit only those that were "unavoidable," while I hit bloody potholes that could easily have been circumvented by any bloody driver of rudimentary skill. But as he urged me always to greater speed my driving transcended mere fecklessness and became a kind of diabolical gift. I knew I'd have to answer for it. Dreamily I pictured Muggleton in another life, dressed in the golden coverall and crash helmet with attached halo of the truly skilled and speedy driver. "How many potholes did you hit on the Dakhla Road?" he'd ask rhetorically, having the exact number inscribed on a steel plate from the engine housing. "How many on the road to Dakar?" On that day of reckoning, I thought, I wouldn't have an advocate or a prayer.

The day came when we reached Kidira on the eastern border of Senegal and crossed over the Senegal River again into Mali, once known as the colony of French Soudan and now an independent and impoverished country. There the corrugated Senegalese road dissolved in a cloud of dust and Muggleton decisively took the wheel. For the next week he remained in the driver's seat, presiding with clenched teeth over the swift sad shaking of the vehicle. He drove through rocky fields and endless waves of grass towering above the car, following rough tracks that meandered upstream along the headwaters of the river. It was tricky because, although the track had two ruts like any country road, the grass between the ruts was so tall that Muggleton could see only the rut on the driver's side. I watched the rut on the passenger side and sang out when it was blocked by rocks or holes. Driving became a cooperative effort, like playing "Chopsticks" on a piano. On good stretches we could make thirty or forty kilometers an hour, but often we had to slow down to traverse the rocky riverbed or cross ditches or scout the indecipherable track ahead. Each morning we were awakened before first light by a great cacophony of birds, but by nine o'clock the sun would be high and hot, the sky a bleached white, and the birds still. Only the ground birds—francolins and guinea fowl—spilled into the track before us, driven by fires exploding spontaneously in the bush.

"Do you think this is the real Africa?" I asked in a feeble attempt at humor. But Muggleton didn't laugh.

"I think so," he said. "It bloody well feels like bloody real Africa."

Everywhere people came running, materializing out of the grass to wave and smile and call out cheerily, *"Ça va? Ça va?"* They were friendly, warm, welcoming. They turned their bright faces to us, bemused and always on the edge of laughter, as if our presence was some hilarious joke, as I suppose it was. We came upon tiny villages, mere clusters of round huts woven of reeds like big wicker baskets and plastered over with red mud. Women hurried out, holding aloft their new babies, eager to present them to us. The babies gaped at our hideously white and monstrous faces and burst into stricken howling while the women laughed and laughed. The older children hung back behind the women's legs, quiet and watchful, taking things in. Then we'd be under way again, and they'd wave us on like passing dignitaries. A regal procession. White ghosts passing in the black bush.

Our destination was Bamako. It's a city of three quarters of a million people. It's the biggest city in Mali, which in turn is the biggest country in West Africa, encompassing an area three times the size of California, five times the size of the United Kingdom. Bamako is the nation's capital. An important place. A hundred and fifty years ago, it was the city of Louis Faidherbe's dreams. His grand plan was to build a string of forts running eastward along the Senegal River, eliminating opposition as he went along, then cross the watershed to the Niger River, take Bamako, and use it as a base from which to advance by river on Segu and Timbuktu. Faidherbe never got to Bamako, but his successor Lieutenant-Colonel Gustave Borgnis-Desbordes finally reached the Niger in 1883. He planted the *tricolore* at Bamako, then a Bambara village of perhaps a hundred grass huts. Two or three hundred Bambara came out to watch. Try as I may, I can't imagine what they must have made of the proceedings. Two companies of white French infantry and a host of black Tirailleurs donned their full-dress uniforms for the occasion. Borgnis-Desbordes made a speech. He gave an order, and the air shook as artillery pieces fired an eleven-gun salute.

For several years there had been talk in France of building a trans-Saharan railway from the Mediterranean to Senegal. This mind-boggling idea apparently came easily to politicians in Paris, untroubled by any firsthand experience of the great desert. But Tuareg nomads who called the Sahara home scotched the plan by wiping out the military team sent to survey the line. With Borgnis-Desbordes in possession of Bamako, however, talk turned to a trans-Soudan railroad from the Senegal River to the Niger, a railroad that would open up the interior of French Soudan and facilitate "development." For two decades at the end of the nineteenth century, Paris threw money at the railroad. The governors of Senegal used the railroad survey to mask military assaults that decimated the people who stood in their path: the Tukolor empire, the Bambara, and the armies of the African nationalist Samori Ture. (The push into West Africa bears obvious resemblances to the push into the American West. Cast John Wayne in the role of Borgnis-Desbordes, and imagine the rest.) The French finally finished their railroad in 1904. At twelve hundred kilometers the line from Dakar to Bamako is still the longest railroad in West Africa. The cost in French francs was astronomical, the cost in African blood beyond all calculation. And because they had a railroad, they didn't build a road.

That's how we came to be clattering through the bush on tracks that might have been made—for all we knew—by a passel of cattle or goats. When the river cut to the southwest, we bore away to the east to climb the rocky plateau, the watershed between the Senegal and the Niger, toward Bamako. This plateau was once the heart of the Mali empire, before the French came with their railroad tracks and their Tirailleurs. Now it seemed to be a wild place, bleak and austerely beautiful. We came upon women stripped to the waist and bent over their work, tending fields of groundnuts. They looked up and laughed, astonished to see us, and gestured in the general direction of the far horizon. *"Merci!"* we called out, and pressed on. We came into a country of boulders and deep bush. The tracks we had been following disappeared altogether. We got out and walked back and forth, searching for a clue. When we stumbled upon something like a path, we got back in the vehicle and drove on. The bush closed in around us, smashing our side mirrors and scoring our snazzy blue paint job with racing stripes. Muggleton watched the last fragment fall from the side mirror on the driver's side and muttered, "It's only glass."

Day after day we did this—rattling along at ten, twenty, thirty kilometers an hour over tracks too rudimentary to be called roads. We wandered through bush and bamboo forest, forded rivers, and jounced through fields of rocks. We swam through grass as high as the windows and patches of millet heavy with heads of grain that slapped against the windshield. We watched the roof rack fall to pieces and the radiator stuff up with grass. We bent a wheel and blew a tire. The vehicle jumped and shimmied until it shook loose every screw, smashed all the potatoes in the kitchen bin, pulverized the empty Coke bottles on the floor, and reduced even Muggleton himself to the unthinkable condition of being too tired to eat.

What amazed us most was the dust. Soft, red, fine as sifted flour, it rose around us in clouds. It ascended mysteriously through the floorboards, an emanation of the road, to coat us—clothing, skin, eyes, nose, mouth—with silt as subtle as sunburn. In the course of the day we darkened to a handsome bronze. At each water crossing we immersed ourselves and vanished into pallidity. The dust coated the inside of the vehicle and the surfaces of everything it contained. Our bright duffel bags—purple, green, blue—turned a uniform shade of rust. Try to wipe the dust away, and it rose to fill our nostrils and resettle itself a little nearer than before. Try to wash it away, and it turned to mud—red and gritty—and dried down to the consistency of clay. Open a carefully sealed camera bag and find cameras and lenses coated in the stuff. Take a pull on the water bottle and feel the silt pass over your teeth. In a matter of days we were used to it. It was the way we lived. One evening I wrote a dispatch for the Internet and wondered if it would ever be read. It seemed I might just as well cram a note into a bottle and toss it into the surrounding sea of golden grass to drift toward an infinitely receding shore that we ourselves might never reach.

Our biggest problem was finding food. Moroccan markets had been heaped with gorgeous vegetables and herbs. Senegal had perfect baguettes and prolific harvests of watermelon and potatoes. Even Mauritania had El Frisco Snack. But here in Mali, food of any kind was so hard to find that I couldn't quite believe it. I kept thinking we'd come to a store or market soon, and as a result I never bought enough when I occasionally had the chance. There was little food to be had, even in the farming villages—groundnuts, millet, a pumpkin. In Tambacounda in eastern Senegal we'd bought tiny aubergines and okra and beautiful potatoes, but since then we'd seen no vegetables for sale at all. In the big town of Bafoulabé I saw a man who had a few small plum tomatoes, but he wouldn't sell them. "They are for me," he said. At Meena a woman had a cucumber, but she herself was so thin that I couldn't bring myself to ask her to sell it. What good would the money do her when there were no more cucumbers to be had? Even in big villages, store shelves were empty except for hard soap, paraffin, and sometimes a dusty tin or two of corned beef. In markets in big towns we saw dried fish parts, spices, and sometimes a few tiny chilies. They were meant to season a stew, but where was the stew? I wondered how the people lived here and how long. At Manantali we passed through a checkpoint. One of the guards examined my passport, then called his partner to read what was written there. They looked me up and down. They wanted to know: Could it possibly be true? What amazed them was my date of birth. I, a woman, had lived more than half a century. How is it possible? they asked. One of them took my hand in his and examined my palm, as if he might find the answer there. So much for the damned railroad, I thought. So much for the "development" of the interior.

In Bafoulabé I went up and down the streets asking women where I could buy meat or bread. There is no meat here, they said. No bread.

No vegetables here. You must go to Meena. We found it, a small market town six kilometers away where there were old clothes and plastic pans and basins for sale, and more paraffin and brown soap, and an actual bar serving warm Cokes and Fanta and beer. But there was little food— a few blackened bananas, a handful of tiny oranges, and at a small butcher stand under a tree, hanging from a branch, a hunk of desiccated meat, black with flies. No bread. But by then I'd learned my lesson. Despite the promise of the Meena market down the road, I'd bought what I could lay my hands on in the dingy little store at Bafoulabé. One day a woman working in a field, an old woman with long flat leathery breasts, had extended her hands offering fresh groundnuts. Now we lived on those groundnuts and Senegalese potatoes and the tinned herrings I'd bought in Bafoulabé, stamped with the label A GIFT OF THE FEDERAL REPUBLIC OF GERMANY.

To keep us going, I decided that I must tempt Muggleton with a good dinner. Boldly I walked into a cluster of mud huts where I had seen chickens scurrying to have a chat with the senior wife. She would be in charge, I knew, for all the able-bodied men had vanished— gone someplace else in search of work, I supposed, or food—and only women, children, old men, and blind people remained in these tiny villages. The head wife was a wiry woman, wrapped in a yellow cloth, roasting groundnuts in an iron kettle over a charcoal fire. I flapped my arms and clucked, doing my best chicken imitation in hopes of getting some eggs for a nice omelette. Instead, she waved a bony arm and murmured an order to the children. They erupted in hot pursuit of the poultry—in and out of huts, round the fire, over the fence and back again. Chickens squawked. Children screamed with laughter. I was presented with the slowest bird, a mottled gray scrawny creature, already beginning to shed her feathers for the pot. I gave the senior wife a thousand CFA—about $2. She broke the chicken's neck and shook my hand, sending a sharp spasm of remorse through my vegetarian heart. The whole village followed after me to see the limp bird loaded into the back of the Land Rover. Even the old blind men followed, led by little children who tugged at their canes. One of the old ones wanted madame and monsieur to know that in his youth he had served in the army of his mother country, France. He drew himself up proudly, throwing his shoulders back, and Muggleton reached out to shake his hand. Much later, after we'd made camp and I had plucked and butchered and stewed the poor hen with the last of our rice and tinned tomato paste, Muggleton looked into the pot and said without enthusiasm, "Good effort."

He ate his dinner and wrote in his notebook in a road-weary, barely legible scrawl: "Flashing greens, streaking yellows, grating roof rack, metal on metal, bumps, dust, crops, thorns, branches, broken bridges, deep rivers, steep hills. Small track, thin piste, straining vehicle. And we're still not there. This is the road to Bamako."

THE ROAD NOT TAKEN

Bananas. Grapefruit. Oranges. Lemons. Pawpaws. Aubergines. Courgettes. Green beans. Tomatoes. Peppers. Potatoes. Radishes. Onions. Scallions. Carrots. Parsley. We found them all in the teeming Dibida market, where the road to Bamako ends. Gradually the dusty track we had been following gathered itself into a real road and then cascaded in a series of switchbacks from the high plateau to the bank of the broad blue Niger River. There the road fanned out into the leafy avenues of a sleepy overgrown village. Bamako. Broad boulevards opened before us, lined with weathering pink French colonial villas set well back from the street, as if this were some garden suburb and not the nation's capital. The boulevards led into the heart of the city, and the heart of the city was filled with food: all the food we'd failed to find along the road to Bamako. Muggleton turned a corner into the market, and a new aroma filled the air. "Stop!" I shouted. "Stop! It's parsley!" And it was. Great piles of it. Honest-to-God broad-leafed Italian parsley, deliciously fragrant and beautifully, heart-stoppingly green.

Along the streets of the market, women sold fried plantains and millet cakes and bowls of rice with chili sauce and brochettes of beef cooked over charcoal braziers. Men presided over tiny portable shops—a plank and a bench long enough to seat three or four patrons—selling tea and Nescafé and café au lait made from canned condensed milk laden with sugar. With big knives they lopped hunks off crusty baguettes. On one corner stood a chicken abattoir, where squads of men worked furiously to kill, scald, pluck, gut, truss. Steam rose from a huge cauldron of boiling water, and reeking piles of wet feathers mounted up. The whole of Bamako seemed given over to the frenetic effort of feeding itself.

Where was all this food coming from? Not from the land we'd traveled through. Even in the best of times only twenty percent of the land in Mali is arable, and the country is plagued by recurrent droughts, sometimes lasting years. Then there's the French factor. The French were busy colonizers, reshaping West African economies to feed Parisian tastes and pocketbooks. They turned black Malians into cash-crop farmers, monotonously producing cotton; and where cotton is planted, food crops are not. Since Mali became independent in 1960 there'd been little to eat and little to trade. Some blamed drought. Some blamed government mismanagement. Governments in Bamako had fallen for lack of food. I had grown thin just passing through Mali, and Muggleton positively skinny, yet we found ourselves in Bamako in the midst of a perishable plenty. Folks in Bafoulabé and Meena could have used some of the vegetables piled in the overstocked markets of Bamako, but shipped over the roads we'd traveled they'd reach their destination as gazpacho. "They could easily ship food on the river," Muggleton said later, when we were admiring the skill of boatmen on the Niger handling their pirogues. But downriver to the north, beyond Timbuktu, where nomadic Tuaregs were fighting a hopeless battle for an independent state, Tuaregs were starving in refugee camps. What could we do? It shames me to say it, but we ate.

We searched for the so-called Mission Libanaise in the Rue Poincaré, a shabby refuge for overlanders. We drove through the gate to be greeted by Georges Frances, the PDG—président directeur général— of the Mission Père Frances. Portly and complacent, one of a substantial community of Lebanese businessmen in Bamako, Georges was fresh from the shower, his ample belly slung in a large pink towel. Judging by his appearance, he had never missed a meal. "Welcome to Lebanese Mission," he said, grinning. He wound up a pudgy hand to extend it for a shake. "All Europeans is my friends," he said. "You have something for me?" What he wanted was six thousand CFA—$12—the price of parking our vehicle and pitching our tents for the night on the broken concrete of the courtyard of what used to be a genuine Catholic mission before the priest, Georges's uncle Père Frances, fled to Paris and Georges went into the tourist business. Too tired to bargain, we gave him what he asked, put up our tents, and turned in.

When the muezzin's call to prayer woke me at four-fifteen in the morning, the air was chill and already thick with the smoke of thousands of tiny charcoal fires. It was still dark, but the citizens were already cooking, already eating. By six o'clock the street beyond the mission gate was abuzz with shoppers headed for market and vendors hawking food. These people seemed to shop and eat with the intensity of the condemned, for whom any meal might be the last. I threw on my clothes and hurried out into the street to get some breakfast before it was all gone.

We spent what overlanders call "a day at the beach"—which means we dragged everything out of our filthy dust-crusted vehicle and scrubbed. By day's end our gear was stowed away again, covered by only a thin veneer of red grime. While I shopped for more food and supplies, Muggleton fixed the flat and rotated the tires again and tuned the engine and tightened a row of reluctant screws to cure a problem that had begun to afflict our vehicle. We called it wheel wobble. Then we were ready to hit the road again.

I opted for a diversion north to Timbuktu. The name alone had exploded in the midst of my grim childhood like a pheasant from a dead field, feathering my imagination with fantastic images of a place more exotic, more remote, more inaccessible than any other place on earth. Recently I'd read my guidebook and adjusted my expectations downward. I knew that Timbuktu had shrunk to just another scruffy outpost on the desert frontier. Still, I yearned to see it. It stood far to the north on the northernmost bend of the Niger, just where the river humped its back into the Sahara. It owed its place in history to its place on the map.

Not long after the time of Christ, nomadic Berbers came to the Sahara with a new and miraculous technological innovation, a concept so advanced and so perfectly suited to the desert that it revolutionized transportation and trade, transformed cultures, and totally eclipsed the wheel. It was called a camel. It came originally from North America by way of Asia and the Arabian Peninsula, though where the Berbers themselves came from—those nomads, neither black nor Arab, who peopled North Africa—nobody knows. The camel could work for nine days without water, and even longer without food. It could carry a heavy load and easily cover vast distances: a thousand kilometers in ten days or twenty-five hundred kilometers in a month of steady travel, according to Lawrence of Arabia. And it required no road. Soon thousands upon thousands of these miraculous beasts were trekking out of the Sahara bearing slabs of salt, a commodity so valuable that it could be exchanged in equal measure for gold. They converged at the crook of the Niger, which flows eastward and south to empty into the Atlantic at the Bight of Benin. The trading post there at the juncture of the trans-Saharan caravan route and the greatest waterway in West Africa was Timbuktu.

For centuries African economies and cultures hung upon the trans-Saharan trade, which in turn hung squarely upon the hump of the magical camel. In the thirteenth century at Timbuktu the leader of the Malinke people, Sundiata Keita, founded the Empire of Mali, which controlled the lucrative trans-Saharan trade for more than a hundred years. In the fifteenth century, control passed to the Songhai Empire farther down the river at Gao in what is today eastern Mali. Historians say the trans-Saharan trade ceased to be important in the seventeenth century, when European sailing ships trading along African coasts eclipsed the "ships of the desert." But even in the nineteenth century, tales of the riches of Timbuktu and Gao and Segu inspired French dreams of finding a new India on the Niger. And in our own time Arabs and nomadic Tuaregs still come out of the desert with caravans of camels laden with precious salt. They still come south from the old mine at Taoudenni, eight hundred kilometers along the ancient trail, across the Sahara to Timbuktu.

All this information I'd dropped into my conversations with Muggleton over many days, planting little seeds of thought, gently, bit by bit. I'd hoped they might take root in his mind and grow into a single brightly blooming idea: "Let's go to Timbuktu." But at last, as we got ready to leave Bamako, I had to say the words myself.

"Are you bloody barmy?" he exploded. It was a rhetorical question. "Are you round the bend entirely now?" I noted the mental crop failure. So much for subtlety, I thought. He paced back and forth, waving his arms, enacting the part of a man driven to distraction by female idiocy. "Do you want to get us killed?"

"I guess you're thinking about Tuaregs," I said.

"Bloody right I'm thinking about Tuaregs. Somebody bloody well better think about Tuaregs." He wagged a finger in my face. "And don't say a bloody word about Blue Men of the Desert."

I didn't. Blue Men of the Desert is a label applied in tourist brochures, presumably because Tuareg men traditionally wear blue robes and blue or black *cheches*—ten-foot-long scarves wrapped about the head and neck and, for that dashing look, the face. Tuareg men are said to be the most highly skilled camel men in the world. Tuareg men are said to be brave warriors. (Tuareg women and children are less celebrated.) But I knew the other side of the story too. Their traditional social structure was offensive: a hierarchical arrangement based on color, with light-skinned aristocrats at the top and black slaves at the bottom. So was their chief occupation: banditry. For centuries they lived by preying upon the trans-Saharan caravans. They'd cozy up to a caravan, single out a weak victim, then do him in and take his goods. The ethic of caravans—every man for himself—made them easy pickings. During the long Saharan crossing, the Tuaregs might strike again and again. They even developed for their purposes a low-slung, long-backed modified camel, the *merani,* that had room for a saddle low down in front of the hump, a position that brought pedestrians and horsemen within easy range of the mounted Tuareg swordsman.

"You do know there's a war on," Muggleton said. "You do know that Tuaregs have been massacred up there, and in Niger too."

"So I've heard," I said. Tuaregs had been massacred by the French too, but they'd always been able to withdraw farther into the Sahara, where no one was more at home than they. Ironically, independence put an end to that. West Africa fractured along the "national" fault lines imposed by the Europeans' map, and the freewheeling Tuaregs became citizens of Niger or Algeria or Mali, some in each country, liable to be thrown back when they crossed a border for refuge. Eventually, in March 1996, the Malian Tuaregs would sign a peace treaty at Timbuktu and make a bonfire of three thousand weapons. Many would be converted from banditry to soldiering; enrolled in the Malian army, they would draw paychecks that (in theory at least) would enable them to buy food. But that resolution was months away. At the moment, the fighting was still going on.

"You do know those Blue Men of yours may take revenge on anything that moves," Muggleton went on. He was in full-throated lecture mode now, his flexible British accent funneling into the pinch-nosed nasality of the hoity-toity. The Blue Men had become *my* Blue Men, although it was actually the Tuareg women I wanted to meet. I knew it was hopeless. "And you want to drive to bloody Timbuktu and meet these bloody chaps, eh?"

"Yes, I do actually."

"Bloody tourist!" he sneered. It was his worst insult.

So we didn't take the storied and strife-torn track north to Timbuktu. Instead, we hit the road that would more expeditiously carry us to Zaire. This time it was a highway. An actual paved highway, relatively free of potholes and bordered amazingly by gravel shoulders. It carried us over the broad Niger, deep blue in the morning sun, and due south to the border of Côte d'Ivoire, where—astoundingly—it fed into an even better highway with paved shoulders, a white line down the middle, and a posted speed limit of 120 kilometers (seventy-five miles) per hour. The speed limit was irrelevant to our old Land Rover, which could barely reach eighty kilometers an hour, but a fast road can give eager minds the illusion of velocity. "This is more like it," Muggleton said. "We can make up for lost time." He relinquished the wheel to me and lounged in the passenger seat—insofar as lounging is possible in a 1980 Land Rover—eating red licorice. He'd brought a big bag of the twisty sticks from England. He had that hell-bent-for-Zaire look in his eye again. "Parnelli Jones!" he said to me approvingly as the Land Rover began to shudder and I eased off a little on the gas. He gave me a big grin. He was happy.

My imagination drifted north—back over the river, over the desert—while I drove steadily south, strapped in this sky-blue and creamy capsule like an astronaut in unrelenting orbit. Beside me, also strapped down, sat my constant companion, sucking a red licorice stick. He loved licorice. I loathed it. He ate licorice. I didn't. Was this what remained of my individuality? This negative choice? Here was the dimension of our journey that I hadn't foreseen: the togetherness, the tight confinement to this tiny space that seemed to close in around us like one of Poe's horrific shrinking chambers. Africa rolled by in the background, like a distant view of planet Earth seen from a space capsule, but always in the foreground, eclipsing the scene, was my fellow voyager. He took up more space than Africa, certainly more space than I. And even as his hand disappeared again into the bag of licorice, it seemed to rest on the controls. I cajoled, I argued, I fought chin to chin, and always our vehicle seemed to proceed on the course of his choosing, as though he held it in orbit by the sheer force of his personality. "Are you sure you don't want some licorice?" Muggleton asked, holding up the bag. How was the Lovedu Queen able to rule a whole people when my choices seemed to come down to this? "No, thanks," I said. "I'm sure." I felt a new urgency to meet the Queen. I put my foot to the gas pedal and held the Land Rover on that fine edge between speed and disintegration.

We rolled easily through Côte d'Ivoire, a country long known as the jewel of West Africa and touted until quite recently as one of the best examples of stability, prosperity, and modernity on the continent. Along the highway stood real modern houses faced in stucco with tall louvered windows. New cars and trucks passed by, as on any ordinary American highway, though a large number of the really big trucks had finished in flames upside down against trees at the side of the road. As we sped south out of the dry savanna into the tropical rainy zone, the vegetation thickened, but it had the spare scruffy look of decimation. Here were the shreds of rain forests once so thick and lush as to seem impenetrable and so vast as to shield the country from would-be explorers and colonizers. The forest canopy had been breached, the big old trees trucked away, and now only the palms still stood, like pinfeathers on a plucked bird. It was a dispiriting sight. Then the highway cloned itself to become a divided superhighway—officially a "Motorway"—and we felt ourselves worlds away from the dusty path to Bamako, the still forbidden track to Timbuktu. We sped along once again through modern life.

REAL AFRICA

"Bloody hell," Muggleton shouted over the roar of the flat-out engine. He lifted his sunglasses and peered through the windshield. "What the hell is *that*?" An immense shape loomed on the horizon—an oversize elephant perhaps?—and gradually took form as a great round-shouldered hulk of a building. "The Taj Mahal?" Muggleton speculated. "The Kremlin?" We drew closer. "I've got it!" he crowed. "It's Saint Peter's." I laughed scornfully and looked again. He was right.

The motorway led into a parkway that led into a boulevard broad enough to host Macy's Thanksgiving Day Parade while the Rose Bowl pageant passed in the opposite direction. This was Yamoussoukro, the capital of Côte d'Ivoire, a city purposely built for presidential pomp and circumstance. Félix Houphouët-Boigny, who led the country to independence in 1960 and served as president until his death in 1993, was born in this place in 1905, when it was a little village named Ngokro. Educated by the French in Dakar, he returned to Côte d'Ivoire as a doctor, became a public health official and a successful planter, and began his political career in the 1940s, when he formed the country's first agricultural union to lobby on behalf of farmers. He went to Paris after the Second World War to represent Côte d'Ivoire in the French parliament and soon became a cabinet minister, the first African to hold such a post in a European government. He returned to his homeland in 1958, after twelve years in France, and in 1960 became the first president of independent Côte d'Ivoire, although he considered the country not yet ready to make its own way. As president he resisted the wave of anticolonial African nationalism sweeping the continent and instead threw open his doors to French expatriates and foreign investors. When the country prospered, he renamed his hometown Yamoussoukro in honor of his mother, Nana Yamoussou, and created an imperial city complete with modern roadways, brilliant streetlamps, imposing government buildings, spacious college campuses, luxury hotels—one with an eighteen-hole golf course—and a presidential palace set amid ponds full of crocodiles. All that was missing in Yamoussoukro was people. Public squares stood empty and sidewalks vacant, as though the city had been blitzed by some Star Wars weapon that vaporized the population but left the buildings untouched.

I eased into a huge empty parking lot and stopped before a tall fence of iron bars. Beyond the fence stood Houphouët-Boigny's last great architectural project: the Basilique de Notre Dame de la Paix. It was in most respects a carbon copy of Saint Peter's Basilica in Rome, but in place of Michelangelo's transcendent dome it sported a shorter, squatter dome topped with a tall golden cross, rather like a derby with a feather. It stood in the middle of a great empty field. "Not very inviting, is it?" Muggleton said, gaping. Armed guards eyed us suspiciously and demanded that we surrender our passports at the gate, as though we were passing into another country.

"It's easier for a camel to pass through the eye of a needle than for a visitor to pass into this church," I grumbled.

"It's probably easier to get into heaven," Muggleton said.

I consulted the guidebook. "It's the largest Catholic church in the world," I told him. "It's meant to seat seven thousand worshipers, with standing room inside for twelve thousand more, and on the terraces outside for another three hundred thousand."

"That's a lot of passports," Muggleton said.

"There aren't that many Catholics in the country," I said. I consulted the guidebook again. "Construction started in 1986," I reported. "It was consecrated in 1990. The pope came to handle the kickoff."

"I hope he brought his passport."

Inside, dwarfed by pillars of imported French concrete and acres of stained glass, I felt my spirits sag. At a time when his people needed food and health services and better schools, Houphouët-Boigny spent more than $150 million—$360 million, some reports say—on *this*. Critics challenged his priorities, but he replied that there were poor people in Rome too when the original Saint Peter's was built, and in

London when Saint Paul's went up. Besides, he said, he was a devout Catholic and he'd paid for the basilica out of his own pocket. He didn't say where he got the money.

"Brilliant, eh?" Muggleton said. "Could this be the real Africa?"

I gave him a feeble laugh, but I was crumpling under the weight of all this French-concrete evidence that Houphouët-Boigny had bought the whole egocentric Western package: capitalism, Christianity, modern technology, monumental architecture. Other African leaders in exile in Europe had begun as early as 1900 to meet and discuss plans for a pan-African future, envisioning a postcolonial era when Africa would erase the boundaries of the white man's map and return to its own system of ethnic and regional alliances that arose naturally out of the configurations of kinship and the land itself. Somehow at independence Africa got trapped in the map, but still the new nationalist leaders planned a cooperative pan-African union. In 1958, the year Houphouët-Boigny returned from France wearing a three-piece suit and a homburg, the Pan-African Freedom Movement of East and Central Africa convened in Mwanza, Tanzania; and Prime Minister Kwame Nkrumah hosted representatives of twenty-eight African territories at the First All-African Peoples' Conference of Independent African States in Accra, Ghana, right next door to Côte d'Ivoire. But Houphouët-Boigny set his own course. He'd go it alone. He laid his country open to "development," trusting that some of the profits made by exploiting its natural resources would stay at home.

Tens of thousands of Frenchmen flocked to Côte d'Ivoire, drawn by the president's generous economic policies. The forests were cut, and the land was turned to coffee and cocoa production to feed the tastes of France. The country seemed to thrive. In little more than a decade Côte d'Ivoire was acclaimed abroad as an economic miracle, and Houphouët-Boigny as a great and prescient leader. But the profits went abroad or fell into the pockets of a small Ivoirean elite and a larger group of French expatriates, who held most of the white-collar jobs and controlled the lion's share of industry and trade. Then the forests were gone, thanks in part to an $80 million "environmental" loan from the World Bank in 1990 that accelerated logging and dislodged between forty thousand and two hundred thousand people. Coffee prices fell, and cocoa became a glut on the market. French patronage vanished. The IMF, acting as enforcer of World Bank loans, stepped in to demand economic "adjustment," a process that usually requires the debtor government to reduce public spending and open itself fully to unrestricted free-market economics. A process that usually requires the debtor government to take out additional "adjustment loans" to repay the interest on its original loans and keep it afloat amid vain dreams of eventual solvency. A process that looks suspiciously to the nonfinancial mind like what my grandmother called throwing good money after bad. By mid-1995, Côte d'Ivoire's adjustment loans totaled almost $1.5 billion.

Not long after the Basilique de Notre Dame de la Paix was completed, austerity measures were declared. Citizens protested. The military protested. Students demonstrated. Political opposition grew. When Houphouët-Boigny died, money fled the country in the pockets of all those French expatriates who chose that moment to go home. The great man, so steeped in Western ideas, left his country in confusion—hopelessly in hock to the fiscal agents of the very Western nations that had "helped" Côte d'Ivoire "develop," consumed its resources, and praised its economic "progress" when it was one of Western capitalism's darling boys.

And this was the president's self-immortalizing legacy—this concrete copy of Rome's biggest church. It stood in the middle of Yamoussoukro, in the middle of the country of the Baoule, a people famous throughout Africa for their exquisite goldwork, their carved and painted masks, their ceremonial costumes—art that is truly African and truly beautiful. But Baoule artists didn't work in concrete or marble or stained glass. President Houphouët-Boigny was a Baoule himself, the son of a Baoule chief, and African enough always to honor his mother; but he had learned in Dakar and Paris to tell the difference between what is beautiful and grand, and what is not.

We fled to the Motorway and drove south to Abidjan, the commercial center and former capital, a modern metropolis of high-rise concrete and glass—a small-scale New York City, once famous for its fine French restaurants—in the midst of garden suburbs set among blue lagoons. We drove to the southern edge of the city and camped on a palm-fringed coast beside a roaring unswimmable sea at a campground called Les Vagues de Vridi. (It was that inhospitable coast of the Gulf of Guinea, scoured by riptides, that kept foreign exploiters out of Côte d'Ivoire long after other African countries succumbed to "exploration.") A reggae band was practicing lethargically on the beach. Reggae in slow motion. Tropical weather slows everything down.

It grew hotter. The air was heavy and thick with damp. We were drenched in our own sweat, as though life were a sauna. We took the bus into the city and trudged the busy modern streets of Plateau, the central business district, seeking visas: Ghana, Nigeria, Zaire. It was a tricky business, getting visas, for African capitals held the consulates only of their current allies, and alliances often changed. Like food, you had to grab a visa when you had the chance. DO NOT LEAN ON THE WALLS, said signs posted in the Nigerian Embassy. There were no chairs. KEEP OUR WALLS CLEAN! But the heat wilted me. My sweaty shirt clung to me. What if I were to set my wet back against the wall and slide slowly down their creamy paint job, leaving a murky trail of sweat? Would they deny me a visa if I did?

All through the steamy weekend, as we waited for our visas, I pondered heavy things—like my own mission in Africa. I'd come in search of the Lovedu, the tribe where women rule a prosperous land by peaceful diplomacy. But what I'd found—everywhere—was women in charge mostly of hard work. I'd been reading *The Africans* by David Lamb, who noticed the same thing. He writes that if work is what liberates women, African women are the most liberated in the world. Their labor is the one great constant force of the continent. They feed Africa, producing something like seventy percent of the food. They sell to Africa, running the market economy of village and town. But their work has grown harder over the years thanks to colonial administrators, missionaries, bureaucrats, and "experts" of international-aid and technical-development projects—all advancing theories of social progress that discount women's work, preclude women's education, set women back. Colonial governments and missions established too few schools for boys, and in seventy or eighty years of colonial administration almost none for girls. Colonial development projects set up monocultural cash-crop plantations with men in charge on lands where generations of women had run subsistence farms. Postcolonial aid organizations still give agricultural grants to men to buy modern farm equipment. Never mind that it's women with hoes who tend the *shambas*.

In the cities, among educated people at least, life changes. Young women speed to work or to the university on their motorbikes—at least some young women do. On the bus in Abidjan two girls stand on opposite sides of a handrail. Up front is a plump schoolgirl in her smart uniform: navy blue skirt, crisp white blouse. She wears neat suede loafers and gold earrings and carries an electric-blue backpack full of books. On the other side of the rail, on the back platform of the bus, stands the other girl with her mother. She is very thin and wears a simple African print dress, dingy from many launderings. On her feet are plastic sandals, well worn, the backs broken off. On her head is a coil of cloth used for balancing a load. When she gets off the bus at a neighborhood market, following her mother, she hoists a tin basin to her head—a basin containing cloths and dishes and a plastic container of cooking oil. She is going to help her mother sell fried plantains in the market. The student remains on the bus until it reaches an area of small well-kept bungalows near the sea. Two girls. The same age. In the same city. Yet their lives are generations apart. In the complicated context of Africa, who can say which girl is further "ahead"?

Outside the cities, women in bright print cottons walk along every road, carrying basins and calabashes and firewood on their heads, going to the river to do laundry or to the village market to sell fried fish or bananas. Almost everywhere women sit by the side of the road, selling mandarins or groundnuts. In the bush, in tiny villages, women work the fields and look after many children and a few old men. The younger men, in need of cash to pay school fees and taxes, and displaced from their land by development projects and structural adjustment policies, have gone to the cities, where most of them will be unable to make a living still; the crops and huts and animals, the young and the old, are left in the care of women who will never leave the village. Under pressure of the new world economy, the African extended family comes apart, and as the lives of women and men diverge, it's women who are left "behind." This is not necessarily a bad thing. Left out of development projects, women help themselves and one another as they have always done, building the local economy on bonds of kinship and affection—the system Nelson Mandela calls the "natural socialism" of the African.

But even natural socialism can break down along gender lines. One day in Mali, when we were on the road to Bamako, we stopped at a village and I jumped out to ask directions. A young woman, smiling, with a baby in her arms, came forward to greet me. Suddenly a little wiry man leaped out of a hut and rushed between us. He turned on her and pummeled her about the head and neck with his fists and forearms. He hit her resignedly and hard, the way I'd seen Africans club their donkeys on the head and neck to make them turn, as if this were the only signal the stupid beasts might understand. The woman did as the donkeys do: she hunched away without a sound. The man turned to me then, extending to me the same hand that had just clubbed his wife. *"Bonjour madame,"* he said cheerily. *"Ça va?"*

Muggleton, for his part, could not afford the luxury of reflection on topics heavy or light. He had work to do. He was committed to the deadly serious business of being an adventurer. He immersed himself in the German overlander's Bible, *Durch Afrika,* a dense compendium of motoring information. He made plans. He pored over the Michelin map, calculator in hand, figuring routes and distances. What would the road surface be? How many kilometers per liter could we average? Where would we get petrol? How many jerry cans would we need? Should we buy more? Where could we put them? What would the additional weight do to our fuel consumption? How many days would we need between here and there? Where were the ferries? Were they running? Would it rain? And most of all: How bad would the mud be in Zaire?

The Land Rover was our lifeline now, and we had mixed feelings about it. "Brilliant!" Muggleton proclaimed on his good days. "Bloody albatross," he snarled at times, especially in cities like Dakar and Abidjan, where it was an easy target for thieves. The Land Rover made our journey possible—especially the journey that lay ahead through Cameroon, the Central African Republic, and the rain forest of Zaire. But it also encapsulated us and absorbed our thoughts. Would the vehicle make it to South Africa? To the Transvaal, where supposedly the Lovedu last lived? Would we make it? And if we did, worn down by dust and heat and mud and the incessant shudder of the old Land Rover, would we give a damn about the Lovedu or one another or anything else?

"I worry about you," Muggleton said as I slumped into the campground after making another round of embassies in Abidjan. "If you can't hold up in this weather, what are you going to do when it gets really hot in Zaire?"

I didn't answer. It was too hot to answer. And anyway, the only conceivable answer was "Perish!" I brushed past him and walked into the

shower with my clothes on. Later I found the ever-resourceful Muggleton puttering in the vehicle again. He'd cut up a heavy, heat-reflective
emergency blanket from the medical kit and was installing it in the well
between the engine and the passenger seat. "Maybe you'll be cooler," he
said. I must have looked ashen and terrible. He stared at me. "Or
maybe not."

In this manner we waited out the weekend, venturing out in the evening, when we imagined it to be slightly cooler, to *maquis* (open-air
restaurants) to feast on yam chips and *kedjenou* (chicken braised with
chilies and tomatoes). Aka, the amiable Ivoirean proprietor of the
campground, went with us, and we talked far into the night. He told us
about Houphouët-Boigny—the greatest man in the history of Côte
d'Ivoire, he called him. Aka admired the president for leading the
people to independence and then setting the nation on the path to agricultural self-sufficiency and development. Aka wasn't sure just what
went wrong, but somehow, under the pressure of the new "adjusted"
economy, his family—like so many others—broke apart. He used to
tend his small plantings of coffee and cocoa upcountry, but prices kept
going down, he said, and profits. So he left his wife and two children
and came to town to start Abidjan's first campground. His wife tended
the plantings now, and his children helped after school. Aka was a sweet
man and a hard worker. He tried to keep his campground clean and
pleasant. He swept the sand around our tents. He zipped up our tents
for us if we were away when the rains came, as they did almost every
morning. He invited us into his tiny kitchen to make tea. He missed
his wife and children very much. So he took us to the *maquis* in the
evenings and talked—about the president, about his wife and children,
and about his father, now dead, a famous practitioner of traditional
medicine. Aka had not learned the art himself, for he knew that Westerners frowned upon such things and he wanted to be modern and up-
to-date. But he had learned from his father that all races and tribes must
live and work together in peace. "Life is so short," he said. "You have
life, and then you die. There is no time for war." Aka taught us to say in
Agni, his native language: "Come, eat meat."

One morning, with our visas at last in order, we stood under the
trees with Aka and endured the moment of goodbye. Then we drove
out of Abidjan, heading east. It was a landmark day. After two months
of driving south, we had turned a corner at last to begin our journey

across the belly of Africa. Muggleton had been thinking all along about things that lay ahead, but now I began to think about them too. Zaire, for example. And mud. I began to worry, as Muggleton was worrying, about the degenerative disease that continued to afflict our vehicle. The condition we called wheel wobble. Every time we hit a substantial bump—a frequent event in Africa—the wheels lurched to the left, then to the right, then to the left, and so on in a kind of frenetic cha-cha-cha that left me breathless, especially when I was in the driver's seat, operating what I now jocularly referred to as "the controls." These thoughts filled us both with trepidation.

When we crossed the border into Ghana, a police officer asked, "Where are you going?"

"Cape Town," Muggleton said. He had to laugh out loud at the improbability of it. "We're driving to Cape Town."

The officer laughed too. "Well, then," he said, "you'd best be on your way."

WHITE BREAD

As we drove along the coast of Ghana we were ambushed by admonitions: SLOW DOWN! USE CARE! SEEK JESUS! The signs were in English now, for when we crossed the border from Côte d'Ivoire to Ghana, we passed from Francophone Africa to Anglophone Africa—that is, from former French West Africa to a former British colony. From the realm of the crusty baguette to the land of pasty white bread. From countries predominantly Islamic to the land of Christian converts. The French had "civilized" their African colonies by military conquest, centralized government, the Napoleonic Code, forced labor, and French schools to teach selected male Africans skills that made them of service to imperial France. The French had proclaimed the revolutionary Rights of Man and set about making faux Frenchmen of the inhabitants of France d'Outre-mer, an area eight times the size of the "home" country. They had soldiered and socialized and slept with the "natives," producing a half-caste population among Africans whose equal rights proved after all to be largely theoretical.

But the British had done things differently. Claiming a special gift for governance, they brought the blessings of British civilization to benighted Africans through trade and the Bible. Their aim was not to produce imitation Englishmen, and surely not to assimilate Africans into the "mother country," for they considered black Africans naturally inferior to white men in general and Britons in particular. Their aim was to develop a stable marketplace for African raw materials and British manufactures, and by example to instruct Africans in the ways of the civilized world, to "lift them up" (as British statesmen and missionaries so often put it) so that eventually, when British business was done, the Africans might carry on by themselves. It seems scarcely to have occurred to either the French or the British that Africans might already constitute civilizations. Or that they might consider the land they lived on to be their own.

The French sent soldiers to Africa. The British sent merchants and missionaries. The French conquered and seized power. The British insinuated themselves and adopted a policy of governing "indirectly" through certain local African rulers upon whom they relied to keep order while British merchants went about their business. The British brought in the Bible and took out precious palm oil that made the soap that kept the godly British nation clean. They brought in cloth and took out gold. Quite often during the nineteenth century disgruntled Africans complained to the English queen about the high-handed tactics of British traders who drove them out of business and cast their people into poverty. Quite often British forces were called upon to silence their complaints and restore order to the marketplace. (This forcible expulsion of African merchant-capitalists from the "free" market, which some historians mark as a turning point in African economic development, seems a sign of things to come.) Once trade along this coast had been under the sway of the Asante kingdom of the Akan people, whose capital lay at Kumasi. They grew rich supplying slaves to the British and Dutch, until the British declared in 1807 that the slave trade must stop and then seized control of trade all along the coast. With righteousness on their side, the British marched upcountry and sacked Kumasi. Later they declared the Gold Coast a British colony in which British merchants and missionaries might carry on business as usual. On the Gold Coast business and the Bible intertwined.

That colony became the country of Ghana in 1957—the first African colony to gain independence from European colonizers. (Although it borrowed the name, modern Ghana is unrelated to the ancient kingdom of Ghana, which once covered what is now Senegal, southwestern Mali, and southern Mauritania.) Modern Ghana's great nationalist leader and first prime minister, Kwame Nkrumah, had spent a decade studying and traveling in the United States, but he argued passionately that Africans must establish their own uniquely African forms of government and their own pan-African institutions. At the Accra conference in 1958, Nkrumah declared that Africa wanted to develop its own "community" and an "African personality." "Others may feel that they have evolved the very best way of life," he said, "but we are not bound, like slavish imitators, to accept it as our mold." Nevertheless, like many other African nationalist leaders of the time—most of whom had been educated at mission schools and Western universities— Nkrumah didn't think to seek that community in African traditions and institutions. When he was inaugurated as prime minister of the new nation, one man was conspicuously absent: the king of Asante— who might rightfully have expected postcolonial power to return to him. In retrospect it seems an omen, a kind of moral smoke detector, for the rest of Nkrumah's story might be the denouement of a classical tragedy. Nkrumah looked to the "modern" future, not the African past. He spent foreign aid on industrialization and massive building projects, piling up a huge national debt, and forgot about the peasant farmers. When the people protested, he grew tyrannical. He threw his opponents in jail and named himself president for life. When the military overthrew him in 1966, the people tore down his statues in the streets. He finished his life in exile in Guinea, leaving his wasted country to a modern African history of coups and countercoups.

Four decades after independence, as we drove along the highway toward the capital, the heritage of Bible-toting British businessmen was still plain to see—writ large in English, the official language of a country whose people speak seventy-five languages and dialects of their own. The God Squad had done its work. Scraps of scripture dished out by missionaries were recycled as signboards for tradesmen and shopkeepers along the roadside. GET JESUS SALVATION BEAUTY SALON. ARISE AND GO ENTERPRISE. JUST OBEY FURNITURE STORE. LORD BLESSED MEEK TRADING LIMITED. Scriptures appeared on vehicles too, in admonitions painted on bush taxis, buses, and trucks. On the winding road, it took Muggleton a long time to pass a truck that cautioned PREPARE YE. Then he got stuck behind a *trotro* (a minibus) overstuffed with friendly Ghanaians who waved at him from every window, urging him to pass, signaling that the road ahead was clear. But there across the back of the *trotro*, neatly hand-painted in flamboyant red script, was the forbidding admonition BEWARE HEAVEN BEARS NO LITTLE PRICE.

"What exactly does it mean?" Muggleton asked. "Do you think it means what I think it means?" The pressure was palpable. He was sweating, but it might have been the heat.

"I think we're supposed to shape up," I said.

Muggleton gripped the steering wheel, floored the gas pedal, and shot around the hurtling *trotro* as the passengers waved and cheered. I noticed that his knuckles had gone white.

This might help to explain why, not long after, Muggleton suddenly pulled off the road in Elmina in front of a building that bore the decidedly secular name Hollywood Hotel. "This looks good," he said, although this Hollywood Hotel was no Hollywood hotel. It was a no-frills, cold-water affair, though big-windowed and airy—no small asset on the sweltering shores of Ghana. We got two rooms, each with a double bed, an electric fan, and a private bathroom. A water pipe anyway. And a bucket. This cost us almost $9 apiece. It wasn't that we'd gone all soft and wimpy mid-adventure, but we'd had our fill of tortuous traffic and scriptural admonishment. Besides, we hadn't slept in beds since Gibraltar, and Muggleton wanted to see if he was still up to it. He tried his bed and reported that it was full of sharp slats. That sounded like just the kind of challenge he enjoys.

The Hollywood Hotel fell under the somber shadow of a fort from which slaves once were shipped to the New World. It was called Fort Saint George, or more commonly Elmina Castle—the first European building erected south of the Sahara. The Portuguese built it in 1482. They had sailed to this coast ten years earlier and anchored off a small fishing village, where they'd bartered with residents who offered them gold. They had come upon the most important source of gold in West Africa; and although the mines were somewhere inland, they knew that controlling the coastal trading center was as good as having the mine—*el mina*—itself. Lisbon dispatched a fleet of cargo vessels loaded with dressed stone, bricks, timber, tiles, and nails; caravels carried one hundred stonemasons and five hundred soldiers with orders to build and garrison a fort at Elmina. This they accomplished, despite the opposition of the local people. By the end of the fifteenth century, Elmina was supplying most of the world's gold, shipping more than half a ton each year to Portugal.

But what were the Portuguese to trade for all that gold? Not horses, which quickly died in the equatorial heat. Not weapons, which were then banned by papal edict. What the Akan people wanted was manpower, and the Portuguese could supply it by buying captives from the Benin and Igbo peoples in the Bight of Benin and the Niger delta, farther east along the shores that came to be known as the Slave Coast.

The Portuguese became the middlemen in an indigenous African slave trade, carrying five or six hundred slaves a year across the bight to the Gold Coast and sailing home with a cargo of gold. Historians say that slavery within Africa was relatively benign: a system of wageless labor that answered the needs of an underpopulated continent always short of manpower. They say that slaves (most of whom were prisoners of war) were taken into the owner's family and might subsequently marry into it or inherit from it. They say that slaves might earn their freedom, and they cite one case of a slave who actually was chosen to be a king. But labor was wanted in Portugal too, and Spain, and in new possessions in the Caribbean and Brazil, where conditions seemed just right for producing what all Europeans were learning to crave: sugar. By 1502 the Portuguese were shipping African slaves to the New World. The new export trade transformed the nature of slavery.

Most European maritime powers soon horned in on the immensely profitable "triangular trade." From Europe they shipped manufactured goods—cloth, copper bracelets, chamber pots—to be exchanged in Africa for slaves. The slaves were shipped to the plantations of the New World and exchanged for sugar, which in turn was shipped to Europe and sold for cash. Every exchange put money in the pockets of merchants on all three continents. For more than three hundred years the Atlantic slave trade prospered, driven by greed and the European sweet tooth. At its peak, in the eighteenth century, more than sixty thousand slaves were shipped each year from African shores; even at the end of the nineteenth century, almost one hundred years after the trade was officially abolished, more than thirty thousand slaves were shipped out each year. Historians put the total "export" from Africa between 1500 and the late 1800s at eighteen million people: eleven million from West Africa, five million from the savanna, and two million from the east coast. They keep revising the number upward, and they point out that, given high mortality rates among slaves on the long march to the coast, the number of Africans seized must have been far greater than the number actually exported. Untold millions were lost who surely would have changed the face of their continent. And even when the intercontinental slave trade ended, slavery *within* Africa actually increased; for by that time Africa was enmeshed in the "legitimate" export trade, producing items of European desire—tropical timber, palm oil, cocoa, rubber, and gold—with indigenous slave labor. What the numbers mean, according to historian John Reader, is that every village must have been touched at some time, and every person must have come to expect that some friend or relative would inevitably vanish one day without a trace. For four hundred years—twenty generations—this was life in Africa.

"The guidebook says they're turning some of these old slave forts into tourist hotels," Muggleton said as we stood looking up at the great stone walls. We had walked across a bridge over a lagoon, where scores of longboats filled with fishermen lay ready to ride out on the tide, and had climbed the promontory where the fort stood, fronting the Atlantic. Palms lined the promenade, rattling in the wind off the sea. "Bloody awful idea, if you ask me," he said. "Who could sleep?" We crossed over a moat and through the gate and wandered the stone corridors in silence. We were the only visitors, and our footsteps echoed in narrow passages. We felt our way down winding stairways into utter darkness where dungeons lay, and scrambled up again toward the light. We peered into shadowed rooms—kitchens, a mess hall, barracks, a chapel that served also as a slave market—and high up, commanding a sweeping view of the sea, an airy chamber, full of light, for the governor. We stood there for a long time looking out. And then we made our way back across the lagoon from which the boats had sailed and through the broken streets of Elmina to the Hollywood Hotel.

"Who knows when we'll see a bed again?" Muggleton said. He was grasping for an excuse to justify our spending the night in a hotel when by rights we should have been out in the bush. "At least we're not staying in some bloody fort," he said. Was he feeling guilty? Or was it just that he took pride in depriving himself, as only those not truly deprived can do?

"It's okay," I told him. "It's just a hotel."

"Togo, Benin, Nigeria," he said, thinking ahead. "We must get some spare parts for the vehicle. In Accra, perhaps. We should find spare parts in Accra."

After Accra we would pass beyond the red lines on the Michelin map, beyond phone and fax and DHL Express, which so far had carried my dispatches back to the Internet. I'd already notified my editor at America Online that I'd be out of touch for the next four or five weeks. And Muggleton spoke of the onward journey through Central Africa as though we were astronauts about to venture round the dark side of the moon.

"It's refreshing to have a proper shower," he said, speaking of the pipe and bucket in the corner of his room. We sat side by side on the veranda of the Hollywood Hotel, eating our dinner of tomato sandwiches made with Wonder Bread, and gazed out into the parking lot, where the battered Land Rover stood like an abandoned but faithful dog. Stars appeared overhead, and the looming walls of the fort receded into the night.

NO CONDITION IS
PERMANENT

N O CONDITION IS PERMANENT. So said the sign on the back of a *trotro* in Tema. I saw the same sign again on the dashboard of a taxi in Accra. It's a popular sentiment in Ghana, or for that matter, in Africa. For the Igbo of Nigeria, it's a slogan that expresses their traditional understanding of life, as novelist Chinua Achebe has said. A worldview on a bumper sticker. What it means, I guess, is that everything passes, both bad fortune and good, both intolerable misery and bliss. Achebe writes: "In Igbo cosmology even gods could fall out of use; and new forces are liable to appear without warning in the temporal and metaphysical firmament." *No condition is permanent.* Travel for a while in Africa, and you understand it. In the United States, if you don't like conditions, you try to change them. In Africa, you accept. In Africa, you wait for the change that must eventually, inevitably, come.

In Abidjan, in sweltering heat, I waited an hour and a half for a bus. Toward the end, there were close to a hundred people in line. They stood in perfect quiet, looking around aimlessly, daydreaming, woolgathering—waiting. Nobody grumbled. Nobody looked impatiently at a watch. Nobody examined the bus stop in search of a printed schedule. Nobody peered anxiously up the street in anticipation of the bus. Nobody but me, that is. I turned to the African behind me, a middle-aged man in a dark well-tailored business suit who looked perfectly calm and cool despite the blistering heat. "Is this normal?"

"Normal?" he said, puzzled.

"I mean, do you usually wait this long for the bus?"

"Sometimes," he said. "Sometimes long. Sometimes short." He smiled a friendly smile. Reassuring. That's the way things are.

The average African is a past master at waiting—for the bus to come or the drought to pass or the government to fall in another coup d'état. I, on the other hand, am not good at waiting at all. And Muggleton is hopeless. A man of action, he goes crazy sitting still. For some time he'd been growing increasingly impatient with the slow pace of our progress, the countless delays. We'd been held up time and time again—waiting for the convoy in Morocco, searching for roads through Mali, waiting for visas in Côte d'Ivoire. We'd been on the road two months, covered twelve thousand kilometers or more at what seemed to me relentless, bone-jolting speed, yet gradually, almost imperceptibly, we had fallen weeks behind what Muggleton still referred to as "the schedule." No schedule is permanent either.

"You're where? Ghana?" said my friend Joan when I phoned home. "I thought you'd be in Kenya by now. What's taking so long?"

"I don't know," I had to say. "Everything. Africa. Life."

Muggleton and I checked out of the Hollywood Hotel and set out at the crack of dawn on a Friday morning to race from Elmina into Accra, the capital. Our plan—we were always making plans—was to reach the French Embassy at nine o'clock, when it opened for business, obtain our visas for the Central African Republic, exchange some money at the bank, and be quickly on our way east. Toward Zaire. Muggleton insisted on driving. Having psyched himself up to ignore the God Squad slogans displayed on other vehicles, he drove as if he were on the course at Le Mans. I navigated brilliantly, if I do say so myself. It was one of those glorious days when our teamwork was impeccable. We pulled up in front of the French Embassy in Accra at precisely one minute after nine. That's when we found out that it was National Farmers' Day in Ghana. Farmers celebrate National Farmers' Day. So does the French Embassy. So do the banks. So does everyone in Ghana. On National Farmers' Day, the whole of Ghana goes to the beach.

What else could we do? Who could grumble about a day set aside—probably not by Kwame Nkrumah—to honor Ghana's struggling farmers? About fifteen kilometers beyond Accra we came upon the Coco Beach Resort, a popular retreat for locals. There, in a small camping area on the grounds, we pitched our tents—midway between a Highlife band on the beach and the African System Reggae Band on the resort's outdoor bandstand. The beach was packed, the water crowded with holidaymakers. Young women bravely held their noses and suffered their gallant husbands to boost them above the breaking waves. Muggleton vented his frustration by swimming off briskly in the general direction of England.

"White man! White man!" the lifeguard called to him when he reappeared on the crest of a big bodysurfing wave. Muggleton coasted onto the beach. "Why you go so far out, man? I'm hurting for you, man," the lifeguard said. "You be in trouble."

Muggleton laughed. "No worries," he said. "You can save me."

"Me?" The lifeguard was astonished. "No, man. You kidding? Don't you know I can't swim?"

"Can't swim!" Muggleton said. "How can you be the lifeguard?"

"Hey, it's easy, man. Don't you know nobody can swim?"

Bodysurfing amused Muggleton for about twenty minutes. Then he was restless again—waiting for Monday, when the Embassy and the bank would reopen. It seemed a long way off. I could hear him in his tent at night, sleepless, *psssshhhht*ing mosquitoes with a politically incorrect aerosol can of heavy-duty insecticide I'd bought him in Abidjan. It was called Laser. Muggleton was paranoid about mosquitoes, having suffered a near-lethal case of malaria a few years before. He didn't want to get it again. So each night at sunset he zipped himself into his tent—it was an REI expedition tent equipped with a mosquito net so fine it barely let in air—and if I wanted to talk to him, I had to sit outside and speak through the wall. (There seemed to be some tacit understanding that I was less susceptible to mosquitoes than he, or perhaps I was simply more expendable, which from Muggleton's point of view was certainly true.) Despite his precautions, mosquitoes got into his tent. Not ordinary mosquitoes that whine in your ears, but the deadly silent kind that sneak up and bite you before you know they're there. They sent Muggleton into a frenzy. He lashed about, swatting, slapping, clubbing. The inside of his tent was a scene of carnage, splattered with blood. "That's my blood!" he cried in dismay. "*My* blood!" So that's why I'd bought him the Laser, and why at the Coco Beach Resort, when he couldn't sleep, I'd hear the *psssshhhht*ing of his aerosol can. I told him he would die of insecticide poisoning. "Better that than malaria," he said. I thought he'd be dead by Monday.

But the next morning, Saturday, he fell into conversation with the resort's security guard, who stopped to admire our Land Rover while making his rounds of the camp. He was an old man, black and wizened, slow of speech, and apparently half blind behind eyeglasses as thick as Coke bottles. "I've got a problem with the vehicle," Muggleton told him, always eager for an intimate chat about his beloved Land Rover. The old man seemed an unpromising confidant for conundrums in auto mechanics, but Muggleton needed only a willing ear. The old man made all the right moves. He canted his head, indicating that he was prepared to listen and give the problem some thought. "Well, actually, I've got several problems," Muggleton went on, "but the main thing is I've got this wheel wobble. Every time I hit a bump, the front wheels lock up and go *kadug kadug kadug kadug*—like that." Muggleton is good with sound effects. Gestures too. He waved his arms rapidly left, right, left, right, in a violent approximation of wheel wobble. The old man stared. His eyes were huge, magnified by his thick glasses. *"Kadug kadug,"* Muggleton said again. "Like that." The old man nodded and stared.

"Kadug," the old man said.

"That's it," Muggleton said. *"Kadug kadug."*

"Kadug kadug."

"Right!" Muggleton said. "It's a problem."

"Right," the old man said. A long slow syllable. He turned to walk away, shaking his head.

"Kadug kadug," Muggleton said again.

The old man turned back to him. "Sounds to me," he said, "like the swivel ball joints."

The next thing I knew, Muggleton and I were on our way into Accra to scout up a Land Rover parts dealer on the Kinbu Road. Yes, they were open on Saturday. Yes, they had a carburetor repair kit. Yes, they had a clutch plate. Yes, they had a steering relay unit. And yes, they had the swivel ball joints—all six of them. No problem at all. They could even provide new glass for the side mirrors we smashed to smithereens on the road to Bamako.

By afternoon we were back at camp, and Muggleton fiendishly began to take the vehicle to pieces. The hood went up and the carburetor came out and disintegrated under Muggleton's feverish hands into dozens of infinitesimally tiny bits and pieces. The front tires came off and went underneath the vehicle to hold up the chassis. Then the wheels came off and the steering rods and the relay unit and the swivel ball joints. Wrenches and spanners were everywhere. One minute Muggleton was nearly cross-eyed, ratcheting down a microscopic screw with the tiny screwdriver I carried to repair my eyeglasses. The next minute he was winding up to swing two-handed with a sledgehammer at the swivel ball joints. I couldn't watch. I wondered how much we could get for the scrap, and if it would be enough to help with the cost of a flight home.

I took myself off down the beach to watch the local fishermen return with their catch. Most of them were in longboats lying just beyond the line of the surf, waiting. When the time was right, the rudder man would guide the boat through to the beach. Women were there with basins, waiting too. They hitched their skirts up to their hips and waded to the boats to have their basins filled with small silver fish. Then the boats hit the beach and crews leaped out to put wooden rollers under the heavy craft. They put their backs under the hull and heaved in unison while the smallest of them kicked the roller home under the keel. Then, chanting a work song, they dragged the boats, little by little, up the beach above the tide line.

Other fishermen sat in groups on the sand. These were young boys and old men, some of them blind, who didn't go to sea anymore. They'd placed their dragnets before sunup and waited for the right moment, at the turning of the tide, to pull them in. They stood up together, twenty strong, and formed two lines from the beach into the sea, one on each side of the long net. Together they swung their arms forward for a handhold, then stepped back to haul the heavy net across the sand, hand over hand, singing out the rhythm of the job. They could easily see, long before they'd dragged the net home, that it held only a few fish—"small small"—not enough to make a single meal for all the men and boys who'd helped to haul it in.

Late Sunday afternoon Muggleton said, "Should we go for a ride?" He had worked round the clock to put all the bits and pieces—and the new bits and pieces—together again. Miraculously the vehicle was restored. I climbed in, holding my breath. The engine turned over. It didn't stall. The vehicle moved. We drove out onto a rugged washboard road, and Muggleton deliberately hit every bump. The wheels rode up and down like normal wheels. No *kadug kadug*. No wheel wobble. In a rush of relief I felt a new confidence, an absolute certainty, that when we hit the road again in the morning, after our stops at the French

Embassy and the bank, the wheels would not wobble—not once—all the way to Togo.

"You're a genius, Muggleton," I said, meaning it.

"It's good, eh?" he said, grinning.

We drove back to camp in a festive mood. Muggleton's triumph called for a celebration. We cleaned up and strolled over to the open-air restaurant to eat fish and chips and listen to the Sappers Band from the Ghanaian army blast African variations on Bob Marley's greatest hits. We took to the dance floor among well-dressed couples circling politely in their Sunday best, but Muggleton soon slumped back to his chair. "I'm done up," he said, as though it surprised him. "It's all this bloody waiting about. It's got me bloody knackered."

NOT A GREAT COUNTRY

We raced out of Ghana and zipped along the coast road through Togo with Muggleton behind the wheel, hell-bent for Zaire. He was determined to make up for lost time. So I didn't waste my breath reciting tidbits gleaned from the guidebook about the many fascinating things to be seen in the country flashing by so inexorably beyond our windshield. Anyway, Togo and its people looked much like Ghana and its people—no big surprise, considering history. These countries were part of the rich and tasty African cake, sliced up at European conference tables. Germany claimed Togo in 1884, then lost it in 1914 at the battle of Kamina. (It's a curiosity of history that the first Allied victory in a European war took place in Africa.) The League of Nations later awarded the spoils to the victors, one third of Togo to Britain and two thirds to France. Britain annexed western Togo to the Gold Coast (Ghana) while France claimed the eastern part as an updated, pared-down version of Togo. The border they established between them ran straight through the nations of the Adele, Konkomba, and Ewe peoples, leaving half of each nation in one country and half in the other. That's what happened all over Africa when old men gathered in Berlin or Brussels to divvy up a continent they'd never seen. Speaking of contemporary Africa, Nigeria's Nobel laureate Wole Soyinka asked, "What Is a Nation?" In the middle of Eweland, men wearing the uniforms of two different countries and speaking the languages of two different countries not their own stamped our passports—exit Ghana, entry Togo—and we understood that Soyinka's question was not merely philosophical.

We hurried onward through Togo and its next-door neighbor Benin.

The two long skinny countries—shaped a bit like Vermont and New Hampshire—lend themselves to a rapid transit, which suited Muggleton just fine. But the border checkpoints held us up, and the day slipped away. As darkness fell we pitched our tents for the night in the bush of Benin. Muggleton tuned in the BBC World Service for the news. The international outcry against Nigeria continued. The country—which we planned to enter the next day—was reported to be in a state of "unrest."

Unlike little Togo and Benin, the Federal Republic of Nigeria is big—as big as California, Arizona, and New Mexico combined, or four times the size of Great Britain. With more than one hundred million people, it's the most populous country in Africa, and perhaps the most artificial. Three great peoples predominate—Hausa in the Muslim north, Yoruba in the Christian southwest, and Igbo (Ibo) in the southeast—three great peoples with three very different traditions of social organization and governance. (It was the Igbo who declared themselves the independent republic of Biafra in 1967 and lost the ensuing civil war in 1970.) At least 250 other peoples also live in Nigeria's thirty states and speak at least as many languages in perhaps four hundred different dialects. All these disparate cultures were cobbled together by Britain to safeguard British trade along the Niger River and the Slave Coast. For a century British overlords played one people against another to maintain control of their improbable colony. Then, in 1960, they cut it loose. Nigeria has been in a "period of transition" to democracy ever since. In that context, who could guess what troubles lurked behind the simple word "unrest"?

We'd followed the news since our journey began. In early October 1995, when we were still in England packing for the trip, we read reports that Nigerian writer Ken Saro-Wiwa had been convicted of murder, along with eight other members of MOSOP, the Movement for the Salvation of the Ogoni People, of which Saro-Wiwa was president. The sentence was death by hanging. Over the next few weeks, while leaders around the world protested the decision, we inched our way into West Africa, tuned to the BBC World Service. There we heard the story of the Ogoni, a people who had lived peaceably by farming and fishing in the Niger delta until oil was discovered on their land. Enter Shell Oil. Soon Ogoniland—a narrow strip about twenty-four kilometers wide and forty kilometers long—held ten oilfields, more than a hundred oil wells, two refineries, and endless pipelines. Farmlands were polluted and fishing waters clogged with petrochemical sludge. Oil profits—something like $300 billion in thirty years of drilling—flowed to foreign oil companies and to the deep pockets of the Armed Forces Ruling Council in Abuja, Nigeria's new $18 billion capital, where additional billions simply disappeared. While crooked politicians transferred an estimated $25 million a day to foreign bank accounts at the height of the oil boom, little or nothing went to the Ogoni, who could no longer make a living in their own land. MOSOP was organized to protest. Amnesty International and Greenpeace took up the Ogoni cause. So did Jesse Jackson and British actress Glenda Jackson, then a Labour member of parliament.

Enter General Sani Abacha, who seized power in 1993 shortly after Nigeria's first free and democratic presidential election was nullified and the winner, Moshood Abiola, jailed. General Abacha threw Amnesty International and Greenpeace out of the country. He imposed martial law in the delta so the drilling could continue and the plans go forward for a new gas pipeline through Ogoniland—to be financed chiefly by Royal Dutch/Shell and the International Finance Corporation, a member of the World Bank Group, which promised to put up $180 million. (Later Ken Saro-Wiwa wrote: "The World Bank has to accept that its real instrument of torture is its insistence on growth, its economic theorizing at the expense of human welfare.") Abacha sent his goons to the delta, disguised as Ogoni or as their peaceable neighbors the Okrika and the Andoni, to rob, kidnap, ransack, and murder. His purpose was to divide the people of the delta and prevent them from standing together to demand a fair share of the resources of their land, reparations for the damage to it, and representation in controlling its future. Almost certainly it was Abacha's agents provocateurs who, during a public MOSOP rally in May 1994, hacked to death four Ogoni chiefs. This was the crime with which Ken Saro-Wiwa (who did not attend the rally) and eight other members of the radical wing of MOSOP were charged. They were tried before a special tribunal, handpicked by General Abacha, which dutifully convicted them and sentenced them to die.

While we drove through Morocco, nightly BBC bulletins added names to the list of countries, international organizations, statesmen, and celebrities beseeching Abacha for clemency. Only Royal Dutch/Shell—

which might actually have carried some weight with the dictator—declined to appeal to the regime on behalf of Saro-Wiwa and the others. It would be improper, a Shell spokesman said, for the company to interfere in Nigeria's internal affairs. Then in November, as Muggleton and I crawled through the Sahara, came the bulletin: that matter-of-fact Greenwich Mean Time voice reading the news that Nigeria had executed a group of dissidents, including the prominent writer Ken Saro-Wiwa. Then came more reports about the international outcry. Then the expulsion of Nigeria from the British Commonwealth. And now the latest bulletin: that the country was said to be in a state of "unrest."

Other overlanders we'd met along the way were scared and changing plans fast, plotting elaborate new routes to circumvent Nigeria, or buying freighter passage from Abidjan or Accra to send their vehicles south by ship. Muggleton was not deterred. It was no good mentioning the dangers of entering Nigeria at this particular moment in history. Muggleton enjoyed dangers. And he was in a hurry. He wanted to rush into Nigeria only to rush out the other side. We talked things over, and considering his desire for speed and mine for safety, we agreed above all else upon two things. We would *not* drive through Lagos, a city of at least eight million desperate people. And we would *not* drive at night. It was part of the ineluctable bad karma of Nigeria that within the next twenty-four hours we would do both.

I prepared for the border crossing by donning my best official border-crossing outfit—long skirt and clean shirt—and putting in order our fat portfolio of documents. We passed without incident through the checkpoint marking the exit from Benin and drove on. Beside the road stood a long, low ramshackle building of unpainted wood—Nigerian Customs—fallen on hard times, like the country it represented. Muggleton inched the Land Rover through a slew of cars and trucks vying for position in the long line to cross the border while I flung myself into a crowd of clamoring Africans and wormed my way to the Immigration window. There I filled out a blue form, and waited half an hour while a lethargic officer ruffled through desk drawers and cubbyholes in search of a second blue form. When he found it, I filled out that one for Muggleton.

That got me escorted inside—way inside—to a dirty office the size of a closet. It contained a single wooden chair, a bare lightbulb, a 1993 wall calendar, and a woman in a red dress who handed me two white forms. "Write out!" she said. She locked the door. I filled in the blanks with the same information I'd already put on the blue forms. I felt under pressure to do better, but I could see no way to improve upon my answers to "Name," "Address," and "Date of Birth." The room was sweltering. I leaned against the filthy wall and sweated through my official border-crossing clothes while the woman in the red dress compared my answers on the white forms to my answers on the blue forms.

"You wrote both the same," she said.

"Yes," I said apologetically, sorry to have my failure of imagination so brutally revealed. But she unlocked the door and shouted down the hall. A guard appeared. In his hand he carried a pistol that was attached to his belt by a long brown string. With a wave of the gun he indicated that I was to precede him down a long hallway, where a bearded plainclothes man stood with his forearm across the throat of an African teenager, pinning the bug-eyed boy to the wall. The guard put the pistol to my back and prodded me into a larger office, where a fat woman in an army uniform sat next to a big desk. Already she held my papers in her hand, and already she was angry.

"You wrote this!" she said. She held up the blue forms.

"Yes," I said.

"You wrote this!" she said. She held up the white forms.

"Yes."

"They are the same," she said accusingly.

"Yes."

"I! Don't! Think! So!" she said. She spread my papers on the desk and turned away from me in evident disgust. I thought about Kafka and bit my tongue.

Soon a young handsome captain came in and sat down at the desk. He lit a Marlboro and ignored me. He lounged in his chair, comfortable and rude. He looked over my forms. He looked over our documents. He looked at my passport photo. He looked at me.

"You are Jones," he said.

"Yes."

"And where is this Moogleetoon?"

"Moogleetoon is outside in our vehicle," I said. I gestured toward the hole in the wall where a window should have been and pointed out the old blue Land Rover outside.

"What is your mission in Nigeria?" he asked. It would become a familiar question.

"We are tourists," I said. "We are driving from London to South Africa."

"Are you sure?"

"Yes," I said. "We have been driving for two months."

"You lie! You are jou-rrrr-na-li-st-s," he said. The word "journalists" drooled from his lips in six syllables, a prolonged sneer. It sounded to my ears like a criminal indictment. But I knew he was guessing.

"No," I said. "We are professors." I pointed to the blue and white forms. "It is written there."

"Professors of what?" he asked, skeptical.

"My colleague is a professor of . . . communications," I said. I was thinking of Muggleton's business card: F Stop Communications—his photography moniker. Would this guy know what an f-stop is? "And I am a professor of literature," I said. (It used to be true.)

"Are you sure?" he said.

"Yes, of course."

"Li-ter-a-tur-e," he sneered.

"You have many famous writers of literature here in Nigeria, I believe," I said. The name of one the government had just murdered hung unspoken in the air between us. The captain was not pleased.

"Go out!" he commanded. "You! Stay in your car! Send in this Moogleetoon."

I had just time enough to tell Muggleton about our professorships before he got out of the Land Rover. Fifteen minutes later he came back, pleased with himself.

"He was a bit dim on communications," he said. "He wanted an example of what a professor of communications professes."

"Oh, no! What did you say?"

"I told him that I specialize in teaching the methodology of nonverbal communication for the enhancement of personal power." He paused to congratulate himself on this bravura improvisation. "Good, eh?" he said. "I told him that I teach people who want to be taken seriously to sit up straight. Take their hands out of their pockets. Make eye contact. He loved it."

Then it was my turn to face the captain again. "Moogleetoon tells the same story," he said at once when I returned to the office. He was sitting up very straight. His hands were conspicuously placed firmly on the desk before him.

"Yes, of course," I said.

The captain made contact with my eyes. I made contact with his.

"You can go," he said.

And I did.

But that was just the beginning. There were customs forms and tax forms and insurance forms and currency-declaration forms. There were questions and cross-questions in filthy offices filled with the smoke of a million Marlboros. And when, nearly four hours later, we drove away from the border, we were stopped a hundred yards down the road by police, who demanded our passports, and again a hundred yards farther along by narcotics inspectors, and again a hundred yards farther along by soldiers.

"What is your mission?" the big one barked. He leaned against the Land Rover. He rested the barrel of his AK-47 on the edge of the window, pointed casually in the general direction of Muggleton's right ear.

"My mission?" Muggleton said, momentarily taken aback. Rarely is Muggleton suspected of having any sort of mission in life. But he'd read the signs along the road. So he knew what to say. "My mission," he said cheerily, "is the Apostolic Pentecostal Evangelical International Holy Redeemer Christ Chosen Grace of God and Glory World Mission."

"What?" The soldier glared at him and shoved the gun closer. "Your mission!" he snapped again, louder. "What you are doing here?"

"Oh," Muggleton said, smiling viciously. "What I am doing here. What *am* I doing here? I know. I'm a tourist."

"Tourist?" The soldier stared, incredulous at the thought that a foreigner might undertake a holiday in a country from which so many residents had fled. "You lie!" he snarled. "What is your true mission?"

Muggleton tried again. "Honestly, I'm a tourist. And my true mission is to get out of Nigeria as quickly as possible."

That was a mission the soldier could understand. Pleased with himself at having wrung this confession from Muggleton, the soldier demanded only a few of our documents and spent only ten minutes or so riffling through them. We drove on and Muggleton emitted weird strangled cries that gathered volume and burst forth in a kind of primal scream. "Fucking nightmare! Fucking bloody hell!" We were stopped twenty-seven times in the first few kilometers. And during the four days it took us to cross Nigeria, we were stopped so often we lost count. We never traveled more than twenty kilometers without meeting a blockade. The military presence was a measure of the perverse tenacity of General Sani Abacha.

At one roadblock, Muggleton reported to the officer what we'd just seen: a dead woman in the road. She lay sprawled in the right lane, one arm flung out. Her tin basin lay by the roadside, and across the pavement were scattered the oranges she'd been carrying on her head. They had been flattened by passing cars. Even before we saw her—a pretty red cotton wrap stretched over her swollen body—we smelled that peculiar stench of dead flesh. She must have been there for days.

"There's a woman lying dead in the road back there," Muggleton told the soldier.

"Oh, yes," he said indifferently. "They walk in the road and they get knocked over."

Every soldier who stopped us wanted to know only two things: "What is your mission?" and "What have you got for me?" They stopped us eagerly, hoping for a big payoff, but with the dictator determined to prevent a popular uprising, it was their fellow citizens they were out to intimidate. At every roadblock we watched them flourish their weapons and pocket fistfuls of money handed over by their own countrymen. The arrogance of it, and the injustice, turned Muggleton into a kind of Rambo of the road.

"Good morning, officer," he'd say with a big smile. "Are you well?"

"Driver's license!" the officer would snap, waving his pistol in Muggleton's face. "You don't have Nigerian driver's license. You go to jail."

"I don't mind," Muggleton would say, smiling that innocent boyish grin, and stretch out his hand. And every time the fool officer would grasp it. From the far side of the Land Rover I would hear the sound of knuckles cracking and see the flash of pain and dismay cross the officer's face.

"You have a good firm handshake, officer," Muggleton would say, still beaming. "I like that."

Confused, the officer would try to salvage something from the encounter. "What have you brought me for Christmas then?" he'd say.

And Muggleton, always smiling, would say, "I bring you greetings from the queen of England."

Muggleton would laugh. The officer would laugh. They'd have a hearty laugh together, two good old boys—one black, one white, one Nigerian, one British, with a world of bad history between them— sizing each other up, reaching an understanding that even now the *oyinbo,* the white man, had the edge. And Muggleton would drive on, waving, smiling, leaving the officer with a sore, empty hand.

It was the border crossing and the roadblocks that held us up and stranded us in Lagos at night. We made for the motorway that would carry us around the city, but it was near dusk when we found it. We crept along, as traffic does in Lagos, until Muggleton saw a chance to cross a crumbling concrete barrier into a center section of the motorway that was inexplicably empty but for a few cars racing through the void at breakneck speed. He swerved toward the barrier, and I glanced back to see the headlight on the car to our left crumple as the Land Rover cut across its path.

"You've crunched this man's car," I said.

"He should have given way," said the Road Warrior.

Muggleton spurted ahead. The angry driver of the crunched Peugeot spurted after us. I found myself suddenly in the middle of a bad movie. Night was falling fast through hot damp air already thick with pollution. Cars sped past on a motorway laced with potholes big enough to swallow a child. And Muggleton was engaged in a high-speed chase with two men in a one-eyed Peugeot. The car careened around us into our path. The passenger leaned out the window screaming. I could see that Muggleton wanted to slam the Peugeot with the side of the Land Rover, leaving it piled on the concrete median strip in flames. He swung away, then closed in again. The collision would take place on my side of the vehicle.

"We could stop and talk to them," I said.

I watched Muggleton's better nature struggle with this prissy suggestion. And then we were stopped at the side of the motorway and our adversaries were upon us—two young men, hysterical and furious. They were Yoruba, fierce and scary. They screamed at Muggleton and shook their fists. He wrecked their car, and they would make him pay. Muggleton amazed them by screaming back. He did not touch their car, he lied, and if they didn't shut up, he would kill them both. He jumped from the Land Rover, and the two men ran. The two of them together were not as big as Muggleton, or as big as he made himself look at that moment. He spread his arms and walked wide-legged, approximating the stance and demeanor of King Kong. They ducked behind their car and pounded on it with their fists, screaming. Muggleton screamed back: "Calm down! Calm down or I will kill you!"

Suddenly the movie stopped—as if the film had broken or the houselights gone up. Suddenly the actors ran out of steam. Muggleton reassembled the broken light socket for the driver and demonstrated that the damage was slight. The driver said it was his father's car, and he would have to have it fixed. I slipped him an American twenty-dollar bill. He peered at it in the light of his newly reassembled headlamp and grinned. More than enough, he said. We shook hands all around.

Then we drove away again, slamming through potholes in the dark on the unlit motorway. Hours later, when at last we reached the highway to Ibadan, we were turned back by the police. Too dangerous to drive the highway at night, they said. "Robbers! Murderers!" Instead they sent us through the dodgy streets of Lagos to an expensive international hotel, distinguished chiefly by the hot couture of the prostitutes draped in the lobby bar. The next morning, as we crept once again through Lagos traffic toward the highway, I said, "Here's what I think. Right now we should follow the example of God, who certainly has forsaken this country." Muggleton agreed. And that—despite all the roadblocks that lay between us and the far, far frontier of Cameroon—is what we did.

It was only much later, after our journey was over, that I read what Chinua Achebe had written of his native land: "Nigeria is not a great country. It is one of the most disorderly nations in the world. It is one of the most corrupt, insensitive, inefficient places under the sun. It is dirty, callous, noisy, ostentatious, dishonest and vulgar. In short it is among the most unpleasant places on earth." It was only much later, after I'd searched elsewhere in Africa and found the peaceable Queen in a peaceable land, that I read Wole Soyinka's passionate personal account of the terrible disintegration of his country, *The Open Sore of a Continent*. He reports that, like most everything else in Nigeria, the mechanism of the gallows in Port Harcourt was badly deteriorated and didn't function properly when the dissidents of Ogoniland were put to death. Ken Saro-Wiwa, the first of the MOSOP men to be executed, had to be hanged five times before the sentence of death was successfully carried out. Soyinka writes that as Saro-Wiwa was dragged away from the gallows for the third or fourth time, he said, "What kind of nation is this?"

FEMINISTS AND *FONS*

When we were stranded for the night at the overpriced hotel in Lagos, we watched television. The saturation ad for the holiday season on the international channels featured this voice-over: "All over Europe, millions of men are wondering what to get their wives for Christmas." The answer: a Karscher Window Washer, complete with battery pack and recharger. You could send away to Germany for it, and put it on your credit card. The video showed a happy *Hausfrau* bustling about her high-tech German house wearing a Karscher Window Washer on her back like a scuba tank—washing, washing, washing.

"We should get one for the Land Rover," Muggleton said. We had only an old-fashioned low-tech squeegee.

I imagined the faces of women all over Europe at Christmas, opening their gift boxes, donning their Karscher Window Washers, laughing happily in their eagerness to get right to work. "Darling! Just what I wanted!" And I tried to imagine the faces of women all over Africa if they were ever to see this ad. What would they make of it? They didn't have battery-powered Window Washers. Most of them didn't have windows. Or glass anyway. If they eventually came to live in houses with glass windows, would they get Karscher Window Washers too? Or would African women still be smart enough to spot a useless task? Would they still have better things to do? And what of the Queen of Lovedu? In the unlikely event that she lived in a palatial hut grand enough to have real windows, would a queen who specialized in making rain even care if the glass was streaked?

So many Africans seemed like the Igbo protagonists of Chinua Achebe's novels, for whom with changing times things fall apart. So

many African women seemed like Nnu Ego, the heroine of Buchi
Emecheta's novel *The Joys of Motherhood,* who allows herself to wonder,
in her forties, "where it was she had gone wrong. She had had children,
nine in all, and luckily seven were alive. . . . Still, how was she to know
that by the time her children grew up the values of her country, her
people and her tribe would have changed so drastically, to the extent
where a woman with many children could face a lonely old age, and
maybe a miserable death all alone, just like a barren woman? She was
not even certain that worries over her children would not send her to
her grave."

Such thoughts crossed my mind as we drove through the wooded
hills of western Cameroon. Along the road we traveled stood red
mud-brick houses, clustered in tidy and prosperous-looking villages.
There were well-scrubbed children in school uniforms—some girls and
many boys—trooping toward larger villages, where the schools stood.
There were family-planning centers in many villages, and health clinics
too. But at the edge of the roadway women squatted in the dirt and
chopped up manioc tubers with pangas. They spread the pieces to
dry in the sun. The fermenting manioc filled the air with the strong
unpleasant smell of bad cheese.

That evening, to celebrate our liberation from Nigeria, we made
camp at a village near the border and passed a pleasant evening talking
with patrons of the local bar. Jacob was a young doctor, well educated
in England and trained as a surgeon, but his job was to supervise rural
health centers in this remote province. Once he had practiced at a hospital in the capital, but he'd been rusticated for his political views by
Cameroon's notoriously repressive government. He seemed pleased to
have escaped with his life and told us his history without complaint,
merely to explain how he came to be living in a tiny village in the forest.
But he had one great problem, he said. His Western medical training
left him unable to deal with the power of traditional medicine.

"I could tell you of fifteen cases I've seen personally," he said, "where
there was nothing wrong with the patient—nothing modern science
could find—yet the patient died. Why? Because the medicine man had
said he would. The spell is cast, the patient wastes away, and we modern
doctors can't do a thing. I can't explain it. And my colleagues in the
West don't even want to hear about it. It's all voodoo humbug to them."

There it was: the irreconcilable contradiction between the old ways and the new, though in this case it was modern science that fell apart before the force of knowledge much older and more arcane.

One thing we learned for sure as we made our way across Cameroon. In neither the old world nor the new did women rule. Ruling was the job of a tyrannical male president in the capital—Paul Biya had been in power since 1982—and various male chiefs and kings locally throughout the country. In the western part of Cameroon, the kings were called *fons*. A *fon* inherited his office from his father and kept it for life. A *fon* lived in the splendid isolation of his own power. No one questioned a *fon* or contradicted him. No one touched a *fon*. In the presence of a *fon,* one bowed and clapped three times. And no ordinary woman spoke to him, not even his wives—of which he had as many as he liked.

I learned these facts from Ya Wende, the queen mother of Chobe, who had about as much power as a woman could get in Cameroon— the power to speak to a *fon*. A woman of large proportions, Ya Wende wore capacious garments of traditional Cameroonian black cotton overlaid with colorful appliqué and embroidered in red and gold. About her neck she wore a string of red and white beads, the badge of her office. On her head she wore a conical cap that seemed to be woven of fine interlaced braids of human hair. Beneath it her own finely plaited black hair stood out as if charged with energy. She spoke softly and smiled an inscrutable smile even when she uttered the most terrible complaints. What she complained about was the life of the average village woman of Cameroon. Complaining was her job, really. She was not some idle royal—not even a member of the royal family of Chobe—but a kind of civil servant appointed by a progressive ruler: Chief Fobuzi, *fon* of Chobe. Her task was to report to him what his speechless female subjects thought. Without Ya Wende, he wouldn't have a clue.

I ran into Ya Wende at an extraordinary meeting in Bamenda, the capital of North West province. Muggleton and I had set up camp on the grounds of a Presbyterian mission on the outskirts of town; and because Bamenda was a pleasant place, set high among cool green hills, and the market was full of fresh vegetables, we agreed to lay over for a couple of days. Muggleton wanted time to work on the Land Rover, which was wobbling again, and I wanted to attend the women's meeting. It was one of several regional meetings around the country convened and paid for by the government of Cameroon. Its purpose was to draw up a National Plan of Action to improve the conditions of women. The National Plan was meant to accord with the Global Plan of Action enacted at the International Women's Conference held in Beijing in September 1994, the largest women's conference in the history of the world. Hillary Clinton went to Beijing and made a speech. A lot of my friends went to Beijing, and I'd have gone myself if my Chinese visa had been issued in time. But as far as I knew, neither Hillary Clinton nor any of my friends nor any other woman who went to Beijing had ever been invited to make a plan of action for the American government—federal, state, or local. I had to go to Cameroon to find a government that took the Beijing conference seriously. Odd, isn't it, in a country where women seemed to count for nothing at all?

Anyway, when I showed up at the Bamenda meeting, I was seated next to Ya Wende. As we waited for the provincial governor to appear, she leaned her massive presence toward me, smiled her angelic smile, and gave me an earful. What it boiled down to was another massive contradiction: we sat in a room full of well-dressed, highly educated, middle-class professional Cameroonian women, many of whom had driven to the meeting in their own cars, but the average woman of Cameroon had no education, no profession, certainly no car, and virtually no rights at all. Forty percent of them were illiterate. Of all the citizens of Cameroon who had never gone to school, seventy percent were women.

When the men arrived at the meeting—the governor, the mayor of Bamenda, and a phalanx of four *fons* in ornate and splendid robes—the speeches started. The mayor called for a new equal partnership of peace and mutual respect in the family. The governor called for a new equal partnership of women and men in building the nation of Cameroon. The *fons* shook their hoary heads and applauded vigorously. The women delegates called out, "Beautiful!" "Yes!" "We support you!" Ya Wende fingered her beads of office and smiled.

Later, when I returned to our camp, I blurted out to Muggleton what I'd learned from Ya Wende. "Eighty percent of women in Cameroon are farmers," I told him, "but they can't own land. They can't own *anything*—not even their own children." I watched his eyes glaze over.

"Women's whinging," he said. Like privileged people everywhere,

Muggleton believed he'd *earned* his advantages. "Why don't women stop complaining and do whatever it is they want to do?" he said.

"We're trying," I said. "But listen to this: women here have no say in who they'll marry or how many kids they'll have. It's like slavery."

"Don't be bloody ridiculous," Muggleton said.

He ducked his head under the hood of the Land Rover to end the conversation—as he often did when the subject was women's rights. But the next morning he allowed himself to be persuaded to go with me to the conference to videotape an interview with Ya Wende. Reluctantly he set up the video camera on the lawn of the Hotel Ayaba, where the conference was taking place. A chair was brought for Ya Wende and another for the traditional ruler who had appointed her, the *fon* of Chobe, who had condescended to be interviewed as well. Ya Wende spread her magisterial presence before the camera and enumerated in impeccable English the chief complaints of the village women, the majority of women, in Cameroon. They own nothing, she said— no money, no credit, no land, no property, not even their own bodies, which belong by rights to the *fon* or to their husbands, who own the children as well. Muggleton heaved a great sigh of impatience and went on filming as Ya Wende complained of traditional taboos that keep girls at work in the family hut and out of school. Then she went on to marriage.

"Any man can buy a girl or woman from the *fon* and do with her as he likes," she said. "The girl has nothing to say about it."

Muggleton grimaced and raised his head from the camera. "I have a question," he said rudely. What had made me think he could keep his mouth shut? "If she doesn't like it, why doesn't she refuse?"

Ya Wende smiled and said softly, "If she refuses, she will be turned out of the village, an outcast. No one will take her in."

"So? Then what?" Muggleton said.

"She will go into the bush by herself," Ya Wende said.

"So?" Muggleton said again.

Ya Wende went on smiling. "There she will die," she said.

Just then the *fon* of Chobe appeared for his interview, wearing a traditional shirt and trousers of finest white African cotton, richly embroidered in threads of gold. A thoughtful, articulate man, Chief Fobuzi was an anomaly among the *fons*. He was an intellectual and a civil servant, the provincial delegate in charge of education for much of the country. He sent his sons to college in the United States. He had appointed Ya Wende to represent women's interests, and he had come to Bamenda to help draw up the National Plan of Action for women.

"I myself am an example of rapidly changing times in Cameroon," he said. "For example, my father had twenty-five wives and thirty-five children, while I myself have only four wives and ten children." He fell silent, pondering this transformation. "Who knows," he said, "but that my successor may have only three wives, or two?"

To get a clearer picture of the typical *fon,* Chief Fobuzi suggested we visit a more traditional ruler, the *fon* of Nkwem, at his palace in a nearby village. "The more traditional *fons* will be at home at their palaces," he said. "They will not attend this women's meeting."

Muggleton was excited. "This is the photo op I've been looking for," he said. "The real Africa. The real center of tribal power." He dreamed of an exotic and splendid mansion, something on the scale of Windsor Castle. "The *fon* must have many wives," he said, "and a bloody great palace." As we drove out of Bamenda into the hills, he rattled on. "What a break. What a photo op. Think of the art. The masks. The wood carving. The gold. It'll be brilliant."

When the tarmac ended, we followed a red dirt road that narrowed as it snaked deeper into the bush. At last we came to a battered, hand-lettered signboard pointing the way to the Fon's Palace, and we turned into a trash-strewn parking lot. Before us stood a run-down one-story building of faded blue stucco and glass. In the States it might have been, in its better days, a Chinese restaurant in a suburban shopping center. Through dusty windows we could see a large empty room—the *fon's* royal reception hall. At the moment it was locked up tight. A young boy in a black Las Vegas tee shirt emerged from behind the building and told us that the *fon* was at home but not receiving. Not receiving us anyway. Behind the palace we glimpsed a row of huts—the same traditional Cameroonian huts of red mud brick found in every village, but these seemed smaller, jammed shoulder to shoulder like the cabins of some cut-rate motel. The boy offered to show us around. He was, he said, one of the sons of the *fon* of Nkwem.

"How many children does he have?" I asked.

The boy thought and thought. "I don't know," he said. "Many, many. He has twenty-four wives."

Each woman had her own hut, the boy said, where she lived with her children until the children were old enough to move out of the palace and live, as he did, in the village with their grandparents. He showed us through the women's quarters: twenty-four identical mud-brick huts, ranged like cells around the perimeter of a bare muddy lot. Each held a single room containing a dilapidated cot or two and some scattered possessions: a few pots, a yam pounder, a folded cloth of printed cotton that would be the woman's other dress. Over a wood fire in the middle of her room, one woman was roasting ears of maize, another plantains. Five women sat on the bare ground outside under a solitary mango tree, plaiting one another's hair. They wore dingy tee shirts and cotton wraps. Another woman sat alone before her doorway weaving a large basket of raffia and palm fiber. "She is the first wife," the boy said. "She is the most important woman in the palace." Her long fingers moved swiftly, creating an exquisite design. When she was finished, she would put the beautiful basket on her back, much like a Karscher Window Washer, but she would use it to carry firewood from the forest and manioc tubers from the field.

Muggleton was taking photographs, and he was oddly quiet. The shabby palace—so far short of his aristocratic European expectations—left him with nothing to say. The Queen of Lovedu must live like this, I thought, remembering that the once-powerful king of Bamenda lived in a big grass hut. What Muggleton would have called real palaces—the sprawling presidential estate of Houphouët-Boigny, the immense air-conditioned chandeliered jungle palazzo of Mobutu Sese Seko—were architectural bastards conceived in Europe. And the Queen of Lovedu had never been to Europe. Being female, she'd be lucky to have gone to school.

At last we nodded our goodbyes to the women and asked the *fon*'s young son, who of course did go to school and spoke English, to thank the *fon*'s wives, who stayed home and did not, for allowing us to visit them. At the edge of the compound we turned to look back, as if both of us felt the need to hold this picture in our minds. Thin pigs and chickens walked in and out of the houses of the twenty-four wives of the *fon* of Nkwem.

MALARIA AND MISSIONARIES

A t the border the Road Warrior went ballistic again. What was wrong with this man? Usually he stayed in the Land Rover at checkpoints while I cleared our documents with officials. That's what he did while I completed the departure formalities at the Office of Cameroon Customs and Immigration. But a little way down the road, when we pulled up at the entry checkpoint for the Central African Republic (CAR), Muggleton announced, "I'll take care of these chaps." He got bored waiting in the vehicle. He snatched the folder of documents from my hands and disappeared through the open doorway of a little wooden shed labeled IMMIGRATION. Within minutes I heard an African man shouting in Sango and Muggleton shouting back, "The bloody hell you can!"

When I walked in, Muggleton was standing toe to toe, nose to nose, with a big African in uniform. Behind the African, flanking him, stood two more guards with AK-47s at the ready. The African was sweating, and Muggleton had gone all red in the face. They shouted, and spittle flew across the closing gap between their chins. Another man, who stood behind a desk near the door, was muttering something in French about cholera and fanning the air with a yellow paper that I recognized as Muggleton's international health certificate.

Muggleton bellowed, "The bloody hell you will!"

His next move, I knew, would be to bash the African in two or three places simultaneously, using both fists and feet, and send him flying backward to take out both the men who backed him up. I stepped behind Muggleton, caught the eye of one of the armed guards, and circled my finger at the side of my head in the international gesture that says, "You are dealing here with a crazy person." The guard stepped forward and muttered something to the shouting African, who laughed and drew back, while I grabbed Muggleton's belt and dragged him— still screaming—outside.

"They won't let me into the bloody country!" he shouted. "They can't bloody well keep me out!"

"Calm down, Muggleton," I said.

"They told me to go back to bloody Nigeria!" he shouted. *"Nigeria!"*

"Calm down, Muggleton. Calm down, and stay here, or . . ." I cast about for the sort of threat Muggleton himself would use. "Calm down and stay here, or I'll kill you."

I went inside and got the story from the sharp-eyed clerk behind the desk, who had spotted the blank line on Muggleton's health certificate where a doctor should have signed off on his cholera vaccination. Without that signature, the clerk explained, the health certificate was no good. And without a valid health certificate, Muggleton could not enter the Central African Republic. I thanked him, flashed what I hoped was a winning smile at the guards, and took the health certificate out to the vehicle, where Muggleton was pacing and cursing and slamming his fists into the minimally padded car seat. I found a pen and filled the blank line on the health certificate with the first name that came to mind: Dr. Strangelove, M.D. I tried to make it cramped and illegible like the signature of a real doctor. "Good show," Muggleton said with a wink, and went on pacing. I rubbed some dirt over the page for the sake of authenticity, and then I took the certificate back inside.

"I'm so sorry," I said, "but my colleague gave you the wrong certificate. Here is his new one." The clerk examined the new signature and said something in Sango to the guards, who gathered round to look at it as well.

"Très bien!" the clerk said. He was grinning. "That will do very well." Then they were all laughing and slapping my hand—an African high five. They knew what I'd done and seemed pleased that I'd found such a simple way out for all of us. They helped me through the rest of the paperwork and then stood in the road to wave us on our way. Muggleton waved back.

I couldn't resist borrowing his favorite self-congratulatory line: "Good, eh?"

"Yes," he said. "I put the fear in them. I reckon we're getting rather good at this bad cop, good cop routine."

We drove on to Bangui, the capital, and found a walled and guarded campground on the outskirts. Despite its pleasant location, on the Oubangui River, Bangui is a notoriously dangerous place for overlanders, swarming with expert thieves and thugs. If you drive through town in a Land Rover full of gear, you might as well hang a sign on the back saying: STEAL THIS! We'd been warned by overlanders we'd met along the way, and we'd agreed to press on quickly for Zaire, so I was surprised when Muggleton said he wanted to linger. He was tired, he said, and stiff with aches and pains. For two days he lay low, snoozing in his tent. I carried him cold Cokes and half a chicken from the open-air restaurant nearby, but he scarcely touched his food. Then he told me he'd decided to take a course of Halfan. That meant only one thing: malaria.

"Let's go to the French hospital," I said. The French were still a presence in the capital, and the hospital was reportedly a good one. (It was the French who claimed Central Africa in the 1880s and parceled it out, for a share of the profits, to private European concessions that ran their enterprises with forced labor. The French lingered unofficially after independence in 1960, supporting a series of dictators—including the crazed Emperor Bokassa—and maintaining a keen interest in the country's uranium.) But Muggleton bloody well wasn't about to go to any bloody frog hospital. "Let's get you to a doctor," I said. But he bloody well wasn't about to go to any bloody frog doctor or any bloody African doctor either.

"No. No. No. No," he said to every suggestion. He'd had malaria before. He knew what to do. He'd treat it himself.

"At least let's rest up here then," I said. "Let's chill out until you feel better." It was precisely the wrong thing to say. He swallowed some Halfan and started packing. He was ready to go in no time—as cross as a bear and impatient to get back on the road—but when he asked me to drive, I knew he must be very ill. So I was worried and distracted when we set off. Worse, we had to drive our loaded Land Rover to the city center so that I could send out my latest Internet dispatch. In my hurry, when I jumped out of the vehicle and zipped across the street to the express office, I violated two cardinal rules of security: I left my window open, and I left something of value—my laptop computer—in plain view on the front seat. To Bangui's band of highly polished thieves, this was as good as a personal invitation. A pair of them answered the call. One reached through the open window on the passenger side, where Muggleton sat slumped in the corner, and punched him in the face while the other reached through the driver's window to snag the computer. But they hadn't reckoned on Muggleton. Much less a malarial Muggleton in a bad mood. He sprang from the car, decked his assailant with a quick jab, and leaped over the hood in time to see the accomplice drop the computer and run. When I came back, a man with a bloody face lay crumpled next to the vehicle, and Muggleton was slumped in his corner again. "Don't ask," he said. "Let's just get out of here."

So I drove a battered Land Rover and a stubborn malaria-ridden companion out of a capital city equipped with hospitals and drugstores and embassies and an airport into the wilds of Central Africa and Zaire. The quick fight left Muggleton's mind, already riled by malaria, swamped with adrenaline. It's a deadly combination, like alcohol and barbiturates. It didn't kill him, but it flooded his brain with bilious vapors. It sent him into terminal bad temper and borderline dementia. His personality deteriorated before my eyes. He bleated. He whinged. He nagged. He carped. He whimpered. He cursed. I worried about him, but I noted with relief that he was at no stage too ill to tell me what I was doing wrong. When we pulled off the road into the bush for lunch, Muggleton sort of fell out of the vehicle—though I noticed he had the presence of mind to grab the cushions from behind the seat before he hit the ground. There he lay on his back, ashen, sweating, shaking.

"Are the boards all right?" he mumbled. "Check on the boards." It took me a while to figure out that the boards in question were surfboards. We weren't carrying any surfboards, except in Muggleton's mind.

"They're fine," I said. I put up Muggleton's tent, laid out his bedroll, and prepared to wait out his delirium. Late in the day I heard him mewing and found him standing in a clearing, clad only in his towel. Black dirt and leaf muck paraded down his face, across his shoulder and chest. He'd gone into the bushes to vomit and awakened facedown in the dirt. Not to worry, though, he knew what he was doing, he said. He'd just have a bowl of Chinese noodles for dinner in his tent, thank you very much. With maybe some greens thrown in, and a couple of those little green onions. And another round of Halfan. And a Coke would be nice. And maybe a little warm water to wash up? I fetched a bucket of water from the river and fired up the propane stove. Would I find him dead in the morning, I wondered, or would I strangle him with my own hands?

As it turned out, he felt a little better in the morning—well enough to slouch in the passenger seat as I drove on to Mboye, where we planned to get the ferry across the Oubangui River to Zaire. But my driving drove him crazy. Muggleton adheres to the motoring motto "Never slacken, never give way," while I habitually slow down for villages, schools, curves, potholes, pedestrians, bicyclists, oncoming vehicles in a one-lane track, and scenery. Too ill to drive himself, he had to put up with it.

"You're a bloody hopeless driver," he said, groaning. "I should be traveling with my mates."

"You don't have any mates," I said. "You're too mean."

Toward dusk the road grew crowded and tricky to negotiate. Women headed for home, bearing basins of manioc leaves or pineapples or clean laundry. Men rode bicycles freighted with guns and slaughtered monkeys and stalks of plantains. Excited chickens and goats dashed back and forth across the road, apparently bent on suicide. I obliged by clipping a scrawny hen and then a young black goat who threw himself, panic-stricken, under the wheels.

"You take the record for livestock," Muggleton muttered, twisting in his seat to see if irate villagers were giving chase. "I'll give you that."

"Thanks," I said. "As fast as you drive, it must be hard to aim properly, but you could probably get the hang of it with a little practice."

At Mboye we learned that the official border crossing to Zaire was officially closed. "Mobutu," said a policeman. That one word—the name of the man who had been president for three decades—explained almost everything about Zaire. "Gbadolite is just across the river," the officer explained. "Mobutu's home village. Not for tourists. Only VIPs." It would be harder to get into Zaire than we'd thought. Like Houphouët-Boigny in Côte d'Ivoire, Mobutu had transformed the village of his birth and built himself a palace, reportedly a copy of one that belonged to his friend the late Shah of Iran, and an airstrip suitable for the supersonic Concorde he often chartered from Air France; but as opposition to his dictatorial rule grew, it became one of his hideouts. He had shut down the roads, and now the ferry, the way a medieval king might hole up in his castle and pull in the drawbridge over the moat. We were stuck outside.

I set up camp on the grounds of a coffee plantation near the river, zipped Muggleton into his tent, and delivered another bowl of noodles garnished with Halfan to his door. Then I spread my bedroll on the roof of the Land Rover and gave myself over to grim contemplation of our circumstances. Agreeing to leave Bangui with Muggleton so ill, I thought, was the single worst decision I had made in a long life generally undistinguished by wise moves. Would I get him out of here alive? I lay listening to the shrill of a million frogs filling the night with high anxiety. Then I noticed that the grass all around was aglow with fireflies. They hovered over Muggleton's tent like stars.

The next day we had to drive to the ferry crossing at Bangassou, four hundred kilometers upriver. Worse, to get to the main road we had to retrace our drive through the villages I'd so recently deprived of livestock. We'd scarcely gotten under way when we came upon a large troop of armed soldiers in the road. "They're probably investigating the goat murder," Muggleton muttered from his corner. But they waved and let us pass by. Seven hours later at Bangassou we found the border open and the ferry running, but the Customs Office was closed. The chief of Customs had retired to the bar for the remainder of the day. We found him there with his feet well planted on the table. He could not be moved. So we went in search of a place to pitch our tents for the night and found one on a cool bluff overlooking the river.

The sign said BIBLE COLLEGE, and the grounds resembled a cut-rate reproduction of a New England campus: many little redbrick bungalows and huts laid out around a tree-shaded common fragrant with frangipani. In front of a bungalow at the top of the drive stood a couple of kids' bikes and a baby buggy, and a man hurried out the door to greet us. Jerry, the Baptist minister who headed the mission, was a down-to-earth guy who might have been selling farm equipment in Des Moines if he hadn't spent his life selling Jesus in Bangassou. He'd inherited the job from his parents, who had been missionaries here before him and brought him into the world at this very place. Jerry knew Sango, the simple trading language widely spoken in CAR, and said he always used it to speak to Africans. "If you speak French," he said, "they treat you like French." Now he had thirteen students in the Bible College, African men (only) who came to study for four years and then establish churches of their own. Each student lived in a little brick hut, and the student's wife could build a kitchen for herself out back. Actually it was Jerry's wife and four other missionaries who ran the Bible College now while Jerry drove around the bush in a wheezy old Toyota truck calling upon sixty churches under his supervision, all with African ministers, all with congregations numbering in the hundreds. This seemed like success, although the total number of Central Africans converted to Christianity during two generations of Jerry's family's ministry was considerably less than the number of slaves exported annually from this area in the previous century; and the thirty-five Baptist churches in Missouri that supported the work never sent enough money to make ends meet. "My truck is my mission," Jerry said to explain why he spent half his monthly salary of $1,100 on truck repairs.

Jerry and his wife, Lucy, showed us where to put up our tents on the common, and invited us in for a shower, an Aunt Jemima pancake supper with their three kids, and after-dinner Jiffy Pop popcorn and carols with the other missionaries beside a plastic Christmas tree topped by an angel with a white face. Their little bungalow in the middle of Africa was fitted up with cheap American furniture and a Siamese cat; and Lucy, who wore dangling snowman earrings for the occasion, had taught the African house servant to make Christmas cookies shaped like fir trees. Jerry and Lucy spoke with a certain yearning of going "home" soon to Missouri for a year's leave.

"Africans are changing," Jerry said. "My father could tell them anything and they'd believe it, just because he was a white man. And the French knew how to keep the lid on so that white people could live here. Now Africans question everything and challenge and demand. They're starting to think for themselves. When they get democracy, whites will be gone."

"Come on now," Lucy said, to lighten the moment. "Let's all sing 'Rudolph the Red-Nosed Reindeer'!"

Later they saw us off to our tents with a tin of sugar cookies, a loaf of banana bread, and many merry-Christmas wishes. I walked out to the edge of the bluff, from where I could just make out in the moonlight the shimmer of the river far below, and beyond it the deeper darkness of Zaire, where, far to the southwest, lay the old Kongo kingdom, at the heart of the continent. That was the land that Leopold II, king of the Belgians, had contrived to claim—not for his country but for himself. His grand machinations unbalanced nineteenth-century Europe and impelled its leaders to gather in Berlin in 1884 to ratify Leopold's claim and parcel out some other bits of the continent for themselves. The following year King Leopold's king-sized piece became the État Indépendant du Congo—the Congo Free State. It was not a colony but the private domain of one ambitious and unscrupulous capitalist: a wretched and appalling place where, for the better part of a century, white men seeking profits carried out an African holocaust. Their aim was not genocide; they didn't want to exterminate Africans, but to make them work. Leopold's agents first seized ivory, and after the invention of pneumatic tires, they turned in the 1890s to harvesting wild rubber, shipping out eleven million tons a year by the turn of the century. At the same time they hacked a railroad 350 kilometers through rock and forest around the rapids above the mouth of the Congo River, thus connecting more than eleven thousand kilometers of navigable rivers upstream to the sea. All of this they accomplished with the unpaid labor of Africans driven by the Maxim machine gun, the *chicotte*—a searing corkscrew whip of sun-dried hippo hide—and the practice of locking up women and children, without food, as hostages. Africans fought back: the Yaka for ten years, the Chokwe for twenty, the Boa, the Budja, the Sanga—all decimated in the end by Leopold's army of African mercenaries, the Force Publique. To prove their worth and account for bullets spent, the soldiers were required to bring back to headquarters the hands of their victims, carefully smoked over the campfire to prevent rot.

In 1890, a thirty-two-year-old Polish-born seaman named Józef Teodor Konrad Korzeniowski, an apprentice officer on the steamboat *Roi des Belges,* traveled sixteen thousand kilometers up the Congo and back again. Along the way he saw such things, and ten years later, as Joseph Conrad, he wrote them down in *Heart of Darkness.* Literary critics like to say the classic novel is an enigmatic parable of the human condition, but Conrad himself said his story was about specific "experience . . . pushed a little (and only very little) beyond the actual facts of the case." There's no doubt Conrad's portrait of Kurtz, collector of

African heads, is based on an agent of King Leopold. The only question is which one, there having been several who fit the description. No doubt at all that the darkness at the heart of the heart of darkness is white. As Conrad's storyteller, Marlow, says, "The conquest of the earth, which mostly means the taking it away from those who have a different complexion or slightly flatter noses than ourselves, is not a pretty thing when you look into it too much." Perhaps that explains why five hundred white Christian missionaries in the Congo failed to breathe a word to the world of what was really going on.

Leopold enjoyed an international reputation as a great philanthropist, a man of lofty motives who devoted his personal fortune to a noble humanitarian project in Africa to "regenerate" the black man and create in the Congo a "model state." But eventually word of his atrocities leaked out. He tried to save his kingdom by showering plots on influential Americans—the Guggenheims, J. P. Morgan, John D. Rockefeller, Jr.—but in 1908 he was compelled to sell the whole package at a profit to Belgium. In the Congo, business continued as usual with the same officials still in charge and the Force Publique still ensuring a good supply of forced labor for new rubber plantations and for mines producing tin, copper, gold, and most of the uranium that built the bombs labeled HIROSHIMA and NAGASAKI. All the while Africans were dying of starvation, exhaustion, exposure, disease, and murder. White men kept few records of black lives, but ethnographers estimate that between 1880 and 1920 at least half the population of the Congo perished. Ten million people. Ten million people dead of "The horror! The horror!" During that time it's estimated that Leopold *personally* drew a profit from his Congo empire of 220 million francs, or $1.1 billion in today's dollars. He squandered most of it on grand public buildings in Belgium and, after the turn of the century, when at age sixty-five he took up with a sixteen-year-old French girl named Blanche, on palaces for himself and for her. Afterward, generations of Congolese children read in their Belgian schoolbooks about the heroic efforts of noble Belgians who in the nineteenth century brought civilization to the Congo and rescued its people from Arab slavers; but African oral history still remembers the period known in the Mongo language as *lokeli*—the overwhelming.

Independence finally came to the Democratic Republic of the Congo in 1960, and a brief moment of hope in Patrice Lumumba, the nationalist leader and the first (and only) democratically elected prime minister. Political independence was not enough, he said; the Congo must no longer be an economic colony of Europe and America. Lumumba's message resounded throughout Africa—and Washington, D.C., where the United States National Security Council subcommittee on covert operations, which included CIA head Allen Dulles, ordered his assassination. Eisenhower approved. In January 1961, Lumumba was delivered up to his indigenous enemies, in Katanga province, murdered at Elisabethville, and reportedly driven away in the trunk of a CIA car to be dumped in an unmarked grave. The CIA paid off Joseph Désiré Mobutu, army chief of staff and former NCO in the Force Publique; he later visited the White House, where President Kennedy gave him an airplane and a U.S. Air Force crew to fly it.

In 1965 Mobutu seized power in the Congo—richly backed by the United States, France, and Belgium—renamed the place Zaire, and began to reap the profits of selling his country once again to the West. In the next thirty years he pocketed more than a billion dollars in U.S. aid, and more from France, to secure his place as Africa's most successful and enduring neocolonial puppet. He took to carrying a carved ebony walking stick and wearing a jaunty leopard-skin hat designed for him by a milliner in Paris. He visited President Reagan from time to time, and President Bush, who hailed him as "one of our most valued friends." Following King Leopold's example, Mobutu took over the country's gold mines as his own. And he built palaces: in his hometown and in Belgium, France, Switzerland, Portugal, Spain. His palatial villa on the French Riviera was only a few miles down the coast from the estate at Cap Ferrat where Leopold had cavorted with his teenage mistress. Neighbors. Brothers under the skin. Though Mobutu amassed the greater personal fortune: at least $4 billion. It was as if Mobutu, a bright and ambitious pupil, reincarnated the Belgian example of autocracy, atrocity, and plunder in his own stout black person, crowned by that snazzy hat, crafted from the pelt of an African animal, slain and skinned and sewn up in Paris. He renamed himself too: Mobutu Sese Seko Kuku Ngbendu Wa Za Banga. The official translation is "Mobutu, the earthy, the peppery, all-powerful warrior who, by his endurance and inflexible will to win, sweeps from conquest to conquest leaving fire in his wake." Zaireans will tell you it means "Mobutu, the Cock Who Leaves No Hen Untouched."

I thought about these things as I stood on the bluff, peering out into the darkness as if I could actually see the land that hovered there in the shadows beyond the river, haunted by handless ghosts, and I realized that everything I had ever heard or read about the place was unremittingly awful. In the past ten days we'd camped with Presbyterian missionaries at Bamenda, Catholic missionaries at Bouar (CAR), and now Baptist missionaries at Bangassou—and all of them had said they'd pray for us. Would it be enough, I wondered, to make poor Muggleton well? To heal the wounded Road Warrior? Would it be enough to bring us back into harmony? And above all, would it be enough to carry us through Zaire?

STUFFED

At the ferry landing on the banks of the Oubangui we ran into Elmar and Bart, two young Hollanders we had met earlier at the campground in Bangui. They were celebrating their recent graduation from university by driving through Africa in a new Toyota Land Cruiser outfitted with every convenience. For the rough road ahead in Zaire, they were looking for a companion vehicle. "It's crazy to drive through Zaire alone," said Elmar, the cautious one. "Anything could happen." Muggleton could see that I liked the idea, so he took me aside and confided his opinion: "It's crazy to go through Zaire with another vehicle. *Nothing* will happen!" He reminded me that we had crossed the Sahara on our own and insisted that we would have more fun that way. By "fun" he meant trouble, anxiety, and adrenaline. There was no arguing with him. But he agreed, at least, to join Elmar and Bart in negotiating the price of the ferry crossing: twenty-five thousand CFAs (about $55), five liters of diesel fuel, and the loan of the Hollanders' spare battery to power the ferry across the river.

When we reached the far side, we fell straightaway into the hands of the officialdom of Zaire: mercenary minions whose wraparound shades and designer jeans and greasy fingers and state-of-the-art semiautomatic weapons marked them as Mobutu men. They were government officials whose official salaries the government rarely paid, an arrangement that made them both diligent in collecting fees from passing citizens and loyal to the dictator who let them exercise such a free and heavy hand. An hour behind us came four Belgian men in two battered Citroën Deux Chevaux. They told us that in Nouakchott they'd called on the ambassador from Zaire and learned that he had received no money from the Mobutu government for five years. An enterprising fellow, he kept the embassy afloat himself by running an illicit bootleg whisky and beer concession in dry Muslim Mauritania.

All day the eight of us negotiated fees with the resident *chef* and his squad of goons: immigration ($10), camera registration ($10 per still camera, $50 per video), carnet registration ($20 plus $10 supplement because the "offices"—a couple of tumbledown wooden shacks—stayed open during lunch hour), road tax ($100 per vehicle). "Road tax!" we said indignantly and in unison. "You don't have roads in Zaire!" In the end we got the road tax down to $25 per vehicle. Then there were currency declarations to be filled out and stamped and reviewed and stamped again. We watched the day evaporate under the steamy pressure of corruption until, just as we thought we were about to be released, the *chef* announced that the offices must close. He had just received word, he said, that the ferry at the Bili River crossing had been swept downriver and sunk. The route was now impassable. We would have to wait here at the border overnight, and in the morning the *chef* would tell us whether we could go forward or, having paid all our nonrefundable fees to enter Zaire, back again to the Central African Republic.

The Belgians raised a huge four-man mosquito net on the porch of the Customs Office, and we pitched our tents in front of Immigration. We all brought out chairs and cookers and fell to making dinner. Just at dark we saw lights in the road approaching from the forest to the south. A crippled Land Rover disgorged two young Danish aid workers, Hanne and Preben. It had taken them a month to get through one corner of Zaire, a country roughly the size of the United States east of the Mississippi. They looked wasted, exhausted, wan. Their Land Rover was scraped and dented, though they told us it had been new and spotless when they entered Zaire. "The worst was when it fell over sideways," Hanne said. "I didn't know you could pull it back up and drive on." The men wanted to talk to Preben about the condition of the roads ahead, but he fell asleep in his chair. Hanne said, "The mud is so deep. I don't think the Deux Chevaux can make it."

It was Hanne who told me about the snails that live in the banks of the Bili River. She and Preben had spent four days building a raft to ford the river where supposedly the ferry had just been swept away. In fact it had sunk many weeks earlier, and the only way to cross the river now was to make a ferry of your own. "Keep your socks and boots on all the time," Hanne warned. "Even when you go in the water." Otherwise snails will lay their eggs under your skin—in between the layers—and you'll have to dig them out with a knife."

"You're sure it's not larvae?" I said. I'd read about snail fever (schistosomiasis), one of Africa's many death traps, which begins when the larvae of parasitic worms penetrate the skin of people wading in streams, grow in the blood vessels, and work their way into internal organs, causing internal bleeding and death.

"No," she said. "It's eggs. You can see them under your skin." Her worn face wrinkled in disgust. "They're black."

In the morning, most of us were determined to go on. But the Belgians had roused Preben and talked with him about what lay ahead, and one member of their team reluctantly opted out. Like Muggleton, he had been ill with malaria, but he was also older than his partners and afflicted with common sense. He would go back to Bangui with Hanne and Preben and get a flight home to Brussels. If Muggleton also was having second thoughts, this was the time to find it out.

"Bruno is very ill," I said to him. "Like you."

"That's not the problem," he said. "The problem is that he's very old, like you." So that was settled: we would both go on. Despite all our differences, we were in this together.

We plunged into the long dark green tunnel of Zaire. Lush rain forest rose around us, bristling with palm and broken by delicate groves of bamboo. We made surprisingly good time on the rough red dirt track until we reached a bridge made of two logs—giant rain forest logs—laid lengthwise across a river. There was a log for the tires on the left, a log for the tires on the right, and nothing in the middle. Driving across the bridge would be like walking a tightrope, or rather two tightropes—one for each foot. I got out and walked carefully across, trying not to look down at the sluggish stream twenty feet below. I turned to guide Muggleton and the Land Rover onto the bridge and my heart stopped. The logs were too far apart for the wheelbase of our vehicle. The outer edge of each front tire rode on the inner edges of a log. The inner edges of the tires rode on air. As the vehicle reached the middle of the bridge, I saw that the log on the left was slightly bowed. I gestured for Muggleton to inch left, and the left front wheel crept around the bow. The right front wheel moved farther into thin air, and I gestured frantically for Muggleton to ease right. Gently he moved right, creeping by inches, until the wheels again rode evenly on the edge of the two logs. Made it, I thought, and motioned him forward. All at once the vehicle seemed to shrug, and I remembered too late the rear wheels.

"What's happened?" Muggleton hollered.

I told him the bad news. "The left rear wheel slipped inside the bridge. The hub is caught on the log."

Without a word, Muggleton went to work: inching the Land Rover back, snaking the hub along the log—back, back. Just then the Hollanders pulled up behind us. They tied on a rope and hauled Muggleton the rest of the way. Considering how close I'd brought us to disaster, Muggleton was remarkably calm. The Halfan must have worked. He said only: "We have to be able to do this on our own." We knew there were dozens of such bridges—and worse—ahead. On the next tricky bridge I watched all four wheels. I took it slow all the way—too slow for Muggleton, who had to drive the thing—but I got it right.

Seventy-four kilometers and countless chasms later—a long day's drive—we pulled into the village of Monga. Women and children rushed into the road to welcome us and point the way to the Baptist mission, at the top of a hill above the village. It was run entirely by Africans, and the handsome young man who came out to greet us—clad in plaid bermuda shorts, striped tee shirt, and floral-print plastic shower cap—introduced himself as Mr. Tongbo, the assistant minister. Elmar and Bart followed half an hour later, and later still came the three Belgians in their two Deux Chevaux. We were only an hour or two from the Bili River, but we decided to stay the night at the mission. After all, it was Christmas Eve. And Muggleton's birthday, too. He was twenty-nine. Elmar and Bart gave him some Dutch chocolate. The Belgians gave him a colorful glass paperweight—always a useful item on an African expedition. I gave him my share of the Bangassou missionaries' Christmas cookies. But the Land Rover gave him another terrible surprise. As he moved it into the camping area behind the mission, he found that he couldn't turn left. The steering again.

"Maybe there's a goat bone stuck in the gearbox," I suggested. But Muggleton was not amused.

"It's stuffed," he said when he had checked it over. There was a piece broken off the steering relay unit—the new unit we'd bought in Ghana. "Where the hell are we going to get a steering relay piece in bloody Zaire?" he cried. He sounded close to despair. "Without it, we're stuffed. We can't go anywhere. We'll spend the rest of our lives in bloody Zaire! We'll be just like *them*."

He meant the other transients on the mission grounds: a German couple in an eight-ton truck, fully outfitted for camping. We'd already met the man, Karl. The woman stayed inside the truck and spoke to no one. They had been camped at Monga for a month or more. Karl had hoped to recruit volunteers from the village to help him build a raft big enough to float his truck across the river, but the local Mobutu man announced a prohibitive tax for felling trees. The Mobutu man had another plan. He wanted Karl to recruit other overlanders to help him drag the ferry back upriver with his truck and restore it to service. (Poor Karl tried halfheartedly to recruit us, knowing what the answer would be.) He and his wife could have gone back to Cameroon and found another route around Zaire, but instead they had stayed on week after week, bound by the terrible lethargy and inertia of the equator. Walking each morning to the stinking toilet. Walking back to the truck. Gazing hour after hour at the curtain of trees. Karl's black beard had grown almost to his belt, so that when he slumped in a camp chair by the side of his truck, as he did all day, his beard curled in his lap like a cat. Under the truck his Airedale crouched, growling and barking and hurling itself at passersby until it hit the end of its chain and fell back snarling in the dust. The dog had lost its mind in Zaire.

Still, it was Christmas Eve, though the only stockings hung with care were my Thorlo trekkers. I'd washed the mud out of them and pinned them to my nylon clothesline, stretched between the Land Rover and a mango tree. I knew I'd need them the next day—Christmas Day—when we went down to the river to build the raft to float our Land Rover to the other side. I knew I'd need them to keep the snails from laying their eggs between my toes. Bloody Zaire! We had been in the country for only two days and already we'd lost to that squad of crooked Mobutu men who lay in wait for us at the border more American dollars and French francs than I could bear to think about. In two days, we'd almost lost our patience and perhaps—no, it couldn't be true—the Land Rover. All the things we'd need in Zaire: money and patience and a dogged vehicle to get us through. And socks. Luckily, I had managed to hold on to my socks.

But it *was* Christmas Eve, and there was nothing we could do but share a meal with our new compatriots of the troubled road. Together we concocted a dinner of canned ham and potatoes and made a celebratory dessert of the Bangassou banana bread smothered in fresh pineapple and some English custard powder the Hollanders had bought in Nigeria. "You're English," they said to Muggleton. "You must know how to cook it." And he did. Later I lay in my tent and listened to the music from the Baptist church just below: a great drumming and the pulsating chant of African song, and "O Come All Ye Faithful" accompanied by shrill ululations of the faithful. The guardian of the mission had brought me a sprig of bougainvillea, a Christmas present, he said. The flowers, the music, the prayers rising through the night air toward a thin sliver of moon hanging over the rain forest. It was lovely. And it was Zaire. Hanne had given me advice. "Every pothole is one more out of the way," she said. "Every river you cross brings you one step closer. Keep your patience. Keep your sense of humor." But it was a miracle we needed now to keep us on the road. The music rose to a grand finale. I heard the African voices calling to one another in the night: *"Bon fête!" "Bon Noël!"* And then all grew quiet but the frogs and the whirring nightjars. I heard Muggleton talking softly by the tents of the Belgians. They spoke of rivers and rafts and spare bits and pieces for Land Rovers, sharing a nightcap in honor of Muggleton's birthday. In honor of Christmas. Peace on earth, I thought. And please, a piece on earth. I wondered if anyone was still praying for us. And I wondered if my socks would be dry by morning.

MIRACLES

On Christmas morning a miracle occurred. It was only the first in a series of miracles at that. It was also another reminder to be careful what you pray for. Only an idiot prays for the thrill of motoring in Zaire. That morning, as Muggleton lay cursing under the defunct Land Rover, I dressed up in my one and only official border-crossing skirt and ambled down the road to the mission church. My assignment was public relations. The ever lucky Muggleton had already spotted a potential miracle at hand, and my job was to bring it about. Parked in front of the mission, where it must have stood immobilized for years, was an old Series III Land Rover just like ours. And within this vehicle—Muggleton had already checked—was the piece of the steering relay unit we needed. How to get it from that vehicle to ours was the problem I was sent to solve.

Mr. Tongbo greeted me at the entrance to the big mission church and escorted me to a seat of honor near the front of the congregation. People gathered around to welcome me with smiles and handshakes and to wish me *bon Noël*. The place was packed—men seated on wooden benches on one side of the aisle in their best shirts and trousers, and on the other side, women in their brightest print *chitengis* (cotton wraps) and head cloths, and young girls self-conscious in bright red lipstick. (Mine was the only pale face in the crowd, and my long plain skirt distinctly dowdy.) There were several choirs too, seated among the worshipers throughout the church. They wore robes of royal blue appliquéd with crosses of hot pink or yellow, and already they were singing like ardent angels. When the service began, the congregation sang too and slowly undulated from side to side, moving in one mass to the rhythm of the hymns. Mr. Tongbo, resplendent in a flowing white robe, mounted the dais near the altar and stretched out his arms in blessing.

"*Bon Noël!*" he shouted.

"*Bon Noël!*" the congregation answered with a roar.

The senior minister, Pastor Nyete, took his place in the pulpit beneath an arch of palm and bougainvillea. He was an old man with a halo of salt-and-pepper hair and a beatific smile, and when he began to speak softly in Lingala, the congregation leaned forward to catch every word of his sermon. They nodded from time to time and raised their voices in affirmation. I listened intently myself, and though I scarcely understood a word, I found it comforting to be here among these generous people who so honored their small leader. He had a splendid warmth and dignity, and what he said made the people glad.

"*Bon Noël!*" shouted Mr. Tongbo again when the sermon was ended, and the congregation roared again, "*Bon Noël!*" The choirs scattered throughout the big church sang again, first one and then another and then all together, while the worshipers danced forward one at a time in long, slow, sinuous, shuffling lines—children first, then men, then women. Every man reached deep in his pocket. Every woman painstakingly untied a knot in the corner of her *chitengi* and brought out a few tightly folded bills—nearly worthless *nouveaux zaïres*. (At the time it took fifteen thousand NZ to make a dollar, and the rate of inflation was 150 percent.) For an hour they danced their way to the altar and back again to their seats, offering up their hard-won Mobutu money to the Monga Mission Church. "*Ogami gutu te,*" they sang in Lingala. "*Ogami gutu te.*" Don't weep anymore.

Afterward, while church elders smoothed out crumpled bills and counted them into bundles, I talked with Pastor Nyete about the service and about his work with the hundreds of faithful in his charge. "My people are not rich," he said, "but here in the bush we are blessed with good things to eat. In the cities, the people are also poor, and there is no food. In Kinshasa people eat only every other day."

The schoolteacher, a serious young man named Simon, explained: "It is Mobutu. He has all the money. He cares only for himself—not for the people, not for the country." Simon said that his own salary was supposed to be twenty-five thousand NZ per month—a dollar sixty-five—but usually he was not paid at all. "The parents of my students give me food," he said when I asked how he managed to live.

Pastor Nyete added, "He honors us by residing at the mission."

"When Mobutu dies," Mr. Tongbo said, "ah, then there will be such feasting!"

"That is the truth," said Pastor Nyete. He smiled his beneficent smile. "Then the land will rejoice and the lamentations of the people will be heard no more."

Later the conversation turned to our broken Land Rover and to its twin, which rested coincidentally in Pastor Nyete's front yard. "Maybe we can help you," he said, as if he had just thought of it all by himself. "We would enjoy to help you."

That afternoon, Muggleton crawled under the hood of the mission's ancient, rust-encrusted Land Rover and struggled to remove the piece we needed. Pastor Nyete looked on, comfortably seated under the grapefruit trees, sharing the fresh fruit with Mr. Tongbo, Simon, and the church president, all of whom had given up their Christmas afternoon for our sake. The church president wore green-and-yellow-plaid golf shorts, a red "Bill Clinton" tee shirt, and on his head a pale blue crocheted tea cozy with pink stripes—a fashion statement rivaling Mr. Tongbo's shower-cap ensemble of the day before. The teacher wore old red high-top sneakers that had been sewn and resewn with all the colors of the rainbow, but his shoes testified to poverty, not fashion. The pastor said that he couldn't sell us the steering relay unit because he expected to have his own vehicle up and marching any day now. He did agree to rent it to us for $40—but only as far as Bondo, 120 kilometers down the road. Then we were bound to send it back. I pondered the wisdom of renting an engine part only to go deeper into the wilds of Zaire, but Muggleton read my mind. "We'll face the next problem when we get to it," he said. He installed the rented piece in our Land Rover, and we set off after the Hollanders and the Belgians down the Bondo road, powered by the first in the series of miracles that set us irretrievably upon what the locals call with a sneer *"les routes du Zaïre."*

We drove through bush as thick as a hedge, and soon we were standing with the Hollanders and the Belgians on a platform of lashed bamboo and logs that lay on the bank of the Bili River. The ferry was lodged on the rocks above a waterfall several hundred yards downstream, and we stood on the remains of the raft that Hanne and Preben had built to make the crossing. Some of the logs were nailed together; others were bound with metal bands. The bamboo poles that formed the floor of the raft were tied together with grass and reeds and baling twine. All secure.

"What luck!" Bart said.

"We'll get across this afternoon," Muggleton said. He scanned the far shore, only three hundred yards away.

"Tomorrow anyway," said the cautious Elmar.

"First let's make a plan," Muggleton said, taking command. "Let's get out our kit and see what we've got to work with. Then we'll put it all together."

But the Belgians proposed to have lunch first. And the Hollanders proposed a rest from the hot sun. Muggleton was goggle-eyed from another attack of malaria, the others caught in the lethargy of tropical Africa. The hours dragged on. Muggleton announced that he'd feel better if his hair weren't always crawling under his bloody collar. I went to work with dull scissors that chewed his blond curls down to a punk do. Then Elmar wanted a trim. And Bart. As I sheared them, they talked about flotation and buoyancy. Theory replaced work, and then the day was gone.

In the morning a heavy mist lay over the river. Egrets and avocets fished at the water's edge, just beside my tent. A flight of hadedah ibis winged downriver, squawking alarms, and the camp began to stir. Tents unzipped. Stoves hissed. Pans clattered. One by one the men came down to look at the raft. Each one stared at it, stood on it, bounced on it, stepped back to gaze at it some more, and then walked back toward his tent, head bent, deep in thought. I lay in my tent and watched the parade. Just like *men,* I thought. Women would have put this thing together yesterday, but the men have to make a big deal of it and jockey for command. Then Bart was there beside my tent with a mug in his hand. "Elmar and I thought you might like a nice cup of tea," he said. My heart melted. Here was a marvel: a white man thinking of me. When had Muggleton ceased to be kind to me, I wondered. And why hadn't I noticed?

After breakfast we gathered at the raft and fell into some slow-paced work. To the corners of the existing log frame we tied four empty oil drums we had borrowed from the Monga mission. We took up the center of the bamboo platform and placed underneath it an inflated rubber dingy, also borrowed from the mission. This we secured to the log frame. We spread out our tarps and wrapped them around six inflated inner tubes, although we somehow punctured one of the tubes four times, and each time had to patch it and start all over again. Then we tied the whole package of inner tubes next to the rubber dingy in the center of the raft and secured it to the log frame. We relaid the center of the bamboo platform and lashed the individual tubes of bamboo in place. Disputes arose. Should the oil drums go under or over the log frame? Should a second layer of bamboo—a layer on top of the inner tubes and inflatable boat—go lengthwise or crosswise? Did we even need it? Should the heaviest vehicles cross first or last? While I sat on the raft and listened to masculine egos advance theories of nautical design, I wrapped my precious nylon clothesline around loose logs and tied good strong knots.

Late in the morning of the second day the raft was finished. We pushed it out a few feet from the bank so it wouldn't ground when a vehicle was loaded. We laid sand ladders over logs to make a ramp from the bank to the edge of the raft. One of the Belgians drove a Citroën onboard, and the raft scarcely sank at all. We levered it away with poles, and four paddlers took over, each riding one of the oil drums. The paddlers, who had been chosen for their size and strength, showed little aptitude for the job; but Muggleton, who had once been a rafting guide on the Zambezi, shouted instructions as they moved along. The current took the raft upriver, and then as it reached midstream began to carry it back down. It drifted past the landing on the far side, and Muggleton's voice came back over the water, shouting "Dig! Dig! Dig!" as the paddlers strained toward shore.

Then it was our turn, though the novice paddling crew was already frayed and panting. Muggleton drove the Land Rover up the ramp onto the raft, which immediately dropped lower in the water. I got onboard to film the historic crossing, and as I stood at the back of the vehicle I felt the water rising around my legs. "Wait!" I shouted, but the others pushed the raft away from shore. (My female voice had long since become inaudible in the clamor of male voices vying to take charge.) Muggleton gave orders to cast off. Four crewmen dipped their paddles, the current took us, and the raft began decisively to sink. It tilted backward, and the oil drum at the left rear corner went under. The men paddled frantically backward, but the upstream current carried the raft away into a deep eddy. Desperate, Muggleton leaped into the river, caught the mooring rope on the stern, and began single-handedly to drag the raft to shore, but the back of the Land Rover snagged on over-hanging trees. Then I was in the water too, swimming with my boots on. With my feet I could feel the understructure of the raft being borne down under the limb of a submerged tree. One of the Belgian paddlers leaped in beside me, and together we got a purchase against the under-water limb and pushed. The corner of the raft came free and rose a lit-tle, and then Muggleton was onshore with the rope pulling it in. We formed a chain gang and emptied the contents of the heavy Land Rover onto the bank: bags, tents, cameras, bedrolls, food tins, spare tires, tools. We pushed the vehicle forward a little to the center of the raft. And then, while I stayed onshore and screwed my eyes shut, the crew took the raft out again, paddling like mad, and brought the Land Rover safely to the other side. Another miracle, I thought.

By that time a little crowd of spectators had come out of the forest and gathered on the far side to watch. A few boatmen came down the river in dugout canoes. Muggleton tied a 150-foot rope to a tree on the far side and hired a boatman to carry the other end out to meet the raft as it drew near, enabling the paddling crew to pull the last two vehicles in to shore hand over hand. I hired another canoe and made several trips across the river, ferrying all the heavy gear we'd emptied from the vehicles. In five hours, we moved four vehicles and all our equipment to the far shore, but the paddlers were too exhausted to move on. We pitched our tents in the road, within sight of our camp of the night before—a stone's throw across the Bili. Another full day's travel had brought us only this far. But we dismantled the raft and paid a boatman to take the oil drums and inflatable dingy back across the river, where a man from the mission would pick them up. There was no going back now.

The next day we drove through thick bush that opened from time to time into a cathedral of bamboo or a squat village of mud brick and thatch. The road was the lifeline of the villages, the ribbon that bound them together and enabled them to trade; but they didn't repair it. Per-haps the villagers were amused by the occasional spectacle of a bounc-ing vehicle shaking itself to pieces, for the road was often at its worst in the villages, where it could most easily have been repaired. As we passed they rushed out to wave and laugh at us and entice us to buy. Women asked two thousand NZ (nearly twelve cents) for a luscious pineapple, but half that price would buy a big bunch of yams or a whole stalk of bananas. We traded our empty tin cans, prized items for which the villagers had a hundred uses. Up and down the road went men and women laden with baskets and basins and plastic jerry cans filled with food or paraffin or palm oil to be sold in another village. Those lucky enough to have bicycles loaded them like pack animals and pushed them along. Hunters also passed along the road, armed with ancient rifles or crossbows or bamboo arrows tipped in poison. Their trophies hung on poles in the villages: skinned monkeys and quarters of dik-dik and gazelle. Bush meat for sale. We never bought the blackened meat, though we didn't know then what scientists later concluded: that HIV probably passed from primates to humans in the bush-meat trade.

That day, as we slogged through mud holes and crawled over rickety bridges, the advantage of traveling with another powerful vehicle was obvious. We took turns with the Hollanders, pulling one another out of the worst mud holes; and together we pushed and towed the little Citroëns along. When we were in Mali, searching out a track to Bamako, the presence of other vehicles would have spoiled the fun of independent bushwhacking and dulled our sense of adventure. But here, where the road was clear but nearly impassable, I welcomed the help and companionship of the Dutchmen and the Belgians. Muggleton did not. Too much could go wrong on this road, and did. But the help of others deprived Muggleton of the chance to face disaster on his own, and he began to resent our companions.

It was dark by the time we reached the Norwegian mission at Bondo and made camp on the grounds. In the morning we went in search of Alf, the man to whom we were supposed to return our rented steering relay unit, and found him peddling his bicycle to the machine shop. A long lanky Norwegian, Alf was a carpenter by trade and a Christian by faith. For eight years he had supervised the mission's machine shops while his wife served the mission as a nurse.

"What brings a capable chap like you to Africa?" Muggleton asked. It baffled him that a white man might choose to live among Africans here in the bush.

"I think our Western world is going downhill," Alf said. "Europe. America. When I was a child, you didn't have to lock your doors against your neighbors."

Muggleton laughed. "Don't tell me you don't have to lock your doors here," he said. "Everyone knows these African blokes will help themselves to anything that isn't nailed down."

"True enough," Alf said. "But they're used to sharing. They can't understand why we should have so much when they have so little. I can't understand it myself," he said, fixing his clear blue eyes keenly on Muggleton. "Can you?"

"One thing I *don't* have is a steering relay unit," said Muggleton, changing the subject abruptly, as he always did when he felt uncomfortable. Then he launched into a long, fully detailed account of the Land Rover's history and current internal problems. "So I have to turn over to you the steering relay unit that belongs to the mission at Monga," he said. His voice rose and took on an edge of desperation. "But I ask you: where am I going to get another one in bloody Zaire?"

"Maybe our garage," Alf said. "This is a Christian mission, you know. We specialize in answering prayers. Also we had a Norwegian mechanic here who ordered one of everything."

We followed Alf to the garage, and there among the tidy shelves Muggleton found precisely the part of the steering relay unit we needed, still in its factory wrapper.

"Am I lucky or what?" he crowed. "Look where we are! No stores, no town, no phones, no electricity, no drinking water, no fuel, no McDonald's, no Mars bars, no Coke, but here in the middle of nowhere is a bloody Norwegian with a Land Rover steering relay unit!" Another miracle—the miracle of multiplying auto parts, like loaves and fishes provided even for those of little faith. Another miracle. But that was the last.

CONVOY II

For days we traveled in convoy, moving unsteadily east about three degrees north of the equator. The days were hot, and the air thick with moisture. The Hollanders pulled us from another bridge after I misjudged the footing again. We towed them time and again from mud wallows. Mostly we pushed and pulled the two Citroëns. In this manner we made fifty kilometers one day, seventy the next—too slow by far for Muggleton, who grew increasingly impatient to be off on his own, to test his own driving skill against *les routes du Zaïre*.

On New Year's Eve, we camped together in a feathery grove of bamboo. The Belgians produced a good pair of scissors, and I trimmed them up for the New Year. All the men showered and shaved, donned fresh clothes, and sat down to a spaghetti dinner in the bush, looking oddly clean and civilized. They sat up late to see in the New Year with a bottle of wine provided by the Belgians. I turned in early, slept badly, and dreamed of a burned-out Land Rover (ours) full of tidy men with slick haircuts rolling sideways down a steep mountain. When the wind washed through the bamboo grove and sent a shower of light rain down on my tent, I awakened to the call of whistling birds and the harumph and scuttle of monkeys in the forest canopy overhead. The day came softly—an infusion of light—and with it the New Year and Elmar with a nice cup of tea.

When we reached the Uere River, we could see a big ferryboat on the far shore. The Belgians crossed in a pirogue to find the captain and arrange our passage, but they returned on the ferry under military escort. Two soldiers in faded camouflage walked behind them, their automatic rifles at the ready, while at the head of the party strutted a fat

Mobutu man wearing L.A. Rams blue jeans, aviator shades, cowboy boots, and a big gold watch. He announced that when we reached the other side we must go to Danila to register and pay the district fee. We loaded the vehicles in silence and crossed the river. The Mobutu man mounted a big shiny red motorcycle and directed us to make room for the soldiers in our vehicles and follow him.

"We'd better go," said Elmar, the cautious one. "We don't want trouble."

But one of the Belgians whispered: "The Africans on the ferry told us it's crazy to go with soldiers. People are scared to death of them. They shot some boys at Wamba last week for no reason."

Muggleton turned to the impatient Mobutu man. "No," he said. "We're going to Isiro. Danila is the wrong direction."

"You follow me to Danila," the Mobutu man said. "You register. And then you come back and go to Isiro."

Muggleton laughed. "But if we don't go to Danila, we don't have to register there." The Mobutu man was furious.

"If you don't register at Danila, you will see when you get to Isiro. You will be arrested. You will be sent back to Danila."

"Good," said Muggleton. "That's a plan. We will register at Danila when we come back from Isiro." He seized the Mobutu man's bejeweled hand in his iron grip and shook it. "Thanks, old chap," he said. "Good man."

Confused, the Mobutu man turned on Elmar and Bart and ordered his soldiers into their vehicle. Obediently Elmar opened the door for them, saying again, "We don't want any trouble." The Hollanders drove away in the wake of the Mobutu man, while Muggleton swung the Land Rover in the opposite direction and the Belgians followed us.

"Don't worry," Muggleton said. "I doubt that bloke has a radio."

"I'm not worried," I said. "Do you think Isiro Mobutu men give a rip about Danila? They'll try to make us register *there*."

Nevertheless, after the Hollanders paid fifteen dollars at Danila and caught up with us again, evasion of Mobutu men became our raison d'être. It determined our route and sent us hurtling through the bush at high speed—more or less, given the appalling condition of the roads. Falling back on his Sandhurst education and British army training, Muggleton decisively took command of the convoy. Our transit became a kind of paramilitary operation, with strategy and flanking maneuvers and nocturnal exercises. After Belgian Catholic nuns at a mission warned us about a roadblock ahead, staffed by exceptionally greedy Mobutu men, we barreled around it in the dark with Muggleton blazing the way, manhandling the Land Rover like a kamikaze tank captain.

At the end of another long day we made camp just this side of Poko. Hanne and Preben had warned us that there was a military checkpoint there, so we laid plans to avoid it by driving through town before sunup. We set out stealthily at four o'clock in the morning, but as we crept into Poko, we found the soldiers already on duty. Muggleton wanted to run the roadblock, but somehow the Hollanders had taken the lead. Faced with three soldiers aiming AK-47s at their windshield, they stopped. Muggleton muttered something about "yellow bellies"— a phrase I hadn't heard since World War II—and I feared we might fall into another bad movie. But the soldiers demanded only the name of our destination—and a Bic. These the agreeable Hollanders provided in triplicate—three Bics plus a package of Dutch candies per soldier— and we drove on.

This futile predawn operation—screwed up, as Muggleton saw it, by a couple of university men who couldn't make it through boot camp— put the Road Warrior in a toxic mood. It was futile to point out that we had lost nothing but a little sleep. Futile to suggest that we were not actually at war with Zaire—or with our companions. He flew past "those yellow-bellied Dutchmen" and pushed on alone for Isiro. There, despite the threat of arrest, we had to stop, for this was the town—the only town—where gas was sold, and we needed a two-hundred-liter barrel to refill our tanks and jerry cans. Muggleton haggled with a gang of young Africans over the price. At last the deal was struck, and we set about transferring the gas to our jerry cans. When we finished, Muggleton handed over a stack of dollars—$190, as agreed. But the salesmen demanded $195. Voices rose. Tempers flared. Fists waved. Muggleton revved our refueled engine and drove away. The salesmen pursued in their faster truck and pulled around us into our path to force us to stop. Muggleton rammed the truck and sent it spinning off the road. I'd been in this guy flick before, in Nigeria, and I didn't like the rerun.

"There's a principle at stake!" Muggleton shouted. "They were trying to jack up the price."

"Some principle," I shouted back. "Five bucks."

"Bloody bandits! Bloody fucking thieves!" Muggleton made a run for it, and we flew up the hill out of Isiro. He raced along, looking over his shoulder now and then at the empty road behind us, and soon he was laughing out loud about his great adventure. "High-spirited," he called it.

"Mean-spirited," I said.

"You're just pissed off at me," he said without regret.

"No, Muggleton," I said ponderously. "I'm really shocked at the way you behave."

It occurred to me to wonder what had become of my sense of humor. Muggleton too grew gloomy and drove fast all day—just in case the petrol gang might be gaining on him after all. So that's the last we saw of the mild-mannered Hollanders and the hapless Belgians. From Isiro two roads led to Uganda. We knew that Elmar and Bart and the Belgians planned to play it safe and take the shorter, drier northern route, but Muggleton hesitated only a moment at the crossroads and turned south. With Muggleton's "enemies" in hot pursuit, we didn't even wait to say goodbye. When we reached the little town of Wamba, the shops were closed and the streets quiet, as empty as a stage set before the play begins. Even the checkpoint where Mobutu men held up travelers was deserted. Apparently the report we'd heard was true, that Mobutu's soldiers had shot some boys here last week. Like Mobutu's "civil servants," his soldiers were unpaid and free to do as they pleased. Zaire was a "country" only in the cartographic sense; it had no civic order, no state. In Zaire "citizens" had to fend for themselves, but the soldiers had all the guns. So the townspeople were in hiding, even after the soldiers had gone. We drove south on the road to Nia Nia, heading deeper into the rain forest.

There we came upon the real *routes du Zaïre*. We expected potholes. We expected more pits of muddy water in the road and more flimsy bridges of rotting logs. But nothing had prepared us for the long deep corridor of bottomless mud that stretched before us. Muggleton blasted through one long wallow only to bottom out at the next. Quickly a little crowd appeared from nowhere to study our predicament in silence—a line of African men in tattered U.S. surplus tee shirts and shorts, hungry for work. "This is *our* adventure," Muggleton said. "We'll do this ourselves." We shoveled. We jacked. We laid sand ladders under the wheels. But still the Land Rover stuck fast, and it would soon be dark. At last Muggleton threw down his shovel, and I walked over to talk to the men looking on. Seven of them pitched in to work for an hour. They shoveled. They clawed mud away from the wheels with their bare hands. They laid rocks and logs to make a ramp of sorts from the long deep hole to the top of the great wall of mud that had been thrown up by previous diggers rescuing previous vehicles and had since dried down to the consistency of concrete. Climbing the steep wall of this canyon, the Land Rover tilted on two wheels and seemed about to fall over, but Muggleton wrestled it around and over the top. The men cheered and waved their shovels. I paid them off—ten thousand NZ (sixty-six cents) apiece—and we drove on for almost another kilometer before we came to another canyon of mud walled in by dense forest.

"We can stop here for the night," Muggleton said. "I guess nobody's following us anymore." I didn't laugh.

In stony silence we pitched our tents in the road, this side of the mud hole, just as night and torrential rain fell upon our heads. Muggleton grabbed a can of baked beans and dove into his tent. In a snarl of screeching zippers, we closed ourselves up in our respective domes and listened to the rain pound the vehicle and the trees and the tents and the tall grass. It ran down the red road and poured into the mud hole that lay in our path, filling it to overflowing and flooding in my anxious mind, a single long bottomless chute of mud stretching from here to Nia Nia, sixty kilometers away. Stretching from here to there. From here to the far end of the world.

LES ROUTES DU ZAÏRE

Zaire. Bloody Zaire. We struggled for weeks to get through one small corner of the country. My passport turned black with mildew. My feet shriveled and went gray from the wet. My toenails fell off. My left hand inflated like a balloon from the bite of some diabolical bug. Muggleton was worse off. Wrung out by malaria, he wasted away. He cut a new notch in his belt every week. His hands and legs were a mass of cuts and scrapes from wrestling with sand ladders and shovels in the mud, and the wounds went purplish and septic. Every night he hauled both medical boxes to his tent and doctored himself, but he didn't get better.

The Land Rover was worse still. Both sides were stove in and the blue paint scraped away in long stripes. The lights were smashed and the side mirrors broken off. The front bumper rode at an odd angle that grew more oblique each day. The floorboards jutted up on the driver's side where a log had burst through the steel plates and very nearly through Muggleton's leg as well. The steering rods were bent beyond repair. The passenger window was gone—shattered in a snowstorm of glass—and the steel window frame was torn and twisted, pointing upward like an insolent finger. The interior was crusted with dried mud, and the foot wells and cargo hold were inch-deep in thick red muck, still wet and reeking.

How can I explain the long, slow, withering demise of the Muggleton-Jones expedition on the torturous rack of Zaire? The weather itself was an insult: the days intensely hot and sticky, the humidity a hundred percent. Our clothes dripped with sweat; we washed them and they never dried. The wet earth and air crawled with bugs:

steely-nosed malarial mosquitoes, biting black flies, and huge colonies of poisonous black ants that lived in symbiosis with certain trees. Muggleton stepped into the bush, scouting an alternative route, and jumped back dancing a quickstep, stripping off his shorts, flailing and swatting. Ants in his pants.

Then there were the roads. In the colonial period neither King Leopold nor Belgium wanted to put money into the Congo, but to get the Congo's riches out they had to build some roads. They'd constructed something like fifty thousand kilometers of them by the time the Congo gained independence in 1960. Then the roads dissolved, disappeared, or—worse—devolved into a kind of purgatorial proving ground for people foolish enough to want to go somewhere. In 1980 fewer than six thousand kilometers of roadway were still usable. When we came along in 1996, so few passable roads remained, and they were disappearing so fast, that no one bothered to compile mileage statistics anymore. There wasn't much left—and deliberately so. The disintegration of the roads was not the result of Mobutu's penny-pinching or bad planning, but of his policy to keep the citizenry divided and conquered. It's hard for rivals to trade and prosper when they can't transport goods over the roads. It's hard for rebels to meet and plan and carry out a revolution when they're stuck in the mud. It's hard even to keep your spirits up. Late in Mobutu's reign the roads had almost no function except to demoralize the people of Zaire.

It's what they call "potholes" that wear you down. They're not "pots" or "holes" at all, but interminable chasms of water and mud, some of them a kilometer or more in length. During the rainy season these canyons in the roadway deepen as overloaded trucks sink into the mud and little armies of shovelers try to dig them out, throwing the muck up and out of the track. Sometimes it takes four days to shovel out a truck. Sometimes five, or ten. We came upon a truck that had been on the road from Wamba, sixty kilometers away, for five months; and the driver said he was making good time. Missionaries said a delivery by truck usually took six to eight months, and sometimes a year. As the road sinks under the trucks, the canyon walls rise. Gradually the top of the wall dries out and becomes a path around the flooded roadway, rutted by the tires of overburdened bicycles and worn to the consistency of concrete by the passage of thousands of flip-flop-shod feet. The wisest traveler in Zaire is a pedestrian.

We were on the road to Nia Nia, which—significantly—is pronounced like "nyaaaa-nyaaaa," the sound a kid makes when he thumbs
his nose at you. At another long water-filled "pothole," I saw a man
struggling to push his overloaded bicycle up the wall and along the path
some fifteen or twenty feet above the surface of the bottomless red pool.
As the biker tried to ease his old Phoenix onto the downward slope, I
ran to help him. The bike was piled with yellow plastic jerry cans of
paraffin and big sacks of rice. It bucked under the load and threatened
to dive into the red mud below—into the pit already occupied by our
Land Rover and a squad of muddy men who were remodeling the roadway under the supervision of a road-weary Muggleton. The biker
grinned at me, grateful for the help. "Welcome to Democracy of Zaire!"
he said in English. "All people equal. Road bad for everybody!" Friendly
pedestrians, picking their way along the pathway under heavy loads of
trade goods—palm oil and bananas and cigarettes—looked down at
our vehicle and shrugged. *"Les routes du Zaïre!"* they said—a phrase
that explained everything.

"How's the road up ahead?" we asked pedestrians who passed by our
tents in the morning. We pitched them in the road because the bush
was thick and wet. "Is it like this all the way to Nia Nia?"

"Oh, no," they said. "It's bad only *là-bas*—down there—until
Quarante-Sept [forty-seven], but after that it's *très bien.*" The villages
along the road had no proper names, only French numbers marking
their distance in kilometers from Nia Nia.

"That doesn't sound so bad," we said to one another hopefully, trying to keep up our spirits. "At least we know this can't go on forever."

On our first day south from Wamba, we set out at six in the morning. Each time the road dropped beneath a pool of red mucky water, I
got out to walk through it and assess its depth and the condition of the
bottom—three times. I walked out in the track the left wheels would
follow, and back along the track of the right; then I zigzagged out again,
searching underwater with my feet for any ridge or obstacle in the center that might hang up the vehicle. Muggleton watched and calculated
his course and velocity by the extent of my body still visible above the
water. Nevertheless, within half an hour of leaving Wamba, we were
stuck fast about fifty yards into a great canyon of muck that went on for
hundreds of yards.

"It's *our* adventure!" Muggleton insisted, and we spent the morning under the watchful eyes of would-be laborers. We shoveled the mud out from under the vehicle and from in front of the wheels. Then we shoveled out a place to set down a flat rock (which we carried with us) as a base for the high-lift jack. We jacked up a corner of the vehicle as high as it would go—a tricky balancing act usually requiring many false starts—and when a tire cleared the mud, we sledge-hammered a sand ladder into place beneath it. Then we ratcheted the jack down and repeated the operation on another corner of the vehicle. When both sand ladders were in place and the vehicle was still precariously balanced on the raised jack, Muggleton slid gently into the driver's seat, revved up the engine, and slammed it into gear. The vehicle lurched forward off the jack and hurtled along the sand ladders, spitting them backward into the muck. It slithered a little farther and then bottomed out in the mud. Muggleton got out and walked around the vehicle again, sizing up the new situation, while I retrieved the heavy jack and the shovels. He came back and helped me drag the sand ladders up to the Land Rover. Then we started shoveling again. In this way we went down the road, gaining ten yards at a time.

But it wasn't *our* adventure, and never could be. I was what Muggleton called a "forty-pound weakling" while he—at twice my size and half my age—was thin and weak from malaria. The heaviest work fell to him, and he was in no condition to do it. "Chuck me a sand ladder," he'd say, as if it were the easiest thing in the world—as if the damned spiked contraption didn't weigh as much as I do even before it got clotted with mud. "Right," I'd say, already puffing from the effort of dragging the ladder a few feet through the muck. When he was healthy, Muggleton could pick up a sand ladder with one hand and throw it on top of the Land Rover. I couldn't lift it off the ground, period. So you see what I mean about *our* adventure. Muggleton saw it too, and it made him mad. Not to mention exhausted from doing the work of two. What was supposed to be our adventure became our ordeal. When we sat down for lunch, neither one of us could get up again.

That time it took five strong men three and a half hours to dig us out and build a ramp up onto the bicycle and pedestrian path. With machetes they widened the path through the forest, and then with all of us pushing, Muggleton made a run for it. One by one the helpers and I fell into the mud, but we heard the Land Rover crashing through the forest, and then the cheers of villagers at the end of the trail. The men were jubilant. Muggleton was a lion of a driver, they said. They would carry on with us and help us through one or two (or was it three?) more bad places that lay just ahead—*là-bas*.

And so they did. They advised us which holes we could safely drive through and which we had to skirt on the dizzying edge of the chasm, and they cheered Muggleton on as he drove brilliantly the course they set for him. At last, they said, we'd reached the end of the bad road. It would be good now all the way to Quarante-Sept. We paid the men, double wages this time, and gave them Polaroid photos of the crew posed triumphantly in front of the muddy blue Land Rover. We stopped at a river to wash ourselves and our boots and clean up our tools, and then we drove on in search of a likely place to camp. A small puddle lay before us, no more than ten yards across.

"You don't need to walk this little one," Muggleton said as he headed into it. "I can drive it all right." Just then the vehicle lurched wildly to the left and stuck. "Drive!" Muggleton shouted as he leaped out the high side to throw his weight on the spinning right front wheel. I climbed uphill to the driver's seat and held myself there by hooking my arm through the window. I revved the engine. The vehicle sank deeper. Stinking muddy water oozed into the passenger side—through the floorboards, through the window. Muggleton lost his footing on the bumper and sprawled across the hood, his face just inches from mine on the other side of the windshield. He was still shouting—"Drive! Drive!"—and I was still revving the engine, spinning the only wheel that was not stuck in the mud, as it grew dark. The car filled with muddy water up to my chest, and with huge gray buzzing moths that beat against my face. Muggleton slipped off the hood and stood waist deep in water, shouting, "Bloody Zaire!" as he watched his craft go down.

It took thirteen men that time—thirteen men guided from their nearby village by that sixth sense that draws impoverished people to pocket money. First they bailed all the water out of the mud hole, and then they rebuilt the road underneath. They worked from half-past six in the evening until midnight under the aggressive direction of two women who sat on the embankment and issued orders and sold me cigarettes to dispense to the men. They laughed and sang all the while, and traded jokes with one another, and they worked as hard as if they were actually well-fed and healthy and paid a living wage. Never did men work harder or more cheerfully than the diggers on the roads of Zaire, for it was the only work they had. When they finished, the village chief asked for twenty thousand NZ for each of the men. We offered instead an American twenty-dollar bill, which worked out to better than twenty-three thousand NZ apiece, and another round of cigarettes. Well pleased, the men lit up and set off behind the chief, puffing and singing, for their village. We put up our tents on the spot and fell into them, cold, wet, and exhausted. We'd put in a twenty-hour day—and traveled thirteen kilometers.

In the morning we were on our own again in a vehicle wet and clotted with foul-smelling muck. We topped the first hill and faced another long corridor of murky water and mud. Soon we were shoveling, jacking, hauling, bailing, cursing *les routes du Zaïre.* Two African men stopped to help us and refused the payment we offered. They were ministers of the Kimbanguist Church, they said, on their way to visit a sick member of their flock. Their religion, founded by the black Congolese prophet Simon Kimbangu, was an African version of Christianity rooted in the communal values of Africans and of Jesus. Sharing with others, both blessings and tribulations, was the outward manifestation of their inward faith. Like the good Samaritan, they couldn't pass us by. They stopped again to help us on their way back in the afternoon, when we had progressed three or four kilometers down the road. They invited us to visit their mission, just down the road at Quarante-Sept. They said that only one last yawning mud wallow stood in our way. "We'll see you tomorrow," we said and pitched our tents on the banks of a stream next to the road. We had a bath in the clear cold water and cooked french fries and watched the full moon rise over the trees and pretended that we were not in Zaire, not on the road, not teetering on the edge of another gaping chasm of muck.

In the morning the younger minister, Pastor Alphonse, returned to help us through the last wallow before Quarante-Sept. He was a slight, good-looking man, perhaps in his late twenties, dressed with exceptional neatness in clean trousers and a white shirt. Quickly he hired two other men to help, and within four hours we'd traveled more than a hundred yards down the road. That was when Pastor Alphonse mentioned that there was another mud hole *là-bas* and another and another before we would come at last to Quarante-Sept, the place at which the bad road would end. We struggled on and arrived late in the day at a tidy thatched compound that was both the Kimbanguist mission and the home of Pastor Patrick and his family. There, resting in the yard, were two women who had walked the sixty-four kilometers from Wamba in their worn plastic flip-flops carrying heavy jerry cans of paraffin on their heads to be sold for high prices at Quarante-Sept. The walk took them two days. We'd just driven the same route in five.

Pastor Patrick welcomed us to a thatched pavilion in the yard where he was about to offer evening prayers with a little group of his followers. He gave thanks for many, many blessings, including our safe arrival, which he attributed directly and solely to God. While we put up our tents in the yard, Pastor Patrick's wife, Ana, prepared bucket showers for us in the family bathroom, a reed enclosure behind the house. Ana was a small slender woman, but she bore a bucket full of water on her head as if it were merely a straw hat. Afterward I sat at the edge of the forest with the women of the household—Ana, her sister, and three nearly grown daughters. From a pit where they had buried palm fruits to ferment, they dug them up again and squeezed the ocher-colored masses into fibrous balls. These they placed, one at a time, in a wooden press, and together they did the hard work of ratcheting down the screw. From the bottom of the press dripped the palm oil, red and viscous and valuable. When the pressing was done, Ana brought dinner to the men and me—roasted groundnuts and rice and manioc leaves stewed in palm oil—and retired to the kitchen out back to eat with the women. Afterward the two ministers and Muggleton and I walked through the darkened village, where a dim kerosene lamp burned at each hut and each tumbledown wooden kiosk in the market, these few thin circles of light standing against the immense and total darkness of the surrounding forest. We bought a pound of sugar for Ana, who quickly prepared a thick sweet maize porridge, and while we savored it, we talked of the *très bien* road ahead.

"It's very good all the way to Nia Nia," Pastor Patrick said. "Except for Quarante." This was the first we heard about Kilometer Forty.

"*Vingt-Cinq aussi,*" said Pastor Alphonse. "*Très mal.*" This was the first mention of Kilometer Twenty-Five.

In the end, Pastor Alphonse proposed to accompany us on our journey all the way to Nia Nia. His home was at the mission there, and he had been planning to return home on foot in a day or two. Instead, he said, he would drive with us. He would recruit workers and head work parties should we get stuck. Muggleton would do the driving. And I would test the condition of the underwater segments of the road. I was to continue to walk in my sodden hiking boots through the left track and the right track and back and forth across the center. Most of the canyons, Pastor Alphonse said, would be over my knees in water and well over my submerged boots in muck. It was there, on the road from Quarante-Sept to Nia Nia, that my feet turned the color and consistency of boiled onions and my toenails began to peel.

So Pastor Alphonse was with us the next night when we finally reached Kilometer Forty, seven kilometers down the road. Like a prisoner in a chain gang, he'd worked hard all day—so hard that he'd broken the handle off the pick he'd insisted we buy before we set out from Quarante-Sept. With his machete he lopped off a tree branch, and while I fixed dinner he whittled a pick handle strong enough to last the rest of the journey. I turned my tent over to him and helped him fashion a mattress from our extra tarps; and because his back and arms were sore from shoveling and swinging the pick, I made him a present of my precious container of Tiger Balm. Muggleton helped him rub it on, enveloping Pastor Alphonse in a cloud of eucalyptus from which a small tired voice emerged to speak of Kilometer Thirty-Eight and Thirty-Six and Thirty-Five. With an African's reluctance to bear bad news, Pastor Alphonse would dispense his grim and thorough knowledge of the road only in such small, palatable, nightly doses.

The next night we reached Kilometer Twenty-Five, a remarkable fifteen kilometers farther along. And that's when Pastor Alphonse told us about Douze—Kilometer Twelve. First, he said, we had to contend with Kilometer Twenty-Three and Twenty-One and Twenty and Eighteen and Fifteen. And then Douze. Every evening he immersed himself in our French/English dictionary, studying English in hopes of communicating with Muggleton. He already spoke French, Lingala, and five other African languages, and he had a fair command of basic English by the time we reached Douze.

"I don't get it," Muggleton said. "We've got our own personal expedition Kimbanguisti preacher, and the road is still hell."

Day after day we followed this long red road full of holes through the pages of old *National Geographic*s. Women in faded *chitengis,* with babies at their breasts, waved to us. Women stirred clay cooking pots over smoky wood fires. Women pounded manioc in wooden mortars.

Women bore blackened calabashes of water on their heads, or bundles
of firewood, or stalks of bananas. In bigger towns like Bondo, where
there were two missions (Baptist and Catholic), there was a health center and even an optician dispensing eyeglasses, but mostly this road ran
on and on through a previous century. "The real Africa," Muggleton
liked to call it, like those tourist brochures that advertise trips to see
colorful isolated tribes in remote places: the Himba in Namibia, the
Dogon in Mali. But what we saw along this road was no isolated tribe;
it was a way of life for millions. Missionaries had been here in force.
(*"Vous êtes missionnaires?"* everyone asked, for what else could white
people in a Land Rover possibly be?) There were Christian churches all
along the road and people wearing hand-me-down Western clothing
donated to the missions or resold by Fulani traders. Stanley, the
explorer, once advised his employer, King Leopold, that he could turn
a tidy profit on used European garb, if only Africans could be induced
to wear clothing. Now in this remote rain forest the men wore shorts,
secondhand trousers cut off (or worn down), frayed about the edges or
fringed, with great holes in the rump where the buttocks poked
through—some no more than tattered loincloths that might have been
made of hides or bird feathers except that once they were the gardening
trousers of a philanthropic Baptist in Indiana; once they bore a label
that read "Sears" or "JCPenney." The men wore tee shirts too or polo
shirts bearing the logo of the Chicago Bulls or the L.A. Raiders or the
inscription CLINTON FOR PRESIDENT. The shirts frayed about the edges
and blossomed with holes. The men tied the tattered ends together to
make a kind of African lace.

Once we got through the slough at Douze, Pastor Alphonse told us
that the road would be *très bien* all the way to Nia Nia. We drove on
to Kilometer Five, and there late in the afternoon we stopped at a
beautiful river overhung with weeping trees to bathe and put on clean
clothes in preparation for our arrival in the town. We climbed back in
the vehicle and rounded a curve into another mud wallow. Muggleton
slammed on the brakes, and we skidded deep into the mud. Muggleton beat his forehead against the steering wheel—*bam, bam, bam*—and
buried his head in his arms.

"What is *this*?" he screamed.

Pastor Alphonse smiled, folding his hands across the front of his
clean white shirt.

"Four," he said, in English. And there we pitched our tents for the night.

We finally reached Nia Nia the next day, but only because Muggleton reached a stage of divine exasperation that impelled his driving to new pinnacles of skill. At Nia Nia we delivered a mud-spattered, bedraggled, eucalyptus-scented Pastor Alphonse to the ministrations of his young wife, who hurried in from the fields, still carrying her hoe, to greet him shyly. The whole village turned out to welcome the strange, muddy white people who had carried their young pastor to his door. Roasted groundnuts were served, and glasses of water. Then we shook hands all around and set out for Epulu, deep in the Ituri rain forest—some four or five days away, according to Pastor Alphonse.

But here the terrain was different. The road was full of watery canyons, but there was something like firm ground underneath. Muggleton drove like a man obsessed, for so he had become. I got out to slog through the water time after time, but soon Muggleton's mania took command. Reconnaissance be damned, he said. We came upon a truck stuck in the road, and Muggleton flew up the bike path, teetering on two wheels on the edge of the chasm. The shovelers in the pit beneath the truck screamed and dove for cover. The truck driver scurried to retrieve his teapot from a cookfire in the middle of the path. *Yahoo*ing like a cowboy, Muggleton left them gaping in the road. Where the canyons were deepest, he plowed hell-bent through forest detours made slick by rain, and in that way he shattered the passenger window against a tree. It was a kind of grand finale, an explosion of silvery glass, like a burst of cymbals to mark our arrival in Epulu in a record two days' time.

There we tried to rest and recover beside a wild and soothing river. We stayed in a modest guesthouse at the Epulu Project, an international project headed by Dr. Karl Ruff, a Swiss biologist, to conserve one of the last unspoiled rain forests of the world and its rare inhabitants, the Pygmy and the okapi, a delicate long-necked chocolate-colored creature known as the "forest giraffe." International donors send money to save the okapi, and the incidental beneficiary of this generous concern for exotic wildlife is the endangered Pygmy culture. Every day Pygmies came out of the forest carrying baskets of leaves for the few okapi held in captivity at the station, for they knew precisely what leaves the okapi most enjoyed. One day we walked into the rain forest

with Augustin, a Bantu guide from Epulu, to visit a clan of Mbuti Pygmies. The light was dim and watery under the towering canopy. Big old
trees, festooned with vines and clustered epiphytes, rose from a snarl of
stilt roots; and bright blooms of flamboyant red, gold, and purple
flashed like exotic birds amid the thick green shrubbery of the under-
story. Augustin drummed on the buttress roots of a tree to announce
our coming, and the Pygmies greeted us with shrill cries. The men, who
scarcely stood taller than Muggleton's belt buckle, were sucking greed-
ily on a ganja pipe six feet long and giggling happily as they readied
their nets for the hunt. Marijuana is the Pygmies' traditional—and
legal—drug of choice, and the women were smoking it too, in small
handy pipes that didn't get in the way of their cooking.

High and happy, the men plunged barefoot into the forest, and we
hustled fast to follow them in our clumsy hiking boots. They stopped
to build a small fire and huddled around it, chanting to petition the
spirits of their ancestors who still lived in this forest to bless the hunt.
They beat their backs and shoulders with smoky leaves, smeared their
faces with soot, somersaulted backward, and were up and running
again. Deep in the forest, they told us to wait as they dispersed to the
left and right, stringing six fifty-foot fiber nets end to end to make a
long fence. Silently the women appeared behind us, then disappeared
again between the trees. Soon we heard them yipping and barking from
a long way off, moving steadily toward the nets. Five times that afternoon the men placed the nets and the women drove toward them. But
there were no duiker, no dik-dik. No meat for the pot.

Later we sat by a fire the women had made from wood they had
gathered. We ate rice and red beans the women had cleaned and
cooked. We watched them weave new leaves into the walls of the huts,
making them watertight. The women—as tiny as young girls—went
about their chores, tending their babies, smoking their pipes, while the
men sat together smoking and talking.

"I notice the women are doing most of the work," I said to Augustin.
"They even went hunting."

"Oh, yes," Augustin said. "And if the men had killed an animal, the
women would have carried it home and cleaned it and cooked it and
served the best parts to the men." He paused to reflect upon this division of labor. "That is the way of the world," he said. No wonder Mug-

gleton was mad at being stuck in the mud with a woman who couldn't single-handedly shovel him out.

After we'd eaten, the Pygmies began to chant and sing songs of the hunt, drumming on a log with paddles and sticks. At the edge of the fire circle, dancers clad from head to toe in leafy branches whirled among the trees, round and round and round, spinning through the flickering light. It was late when we crawled into our little hut, woven of sticks and newly papered over with *muggugu* leaves. The Pygmies would make music well into the night to frighten off big animals, the forest buffalo and elephant. They had strewn leaves around the fires, and much later they would curl themselves about the embers and sleep, only to wake an hour or more before dawn to make noise again.

Worn out by work and worry, Muggleton and I had bad dreams. I saw the Land Rover plummet headfirst into a bottomless lake. Muggleton watched a hovercraft tilt and sink backward, like our Bili River raft, carrying his whole family to the bottom of the sea. *Les routes du Zaïre* had all but finished us off. Sick and exhausted past measure, Muggleton hoped for a five-star beach resort with surfboards, while I longed only to rest here among the Pygmies and clap my hands until all the trees began to dance. Instead, in the morning we hiked back to Epulu, emptied out the Land Rover, and drove it down to the river to wash it out. Then we packed up and made a run for the border.

SURVIVAL

On the road from Epulu we met a "European" farmer stuck in the mud, shouting orders at African helpers as if he were King Leopold himself. He didn't hesitate to tell us that he was not what he appeared, that in fact he had been born in the Belgian Congo of a Belgian father and a black Congolese mother; but the fact that he was half brother to the black men he shouted at only seemed to make him shout the louder. "It was a wonderful country before independence," he said. "The Belgians knew how to run this place." American missionaries had raised him and taken him to the States, where he'd worked in factories for twenty years. He'd returned to Zaire to be his own boss (and the boss of black Africans), leaving in the States a son who was a trooper with the New Jersey State Police. "What a weird world!" Muggleton muttered as he secured a towline to the farmer's Land Cruiser. He always took a certain patriotic pride in using the British Land Rover to rescue the vehicles of inferior nations—in this case a Japanese Toyota. But this time the rescue broke the chassis of the Land Rover.

We limped on to Mambasa and found—Muggleton's luck again—an Italian mission that ran a garage to train African boys in auto mechanics as well as Catholicism. As Muggleton arranged for some help with repairs we were accosted by a Mobutu man who identified himself as "Mr. Immigration." He wore the kind of wardrobe—Chicago Bulls blue jeans and flowered silk shirt—that is bought with bribes. He insisted that we go at once to his office in the village to register, but Muggleton angrily brushed him off.

"Just ignore him," Muggleton said to me. "What's he going to do? Shoot us?"

"Hey, it's no joke," I said. "They shot those kids at Wamba. Why do you think everybody dives into the bush when a soldier comes down the road? You know they get snatched into forced labor and raped and shot and God knows what else."

"They're *Africans,*" Muggleton said, as if that explained atrocities. (It's the familiar attitude that guides the African policy of many Western nations.) The Mobutu man strutted around for a while, impressing the students with his magnificence and trying the patience of the priests, and then he disappeared.

Later, when Muggleton crawled under the Land Rover, I walked down the long hill to town to buy supplies. I was headed back again when a soldier stepped into the road in front of me. Zaire's finest. He pointed an AK-47 at my chest. Mr. Immigration appeared beside him and gestured toward an old wooden shack that was his office. I tried to walk past them, but I could feel the gun barrel against my ribs. I turned and walked toward the office, feeling a certain sharp resentment that the gun now prodding me along the path had been paid for by my tax dollars, the United States having supplied Mobutu with enough weaponry for him to keep his own people in terrified subjection for thirty years and arm the FNLA rebels of Holden Roberto in Angola as well. This seemed an inappropriate time, however, to discuss the undeniably awful decisions that passed for American foreign policy in this part of the world. The Mobutu man had money on his mind. He sat down behind a desk and demanded my passport. He thumbed through its mildewed pages, stamped it, and held on to it, giving me a greasy smile. I sat down next to the desk and took hold of the passport too. The soldier stood in the doorway, training the gun on me.

"You pay five dollars," the Mobutu man said.

It wasn't much, and I could see he was only following the advice Mobutu himself once gave his faithful lackeys: "Do not steal too much at a time. . . . Steal cleverly, little by little." But I could also see perfectly well where the money would go, and I was determined not to pay it.

"No way," I said.

"You pay five dollars," the Mobutu man said again. A "registration fee," he called it.

"No," I said. I should have been scared, but instead I was furious. "I paid already—at the frontier."

"You pay five dollars!" The Mobutu man skewered me with his bloodshot eyes and tugged at the passport.

"No," I said, tugging back. "I paid for that soldier's gun too. So that's it. Finish. End of story. *Fini.* Forget it."

The soldier shifted the gun in question, taking a better grip. Was he going to shoot me? I had Muggleton to thank for this. Him and his big bravado. Why couldn't he just register like any normal intimidated tourist and fork over $5? What was $5 anyway? my better judgment asked. But there seemed to be something like a principle involved. At least I knew that Muggleton would think so; and it struck me, to my horror, that I was growing more like him every day. I held on to my passport. I looked up the barrel of the AK-47. And I asked myself: What would Muggleton do now?

We sat in fraught silence for a few minutes, on opposite sides of the desk, tense and angry, while the soldier nervously fingered his weapon. Then we went around again.

"Five dollars," Mr. Immigration said.

"No way."

"Five dollars. You pay now."

"No."

In this way we passed the better part of an hour while I tried to evaluate in my mind the Muggletonian alternatives. He might chop the gun from the gunman's grasp and boot him through the open window, I thought. Or knock Mr. Immigration to the floor with a quick karate kick to his chair and then stomp on his throat. But what could *I* do? I'm no Muggleton—no Road Warrior, no kamikaze commando. Standoffs are not my style. So how had I come to be a pawn in the testosterone wars? This was not my game. I decided that I would not play.

"I'm going now," I announced to Mr. Immigration. I gave a sudden tug on my passport, and it slipped through his fingers. I rose, passport in hand, and crossed the room to where the soldier stood in the doorway. *"Au revoir,"* I said politely. *"Bonne chance."* I heard the Mobutu man sputtering behind me as I walked past the soldier. Then I was in the road. I didn't expect a bullet in the back, but I couldn't rule it out either, so I concentrated on walking steadily up the road toward the mission. When I reached the top of the hill, I was still alive. I found

Muggleton working in a pit under the Land Rover. I had a word or two to say to him about what he'd gotten me into by insulting Mr. Immigration.

"Bloody hell!" he said, momentarily glancing out from under the vehicle. "They can't do that. They can't go rounding up lady tourists at gunpoint when they're out shopping."

"I'd finished shopping," I said, feeling that this was not precisely the point. "I was on my way back."

"Bloody hell," Muggleton said again. He applied a wrench to some gizmo under the Land Rover, then stuck his head out again. He eyed my backpack and asked: "Did you get any of those little doughnuts?"

Eventually, by using an effective slam-and-weld technique, the student mechanics of the Mambasa mission training school managed to reassemble the Land Rover's busted chassis. They fixed our broken window as well, although they had no glass. They installed in its place a plate of sheet metal. "You do not see through it," the foreman said apologetically. "But the rain does not come in. Or the robbers either." The mechanics were proud of what they had accomplished and asked only that if we found their work satisfactory, we make a donation to the mission.

I'm not a believer, but the Mambasa mission, like others we'd visited along the way, was a peaceful place. African boys studied auto mechanics and carpentry, and girls learned to sew, though how they would use these skills to make a living was not clear. "We bring hope," said the old priest who headed the mission. "And the Catholic Church alone speaks in a loud voice against Mobutu."

"Are you not afraid?" I asked.

"We can be expelled or murdered at any time," he said with the sweet smile of one who knew where he stood. "Many missionaries have been killed. But Mobutu's days grow short. In the cities now the conditions are terrible. The people are without food. Things cannot go on in this way."

"And what will be the future of Zaire," I asked, "when Mobutu is gone?"

"I am a priest," he said, smiling, "not a prophet." He gave an Italian shrug. "The United States and the World Bank talk of democracy, but they send money to Mobutu. You tell me: Where can democracy come from when all the officials are corrupt and all the people poor and uneducated? Perhaps somewhere in Zaire are some intellectuals who think about such things, but I have not met them."

"And you, Father? What do you think about?"

"We pray," he said, "and we wait. We wait every day for something to happen. Some explosion."

That night, camped on the mission grounds, Muggleton tuned in the BBC for news of Africa: a coup in one place, an armed rebellion in another, the forcible takeover of a city, the forced ouster of government officials, guerrilla fighting here and there, border war, civil war, massacre, genocide. Sierra Leone, Liberia, Sudan, Somalia, Gambia, Angola, Eritrea, Rwanda. "It's impossible to imagine news like this from Europe or America," Muggleton said. Was that true, I wondered, thinking of Bosnia and Chechnya and Afghanistan. But of course he was right. Africa seemed to seethe. Zaire would be next. Even then the Hutu *génocidaires* who had fled Rwanda before the army of the Rwanda Popular Front were growing fat in the safety of refugee camps maintained by international humanitarian organizations. Even then they were killing the Tutsi of Zaire, the Banyamulenge, in the early days of massacres that would "ethnically cleanse" eastern Zaire, like Rwanda, of resident Tutsi. Mobutu would gain new distinction: the dictator who gave weaponry to foreign fighters to murder his own citizens. But we didn't know then what was to come. Then we knew only the sense of general foreboding that seemed to saturate the air like humidity and make it hard to breathe.

In the morning when Muggleton and I were ready to leave, I went to say goodbye to the old priest. He accepted the money I offered to pay the young African mechanics for repairing our car. They'd earned it. But for camping on the mission grounds he would take nothing. The land was in the hands of the Lord, he said.

"I would like to do something to thank you for your kindness," I said in Italian.

In plain English he answered, "Pray for us."

Muggleton and I made our escape from Mambasa and slithered toward the border, now only about a hundred kilometers away. The road lay through the Kivu district, through what had once been rain forest like the Ituri. It was now a source of timber, and loggers who worked the area had graded the roads. The forest had been clear-cut, as if by a gigantic lawn mower, but only the "good" timber trees had been hauled away. Big trees and limbs rejected by the loggers lay scattered and rotting all along the roadside—too little wood, or the wrong kind, to be of use to wholesale timber merchants, and too much for the cookfires of local villagers. Some great trees had been cut off ten or fifteen feet from the ground, above the spread of their buttress roots; their stumps stood like ruined houses in the ravaged landscape.

"It looks like a war zone," Muggleton said. "Like it's been bombed."

At Mavivi, we inquired for the house of Katina, as the Italian priests of the Mambasa mission had told us to do. Katina had been one of their best pupils, they said. Though still a young man, he'd done well in life and contributed lavishly to the mission, something few ex-mission schoolchildren were able to do in Zaire. He would take us in, they said, and they were right. Everyone knew where Katina lived, and a boy jumped on his bicycle to lead us to the finest house in town, the finest for miles and miles around. In fact, it was the only "house" in a town of mud-and-thatch huts. Katina came running to greet us, plump and cheerful with prosperity. He ushered us inside. The little bungalow was full of Western gadgets: a giant Swatch clock on the wall of the sitting room, a Philco refrigerator in the dining room, a videocassette player with a collection of James Bond tapes. There was a real bathroom with a French bidet, and a generator that powered electric lights in the evening. The village chief came for dinner—the only other honored guest—as young as Katina, high on life and local beer, and as handsome as a film star. Katina's wife brought bowls of stew and greens and mealie-meal to the table and retreated to the kitchen without speaking. Katina poured more beer, and he and the chief told us excitedly of plans for their annual holiday in Europe. It would be Italy and Spain this year.

"Your wives must be looking forward to the trip," I said, as if I didn't know better. The two men stared at me and then at each other before they burst into laughter at the curious notion of taking a wife on a holiday. They howled. They slapped their knees. The chief doubled over, clutching his belly, and thumped his forehead on the table.

"Who would mind the fields?" Katina asked when he had caught his breath. "Who would mind the children? Who would mind the house and the old father? No, no, no. It is not possible."

But how was it possible that Katina himself could fly to Milano for pasta and *vino,* and take the chief along for company? In Zaire, where a schoolteacher earns $1.65 a month and a civil servant nothing at all, here was a well-to-do man. He exported goods to Uganda, he told us. He sent a big truck across the border every week. He named the figure each truckload brought in profit: millions of *nouveaux zaïres*—too many digits for my calculator to comprehend. I could see Muggleton working it out on his fingers under the table, his eyes widening in astonishment. "Bloody good!" he said. "But what is it you sell?"

Katina jumped up, delighted and eager to show off his success. He seized my hand and pulled me out the door and across the yard to a padlocked storage shed made of steel. He spun the dials, threw open the door, and proudly brought out the source of his wealth: a chain saw. I returned to the dining room and reported to Muggleton that our good-natured, generous host was in fact the same evil timber merchant who'd massacred the landscape we'd traveled through. Muggleton stared, pondering this little lesson in the economics of conservation and survival. "It's classic," he said. He rolled his eyes and laughed and thumped his forehead on the table, as the chief had done when faced with an idea he could not bear to entertain.

The next morning we set out for the border, knowing that our path lay through what all the guidebooks call "the most beautiful part of central Africa"—the part we had struggled all this way to see. But rain rolled over the landscape, cloaking it in fog, rendering it all but invisible. Just ahead somewhere, shrouded in clouds and mist, rose the snow-capped peaks of the Ruwenzori. Early British explorers called them "the Mountains of the Moon," but the sensible African name meant "Rainy Mountains." We knew they were beautiful. Their picture was on the label of the bottle of Ruwenzori mineral water Katina had given us when we said goodbye. "It's classic," Muggleton said again. We both felt bludgeoned by ironies laid on with such a heavy hand.

Dark barriers appeared out of the fog. Police checkpoints. I slogged through the mud with our papers—once, twice, three times—to search out the little shacks where officials sat and smoked behind collapsing desks and jotted passport numbers in pencil on scraps of old paper. And then we were over the border. Free of Zaire. "Yes!" we whispered in unison, afraid to say it out loud. "Yes!"

The Land Rover climbed out of the mud and onto a paved highway, shaking itself like a soaked dog. A sign at the roadside said WELCOME TO UGANDA. Miraculously the fog lifted, and the high icy peaks of the mountains materialized to the north. Ahead stood the Ugandan Immigration Office, wearing a fresh coat of yellow paint. The officials wore clean shirts and neckties. They had real desks and real printed forms to fill out with real pens. They spoke proudly of their country. Outside the offices, well-dressed women were selling real food: tomatoes, big green cabbages, and elegant purply aubergines. For more than two decades after independence, Uganda was riven by tribal rivalries fomented by British rule and terrorized like Zaire by corrupt neocolonial tyrants, but now almost everywhere in Uganda people were lively and full of hope. We had passed from the land of Mobutu to the land of Yoweri Museveni, once the leader of the National Resistance Army and now the popularly elected progressive president and architect of the modern nation-state of Uganda. It was as if we'd passed into another dimension—from poverty to prosperity, from despair to promise, from an earlier century to our own.

We camped at Queen Elizabeth National Park, then walked out to see herds of Ugandan kob and waterbuck on the savanna and masses of hippos and Cape buffalo in the waterways. All but exterminated during the terrible reign of Idi Amin (1971–79), when soldiers machine-gunned wildlife for food and profit, the animals were on the rise again. And the elephants, which had fled, were wisely returning from Zaire. I could imagine the great creatures coming on in long files, the matriarchs in the lead, their trunks swaying, their huge feet rising and falling steadily, soundlessly, moving out of the dying forests of Zaire, crossing the border, whispering to themselves as we had, "Yes."

CIVILIZATION

Signs of civilization only increased our appetite for it, and we hurried on through domesticated Ugandan hills, lush with plantations of coffee and tea and bananas, to the capital. There in Jubilee Park, smack in the center of Kampala, stood a high-rise Sheraton Hotel. Muggleton pulled into the parking lot and announced, "I don't bloody well care what it costs!" We thought of the hotel as a sanitarium, a hospital, a rest home, a spa: our prescription for dealing with the lingering effects of Zaire. We opened the list of hotel services and systematically began a two-person effort to exhaust them. We hit the steam bath and sauna first and scrubbed away layers of red mud. Then we sent our mud-encrusted clothes to the hotel laundry and Muggleton lay in bed naked, vowing to drink Cokes and eat chocolate bars until he'd had "enough." Later we visited the health club to pump a little—a very little—iron. We had our hair cut. We read the *Times,* both New York and London. We tuned in CNN. We phoned home. We faxed. We sent off dispatches to the Internet. We lounged by the pool drinking endless Cokes (Muggleton) and cappuccinos (Jones).

"Room service!" It had been a standing joke in our camp ever since Muggleton got malaria and I started delivering meals to his tent—often that African classic: pasta with canned corned beef. Pasta Stanley, we called it. "Room service!" I'd announce, and Muggleton would rouse himself just enough to open a tent zipper—releasing a cloud of insecticidal vapors—and stretch out a limp hand. But this was the real thing. I opened the door of my room in the Sheraton Kampala Hotel, and there stood a waiter with a tray draped in white linen. I stared in disbelief. "Your dinner, madame," he said, and I recovered in time to ask him to serve it on the balcony overlooking the park. Maribou storks sailed the updrafts below me as I devoured a vegetable curry.

In the midst of this period of R and R, Muggleton coasted downhill to a real Land Rover garage and turned over the sad remains of our vehicle for a professional overhaul. Two days later the mechanics were still at it. And little by little civilization gave way to its discontents. Muggleton grew impatient with the mechanics. I grew impatient with a lethargic waiter and snapped at him like any self-important tourist. We grew impatient—more impatient—with each other. We had not been saved, I realized, by all those missionaries who prayed for us. Nor could all the amenities of the Sheraton Kampala restore our equanimity. In fact, they only fed the friction between us, for Muggleton wanted more of the same, and I wanted less.

I spread my sodden tent on the balcony to dry, and it exuded the smells of tropical trees and wood smoke and equatorial rain, the rich seductive aroma of the bush, hinting of bamboo groves and clear, cool rivers curtained by lianas. I buried my face in the tent and conjured up all those days and nights on the equator, all those long unbearably bone-wearying blessed days and nights. What was I doing here, in this posh hotel, with a road-weary companion who wanted nothing more than to be rid of Africa? How had we come to this? Where would we go, I wondered, and when and how?

The next day I sat by the pool—another snapshot of "the real Africa"—and pondered the imminent demise of the Muggleton-Jones Expedition. It seemed doomed, but what would the postmortem reveal? Death by attrition, complicated by massive infections of toxins *du Zaïre,* dangerously elevated levels of viral testosterone, and acute paralytic shock induced by the very shot of luxurious indolence prescribed to revive the patient. A friend of mine says of love affairs: "The end is in the beginning." In retrospect, I believed I had glimpsed the end of this enterprise months earlier, as Muggleton lay under the Land Rover in Guelmim, Morocco, warming up for immigration officials in fake French. I speculated then that some kind of petrochemical grit had worked its way into his central nervous system, clogging the synapses of rational thought. Driving with the convoy of overland travelers through the Western Sahara hastened the process of decay, for every night in camp he was thrown into the company of other men who talked of nothing but points and plugs and gas consumption. By the time we reached Nouakchott, and probably before, he was a complete petrol head. Perhaps he'd been one all along and merely adopted the pose of photographer—as he later claimed the profession of philosopher—for the sake of the impression it made, the envy it provoked among lesser mortals who had toiled as accountants, salesclerks, schoolteachers, to save up for the trip of a lifetime.

After he conquered the Sahara, he set his sights on Zaire—as I've reported—and raced to get there. Once we arrived, he raced to get out. The driving was the hardest he'd ever done, he said, but it brought him no satisfaction because he couldn't drive Zaire, as he had driven the Sahara, all by himself. Sometimes in Zaire when a squad of hired men surrounded our sunken Land Rover, attacking the mud with shovels and picks and bare hands, Muggleton sat inside the vehicle, in the driver's seat, reading a thriller, hiding behind it, blind to the men who rescued him from the mud and so intensified his mortification. He seemed to be elsewhere—in Russia, perhaps, gathering nuclear secrets, or somewhere at sea. It seemed a kind of coma. "I'm young," he said one day, "and I should be happy. But I'm not."

I don't know whether the petrochemical grit metastasized or whether it simply migrated to his brain and imploded there, but he grew suddenly, dramatically worse, which is why I agreed to check into the Sheraton Kampala for a rest cure. I hoped the grit might be flushed out of his system by frequent massive doses of Coca-Cola, but that didn't work. Chocolate didn't help either. Or numbing applications of the BBC World Service. Instead the treatments seemed to produce a secondary inflammation of acute longing for luxurious indolence, which I recognized too late as a terminal case of homesickness. From the Sheraton Kampala Muggleton phoned home. Many times. Soon he announced that his father and brother would fly out to join him for a holiday.

"Good," I said, imagining that their presence might cause him to pause in his headlong flight through Africa. It would do him good, I thought, to take a little breather with men who loved him unreservedly. Men who would laugh at his macho adventures and clap him on the back approvingly. Hadn't I myself been longing for such simple acts of kindness? "Where are they joining you?"

"Vic Falls," he said, naming the city where he'd spent four years rafting, kayaking, filming, hanging out with his mates, working sporadically without a permit, dodging the police—the good old days never long absent from his conversation. His father once visited him there, and they did all the guy things: paddling the river, drinking, swapping tall stories. He remembered it as a bloody good time. Now it was to happen again, and it couldn't happen soon enough for Muggleton.

"When are they coming?" I asked.

"In about ten days," he said.

But Victoria Falls, I reminded him, is in Zimbabwe. Between Kampala and Vic Falls lay the rest of Uganda, Kenya, Tanzania, Zambia—all big countries.

"Yes," he said. "We have to scamper."

The next morning I was awakened at five by the sound of an engine revving in the Sheraton parking lot eight floors below my windows. I peered over the balcony, and sure enough, there in the pale predawn light, was Muggleton, or at least his lower half, protruding from under the hood of the Land Rover. He was making it howl. We'd just spent $400 getting the thing overhauled at a bona fide factory-trained Land Rover garage, but professional mechanics never tuned the vehicle to suit Muggleton. So there he was, tuning it all over again—sleepers be damned. Groaning, I went back to bed, pulled the pillow over my head, and willed myself to dream of life without Muggleton.

When we drove out of Kampala, I noticed a new pallor about his knuckles, as if a new rigor fastened his grip to the steering wheel. I realized, to my dismay, that he'd become doubly obsessed with the vehicle (he'd taken to calling it *his* vehicle), for it promised now to deliver him not into the land of the Lovedu—he'd never been keen to meet that Queen—but into the masculine arms of his family. His eyes locked on the road, his foot on the accelerator, and we flew over the pavements of Uganda. I made a stab at conversation—something about the speed limit, I think—but Muggleton shushed me up.

"I'm listening to my engine," he said.

The new rigor gripped Muggleton's mind as well, setting it in a straight and narrow path along the big red lines of the Michelin map. There were things of great interest nearby: the source of the Nile, Lake Victoria, Murchison Falls, the last of the mountain gorillas. But if a memorable site lay twenty kilometers, or even two, off the main route, I could forget it. Muggleton's vehicle was bound to the highway like a train to its track. We raced on across the border into Kenya, a country where highway accidents are the leading cause of death. Muggleton glared goggle-eyed at the road and pushed the accelerator to the floor.

"Must you drive so fast?" I said.

"Yes," he said.

Somewhere deep inside I heard a distinct ping: the sound of my last nerve snapping. I touched the amulet I'd worn around my neck since the start of our expedition, a tiny blue velvet purse, scarcely bigger than a locket, hand-worked with beads and fringe. It had been given to me by my friend Patricia, a poet for whom life flowers in metaphors. Inside she'd placed a tiny jade tortoise. It was a reminder, she said, to creep at the pace of a tortoise through Africa. *Pole pole*, they say in Swahili. Slowly slowly.

"What about the Lovedu?" I asked.

"Screw the bloody Lovedu," Muggleton said. "How many times do I have to tell you? We have to scamper." As if to underscore the point, he sped around a bus and executed a thrilling two-wheel slalom off the shoulder, affording me in passing an intimate glimpse into the wide eyes of the driver of an oncoming truck.

We stopped for the night near Rongai to impose upon the hospitality of friends of mine, Lucinda and Tristan and their children, Kenyans of British extraction, who live in a gracious old colonial house set among English lawns and stables at the foot of a volcano. Lucinda hurried from the garden and threw down an armful of flowers to embrace me. I remembered: this is what it feels like to be among friends. She helped me carry my things upstairs to my favorite bedroom, just off the veranda that looks out across the great expanse of the Rift Valley. I confided to her a decision I hadn't known I had reached: "I'm not going on with the trip."

"Are you sure?" she said. "It's a marvelous experience, the whole transcontinental journey. Tristan did it, you know. Cape to Cairo. On a motorcycle. It was many years ago, of course, before we married, but he still speaks of it. He had a splendid time."

"Tristan," I said, "was alone."

The long and short of it is that I bailed out in Nairobi. I took my pack and my cameras and my laptop out of the Land Rover. I snatched up my bedroll and my tent and the last functional flashlight. "Bye-bye!" I said, suddenly sad to be parting from the surly Road Warrior after all we'd been through, yet giddy with relief. I gave him a half-baked hug. "Have fun." Muggleton fled before dawn, drove straight to Victoria Falls in three or four days, sold the Land Rover carcass, and jumped off a bridge. Not suicide. Bungee. Just one of the guy things he did with his father and brother. It bounced him all the way back to England, where I imagined him cursing the bleak snows of winter, dreaming of his next inhumanly challenging destination, and calculating how to get there fast.

I bounced back too. Taking stock, I found I was more determined than ever to reach Loveduland. Finding the Queen had once been only a good excuse for an adventure, but now it became a measure of myself—of my ability to finish what I had set out to do. It wasn't that I expected to gain from her some unexpected wisdom, for I already firmly believed in the values of her culture. But maybe, just maybe, I'd find her still presiding over a civilization that contrived to live by them. I went to the Nairobi Auto Show to shop for a new vehicle—one that would run of its own accord, without a resident mechanic—and found the prices higher than the annual gross national product of many African countries. So I sent out word to everyone I knew that I was looking for the loan of a nice set of wheels. Then I had only to wait. One thing I'd learned how to do in Africa is wait.

I settled into a cheap room at the YWCA and went calling on old acquaintances. Nairobi is not just the capital of Kenya but the unofficial urban capital of East Africa. Sooner or later every traveler passes through; every traveler gets acquainted in Nairobi. Two armed African *askaris* (watchmen) swung open the tall spiked steel gates at the turreted suburban villa of the American head of a large international aid organization. A uniformed African maid showed me into the cool air-conditioned parlor. While I talked with my host and his wife, my gaze strayed beyond the tea table to the tall French windows at the end of the long room that gave onto a garden brilliant with flowering shrubs. The windows were barred, and darkened now and again by the shadow of an *askari* pacing back and forth on patrol. In another garden suburb not far off, behind another steel gate opened by another *askari,* I visited a young African businessman I'd met on the Nairobi polo fields. He played on the first all-black polo team in Africa, along with the son of the president, and had commissioned the equestrian oil portrait that hung over the fireplace in his elegant home: a portrait of himself, well-mounted, playing a chukker with Prince Charles.

The next day I caught a city bus to Muthare Valley, a shantytown slum that spread from the road to the horizon and crept on who knows how far. I made my way down a narrow passage between shacks slapped together of old pieces of wood, cardboard, tar paper, and rusty sheets of tin, trying not to tread in the stream of urine that washed down the middle of the path. (I'd been in one of the public latrines that served hundreds of residents; I knew why people preferred to pee in the street.) The pathways were a maze, and the doorways hung with scraps of plastic or faded cloth all looked alike, but I kept asking directions until at last a young girl took me by the hand and led me to my friend. She was a widow who had brought her seven children from the village to Nairobi after her dead husband's brothers claimed the family's land. She'd raised the children here in this tiny windowless room rented from the man who lived in another single room on the other side of a plywood partition. Happily she opened the packages of food I'd brought and put the kettle on the charcoal fire for tea while I sat on her narrow cot and watched her work and wondered anew how she lived.

Surely things in Kenya were never meant to be like this, never these extremes of wealth and poverty. Mzee, the "old one," Jomo Kenyatta, exhorted Kenyans in his big voice: *"Harambee!"*—"Let's all pull together!" He was a great statesman and a great visionary who must have had another future in mind. As a young man Kenyatta spent fifteen years studying in England and the Soviet Union, writing a book about his people the Kikuyu, *Facing Mount Kenya,* and working in Europe for the cause of African nationalism. He returned to Kenya in 1946 to lead the Kenya African Union; and when the Mau Mau rebellion exploded in 1952, the British seized upon him as the most conspicuous nationalist leader. Although historians think he had nothing to do with Mau Mau—some doubt even that Mau Mau was an organized movement—Kenyatta spent seven years in prison and two under house arrest. Even then the people elected him in absentia to lead the new Kenya African National Union. When the British granted independence in 1963, Kenyatta became Kenya's first prime minister; and later, when the government was restructured as a republic, its first president. On Independence Day, he told the people: "Many people may think that, now there is *Uhuru* [freedom], now I can see the sun of freedom shining, richness will pour down like manna from heaven. I tell you there will be nothing from heaven. We must all work hard, with our hands, to save ourselves from poverty, ignorance, and disease." And that is what people did. To this day Kenya is dotted with small local cooperative self-help projects—markets, health centers, schools, light industries—created and maintained in the spirit of *Harambee*. For fifteen years Kenyans worked in the sun of freedom and built a stable, prosperous nation.

Then in 1978 Jomo Kenyatta died. As the constitution provided, the vice president, a soft-spoken nonentity named Daniel arap Moi, took over as interim president for ninety days until an election could be held. But Moi didn't call an election. Instead he stayed in office as de facto president, turned Kenya into a one-party state, began to arrest dissidents and journalists, survived an attempted coup in 1982, and by hook or crook has held power ever since. A strong supporter of Western capitalism, he found generous friends in the United States and the World Bank. Like most African Big Men, he and his cronies prospered personally while corruption, crime, and the gap between rich and poor grew. Early on, Moi replaced Kenyatta's image with his own—on stamps and coins and the walls of public buildings and the homes of party faithful. But my widowed friend still hung a faded photo of Kenyatta on her plywood wall.

After I left her I caught the jam-packed bus to the central city, picked my way over the broken pavements of Kenyatta Avenue and around the reeking garbage heaps near the Nyama Choma market stalls, hurried through the littered grounds of Uhuru Park (where muggers lurk), and climbed the hill to the YWCA. There in the courtyard I greeted fifteen or twenty women who were waiting in line outside the solitary telephone booth to use the pay phone, which usually didn't work anyway. *Harambee!* I thought. *Harambee.*

With more time to wait in Nairobi, I called on a Kenyan program officer with an international aid foundation, from whom I hoped to learn about the status of women in Kenya. When I told him I was looking for a place where women rule, he was too courteous to laugh at me, but he raised an eyebrow.

"Power is decision making," he said. "Women in Kenya, in their daily lives, have very little power to make decisions of any sort." Women in Land Rovers have the same problem, I thought. But he was giving an example: "Women do the farming, but they don't decide what to plant." The detailed description of the powerlessness of women in Kenya evoked disturbing parallels to my own recent temporary residence in Muggletonia. Never again would I refer to a powerless woman as "backward."

"Who gets to decide?" I asked. Silly question.

"Fathers decide, and husbands. And if both father and husband die, uncles or brothers rush in to take charge." Men, men, men.

"But Kenya has a women's movement," I protested. "And educated women in government."

"Just so," he said, "but the state is a male enterprise serving male interests." He tempered that analysis with a wry smile. "The women's movement likes to count the number of women in government. But what do they do there? Only what President Moi tells them to do. Unhappily, this women's movement flowers at the top; it is without roots. Rural women, ordinary women, have very different concerns. And in any case, being queen is not one of them."

A Muslim woman invited me to her home for supper—a modest meal, she said, for it was the month of Ramadan. She encouraged me to eat the rice and vegetables she had prepared, though she took only a little yogurt with cucumber to break her day's fast.

"During Ramadan," she said, "you must think of things more important than food. You must remember all the prohibitions—against anger and hostility, against idle gossip and ill will. In this way you practice spiritual growth."

"Does it help?" I asked.

"I think so," she said gently. "You practice restraint for one month, and perhaps you can restrain yourself a little for eleven months more."

"Perhaps that's what I'm looking for," I said. I had told her about the Lovedu. Now she laughed.

"If you cannot find a place where women rule," she said, "perhaps a place where people rule themselves would do as well?"

. . .

Still waiting for a vehicle to materialize from thin air, I took a bus to Lake Turkana, in Kenya's far north. For five years drought had plagued the high dry desert, and the lake had shrunk into itself: a long gray landlocked sea. Wind raced down barren mountains and across the surface of the lake, sending up great bursts of white water like surf breaking. Flamingos paced the shallows, and spindly plovers and yellow-billed storks; but all around the lake stretched the stony desert, as barren as a plate and strewn with lava rocks, black and porous. Not far from the rocky shore stood a Samburu village of tiny palm-thatched huts like overturned baskets—brown igloos melting into black land. Villagers who had eighty cattle five years earlier now had only eight or ten; those who had forty goats now had four or five. Thin children trailed thin cows across the land, and Turkana camel drivers passed by with strings of dusty beasts, looking for water. Outside the houses sat Samburu women. Beautiful women with close-cropped hair and great collars of bright beads. Expensive women—the average price of a Samburu bride is ten cows, four goats, a sack of sugar, and a sack of maize. In good times, tall, slim, red-robed Samburu men marry as many wives as they please, though in deference to their Catholic faith they take only one wife to church. But how could they marry when their cattle were dead? How could they survive? The Moi government did little or nothing to help them, for what did a "modern" neocolonial African leader, bent upon Western-style capitalism and industrial and urban development, care for these embarrassingly backward citizens still practicing traditional pastoralism and agriculture? "We eat like lions," one Samburu man said. "If we have a bite of goat or fish, we do not need to eat again in four days' time." Stunned, I wandered among scorched villages and talked, as best I could, with women. Samburu women taught me to weave a hut of dry grass just big enough for one. Turkana women taught me to dance fast and quickly trip my male partner, knocking him flat. Such knowledge was bound to come in handy.

Then, still waiting, I went down to the coast for a little breather, a purely self-indulgent dip into blissful solitude. Carol and Lars Korschen had invited me to stay at their place, Peponi, an old family home that had grown into a glistening white hotel wrapped in breezy verandas. It was reputed to be the best hotel in Kenya, one of the best in Africa, and priced accordingly; so the Korschens' kind invitation catapulted me into the *other* Kenya, the one international tourists see, and only top-drawer tourists at that. It's funny how things work out, though. Muggleton wished for a five-star beach holiday—and I'm the one who took it. And in the end, what mattered to me was Carol's simple welcome.

I boarded a bus for Lamu Island, a Swahili settlement that is one of the oldest on the East African coast. "Somali bandits attack the buses," I was warned. "They'll take your money, your blue jeans, your shoes." But my bus carried seven Kenyan soldiers in full combat gear, armed with German automatic weapons; and as the road narrowed to a sandy track through thick bush, the driver went faster than even Muggleton might have wished. Two days later the Lamu ferry—an open boat loaded to the gunwales—transported me safely, still wearing my blue jeans and sandals, to something like a state of grace. The Korschens' hotel stood between the rambling Swahili village of Shela and a twelve-kilometer stretch of beach. A soft breeze blew down that beach, giving Peponi its Swahili name—"place where the wind blows"—and inducing a dreamy torpor. I swam in the warm clear Indian Ocean and walked the empty sands. I went sailing with fishermen in ancient dhows under patched canvas. I helped Carol transplant a nest of hawksbill turtle eggs—one hundred of them—to save them from predation. I wandered the narrow crooked streets of old villages where women swathed in black *buibuis* of Islamic tradition smiled at me and called out the Swahili greeting *"Jambo!"*

In a little fit of sociability, I paid a call on Lamu's most famous resident, Bunny Allen, once a legendary "white hunter"—the protégé of Denys Finch Hatton and Bror Blixen—and later a painter. In old age, he was still a handsome and charming rogue. Amid the tropical foliage of his garden, splendidly attired in beads and a soft sarong, he looked as I imagine Gauguin must have looked in Tahiti. I asked about some of the famous women he had known in the colony, and he filled the cool afternoons with fabulous stories of Beryl Markham, "a long, tall whip of a girl," he said, and Karen Blixen (the woman who became known to the world as Isak Dinesen), "a fine bit of porcelain." We sat sipping fresh lime juice on the terrace of the rambling white villa he'd built for himself and his wife beside the sea, and he embroidered memories of remarkable times in yet *another* Africa, a romanticized colonial Africa where young Beryl still strides to the winner's circle at the Ngong Race Course and Karen still dances under the moon with Finch Hatton at the Muthaiga Club—a romanticized British colonial Africa that lives on in Western imagination and draws thousands of tourists on safari to provide Kenya's chief income. Then Bunny gave me a bit of advice. "You mustn't *do* anything on Lamu, my dear," he said firmly. "Lamu is the place to do nothing."

So I did nothing at Peponi, which turned out to have one of the finest kitchens in Africa. I felt that my luck was changing as I savored a dinner of white snapper prepared in the old Swahili fashion, with garlic and tamarind and mangoes and coconut cream, while at the next table a ruddy Italian beat a large crab into succulence. Afterward, on a terrace above the sea, I sipped rich Kenya coffee—all by myself. "Alone at last," I said out loud. *Alone.* The word had a good solid resonating tone. I leaned back and looked to no purpose at the stars. Things have turned out rather nicely after all, I thought. And then I remembered that I learned that line from Muggleton.

Ah, well.

WAITING FOR TO GO

Y ou come again!" Marie, the uniformed guard, flashed a smile and swung wide the door to the executive offices of United Touring Company. "You come every day—two time, three time," she said, reciting my daily schedule as if we were in it together. She always seemed pleased to see me. "Now you wait," she said. "You wait for to go." She laughed at me and my predicament—waiting for to go—but it was a big warm laugh full of sympathy. Perhaps what amused Marie was the unfamiliar spectacle of a white person kept waiting, a white person trying so hard to wait patiently, after the African example, and having such modest success.

Perhaps that's why they always give you tea. "You take sugar?" the office porter asks. In any good office you always get tea, though only rarely do you get what you came for. But I couldn't complain. The United Touring Company, one of the oldest and largest safari operators in Africa, had offered to lend me the four-wheel-drive vehicle I needed for the journey from Kenya to the Cape. Word had come through from my friend Diane in Zimbabwe. Having introduced me to Muggleton on that press trip on the Zambezi, she seemed to feel responsible for me now that I'd jumped ship; and I suspect she twisted some arms in the Harare office of UTC. I certainly hadn't earned this largesse. A fax from the head honcho there confirmed the offer. He left it to his colleagues in the Nairobi office to sort out the last details—like *what* vehicle? And where was it?

"Something will happen soon. Today maybe. Or tomorrow." That was Mr. Ashanti Sheth, one of the Nairobi colleagues who'd inherited my dilemma. A kind soul with the infinitely courteous manners of an

Indian gentleman, he listened intently as I described my search for Modjadji, Queen of Lovedu, and redoubled his efforts to help me lay hands on the promised vehicle. The trouble was that something was supposed to have happened yesterday. And the day before. I was scheduled to drive out of Nairobi soon, bound for Cape Town. But the days spent themselves as Mr. Sheth, having done all that was in his power, spoke hopefully of what others would do tomorrow.

At least I was no longer waiting alone. One evening I went out for dinner with a friend from Boston who was teaching in Nairobi. She brought along a friend called Caro Hartsfield. Caro was Australian by birth but made her home in London, where for many years she'd been a filmmaker—until she reached a certain age and found herself an anachronism in a world of young men fresh out of film school. She'd find her own work, she thought, and came out to Africa. For a long time she'd been living in Nairobi, making richly detailed documentaries about village life in Kenya and Tanzania. The African film crew she trained gave her the name Caro, honed from her birth name Caroline, and she kept it. She was tall, as thin as a spear, and vibrant with energy, as if Africa had refined her, like her name, to an essential identity. She dressed in a style of her own—all bright colors and long soft shapes topped by a floppy hat of many colors—that set her apart from Europeans and suggested her spiritual affinity to Africa. In Nairobi she'd fallen hard for an African artist named Lazarus Muhonja. He painted big bold canvases pulsing with color, and sometimes—anonymously and at night—unflattering portraits of President Moi and his cronies on hoardings surrounding building sites scattered about Nairobi. She lived with him and loved him and finally took him back to his home village to nurse him through a last long terrible wasting illness that his family attributed to a neighbor's curse. Hundreds of his friends and admirers came to the funeral when they buried him in the front yard of his parents' home. A band played at the graveside, and Caro gave a little speech in Swahili, as was the proper duty of a wife. Now she took the bus upcountry almost every weekend to be with his mother and plant more flowers on the mound that stood in the dooryard, just outside the room where he died. She was at loose ends: between film projects and deep in grief for her lost man, one beloved face among the ever-lengthening line of sub-Saharan Africans shuffling toward the overcrowded Kingdom of the Deads.

Yet life struck her funny, and there was laughter always starting in her dark eyes. I saw it when I poured out to these women—my first sympathetic listeners—the whole long self-pitying saga of the Muggletonian journey that had left me beached at YWCA Nairobi. I ran variations on an old theme: the double standard.

"Let me give you a few examples," I said. "Muggleton said my driving made him nervous; *ergo* I was a bad driver. But his driving made *me* nervous; *ergo* I must be stupid. Then there were his 'wounds'—the cuts and scrapes on his legs that had to be kept dry to avoid sepsis and consequently prevented his ever setting foot in a mud puddle. As opposed to my cuts and scrapes, which luckily were mere 'scratches' that didn't stand in the way of my slogging through mud wallows all day long. Or how about responsibility? When I got food poisoning in Nigeria, he said it was my fault for being stupid enough to eat African food. But when he got malaria—that was not because he'd stupidly refused to take prophylaxis. Oh, no, that was caused by Africa's bad hygiene. Any job he did was automatically billed as 'bloody hard work,' but anything I did counted as 'faffing.' " Caro and my friend Mary were laughing and rolling their eyes in that Where-have-we-heard-this-before? way women have when the conversational subject is male behavior. "Well," I said, "I could go on, but you get the point."

"That's not a double standard," Mary said. "That's a single standard—*his*."

"It's no good trying to reason with these macho types," Caro said. "What you need is a *female* traveling companion."

"Definitely," Mary said. "Especially if you're going to search for the Queen. You really must find a woman to travel with."

"I do need *someone*," I agreed. "If only to help me keep an eye on the vehicle."

There was a long pause devoted to making inroads in the pasta cooling on our plates. Then Caro put down her fork and said brightly, "I could go."

"Do you mean it?" I said. I turned the idea over in my head. Caro looked a likely candidate—older than Muggleton but younger than me, and full of energy. She was smart, warm, funny, and clearly capable of taking care of herself. She could drive. She was good at Swahili, the universal language of East Africa. And she could make films. "Caro," I said, "you'd be brilliant."

"Brilliant, eh?" she said. She raised her wineglass in salute. "Well, that's all right then, isn't it?"

After that, when I waited conspicuously outside Mr. Sheth's door in the UTC office, Caro sat beside me. "We're in Africa all right," Caro said. *"Pole pole."* Slowly slowly. "All you can do is wait."

Celia Muhonja was waiting too—for her passport. Celia was Kenyan, a Luhya woman, and the sister of Caro's dead boyfriend. She had been Caro's guide through the elaborate rituals of death, and grieving for one beloved man had bound them together. Contemplating our journey, Caro couldn't leave Celia behind. Celia could be our translator, Caro suggested; she could assist Caro with filming. But Celia was also a minor civil servant in a government ministry, and as an employee of the state requesting leave to travel abroad, she had a lot to explain. For like all repressive autocracies, the government of President Moi was paternalistic and paranoid. Who knew what motives led these suspicious *wazungu* (white people) to solicit the company of one of the president's lesser minions?

"How will you come back?" the immigration official asked. "What if these *wazungu* take you to Zimbabwe or South Africa and leave you there?"

Dutifully, like any good African accustomed by history to government paternalism, Celia answered every question. "These *wazungu* are my friends," she said. "They will send me back in a plane."

"Ah," said the official in the skeptical voice of an African who knows all too well the ways of the wily *wazungu*. "I must see their bank statements."

We declined the honor of having our bank statements perused by the immigration official, and Caro wrote a letter instead, on some kind of official-looking paper, promising not to abandon Celia Muhonja or any other Kenyan civil servant anywhere in Africa, and the deal was struck. After that Celia had only to wait for her passport application to be processed.

"Something could happen," she said. "Soon."

In the meantime, Caro proposed that we warm up for our search for the Rain Queen by tracking down another important woman: Loise Waithera Nganga, a village housewife turned environmental activist. Caro had heard of her work and wanted to help. We flung ourselves into a packed *matatu,* one of the fleet of battered minivans and trucks

that provide people's transport in Kenya and are never officially "full."
We headed upcountry beyond Thika to an area of red rolling hills finely
patchworked with tiny family *shambas* (garden plots). We found Loise's
neat little house and, in the yard, one of her sons and her husband,
chopping banana leaves with *pangas* to feed two cows.

"My wife has gone to do her work," the husband said. "She is never
home. Only I am staying home to support my wife's work."

"And I," the son said. "I am lucky to have such a mother."

They pointed out the direction Loise had taken, and we soon caught
up with her—a small sturdy woman in rubber flip-flops, the mother of
six grown children—walking along a gravel road, stopping to talk to
passersby. To everyone she met she explained why the river was going
dry, or why women mustn't do their laundry in the stream, or why they
mustn't cultivate gardens on the banks, or why they must plant grass on
the hillsides and along the roads, or why they must plant trees everywhere. Loise took us to a cooperative nursery—a *Harambee* project—
where women volunteers tended tiny seedlings to be planted eventually
around the *shambas* and along the roads. "Trees are our mothers," Loise
said. "With their wood we cook our food, we build our house, we build
our cow *boma* and our school for the children. They give us fruit and
leaves to feed our cows and cool shade when we walk along."

"How did you learn about these things?" Caro asked. "Where did
you study?"

"In the city people must study about the land," Loise said, "but I live
here." She didn't laugh at our earnest questions, but explained patiently.
"I saw the river dry up. So I asked myself what we do to make it dry."
When she figured it out, she started canvassing on foot, convening
meetings, explaining to others "what are our problems." In the past
three years, she had enlisted her neighbors to start nurseries and plant
hundreds of trees and acres of soil-retaining napier grass. She had organized thirty groups of men and women to rehabilitate thirty silt-filled
wells. She had persuaded two coffee-processing plants to stop dumping
waste in the river. "You can't put everything on God and the government," she said. "You have to take care of the world—like your *shamba*.
When people know what their problems are, they will work on them;
and the people here, they understand now that the river is their problem, and the trees."

"Where do you get the money to do your work?" Caro asked as we walked along.

Loise snorted. "Money!" she said. "I am waiting for that."

Caro and I chipped in, keeping back just enough to pay our fare on the *matatu* that hurtled us back to Nairobi. But when we appeared again at the UTC office, we learned that our vehicle had not yet materialized. Mr. Sheth felt bad about making us wait. "Why don't we send you to Larsen's Camp?" he said. "It's the best tented safari camp in the country."

"Why not?" Caro said. "If we're going to camp on our expedition, we should find out how it's done with proper style." So we flew north to Samburu National Park to lounge in a spacious and airy walled safari tent on the bank of the broad Ewaso Ng'iro River, crawling with crocodiles. Caro liked the full bathroom—basin, flush toilet, hot shower— built into the rear of the tent and equipped with rosy-colored plush bathrobes.

"Could we order tents like this?" she asked. "Robes would be very nice too. I do like pink."

"Sorry," I said. "Our camp won't be quite up to this standard."

She laughed. "Neither is my room in Nairobi."

Just at cocktail time an enormous crocodile crept out of the dark river and climbed the bank, lured by the meaty thigh bone of a cow. The spectacle had been arranged for the delectation of guests who clustered on the riverside terrace of the Crocodile Bar, juggling point-and-shoot cameras and chilled Tusker beer. The croc turned an eye on fleshy Western tourists protected from him by only a low fence. I'd have gone for one of them myself, what with their loud bad jokes about handbags and new shoes. That and the fact that the cost of their drinks alone could have supported Loise Waithera Nganga's work for a year.

"Look at him," said a ruddy-faced Briton, exhaling the smoke of a ghastly cigar. "These blighters haven't evolved in twelve million years."

"What does it mean exactly?" his portly wife asked. "Evolve."

"Evolve," he said again in a professorial tone. "That is to say—grow to look like us."

We dined under canvas while a long-toothed "white hunter" at the next table talked loudly about the good old days in Kenya, before the ban on shooting animals. After dinner, for the further entertainment of guests for whom unembellished Africa seemed insufficient, Samburu tribesmen performed "traditional dances"—the hunting dance, the lion dance, the honored warrior dance, and, for a change of tempo, the love dance. Samburu are tall, elegant, pastoral people like their Nilotic kin the Masai, and Samburu men do similar dances, emitting grunts and whoops that blend in a syncopated chant while they leap straight-legged into the air. From a standing start, a good Samburu dancer can spring three feet or more off the ground. Like his beaded jewelry, his plaited and ochered hair, his ears riddled with holes, and the fringe of scars carved across his chest, his jump is a sign of his manhood. Samburu girls don't jump.

A Kikuyu guide named Hosea chauffeured us in a Land Rover through Samburu National Park, pointing out lions and elephants and Cape buffalo and leopards close at hand, like the Discovery Channel come to life in a series of heart-stopping spectacles. We watched the birth of an impala—up and running in eleven minutes flat—and the death of another, brought down by a cheetah, who devoured his catch ravenously as the air shuddered under the wings of gathering vultures and marabou storks. Caro had never seen anything like it, though she'd lived in Kenya for years. Like the average Kenyan, she couldn't afford a safari.

But we had been airlifted courtesy of UTC back into the tourists' Kenya, into the great expanse of a national park where well-fed foreign visitors in stiff safari clothes live out their lifelong fantasies in the presence of "game" and a few black Africans. (Back in Nairobi they'd be sure to visit the Carnivore Restaurant to make a meal of the wildlife they'd come so far to see.) And there just beyond the park boundaries lay the other Kenya, the Kenya with too many people and not enough food or clean water. One afternoon we sat in a tree house above the water hole near Larsen's Camp and watched the sky as if our lives too depended on the weather. "Maybe it will rain today," Hosea said. "Or maybe it will not rain." Clouds had gathered slowly during the day, and in midafternoon they turned gray and rain came down in great wet drops that bounced off the dry land, leaving tiny craters and sending up little poufs of dust. The sun reappeared, clearing off the clouds and circling the horizon in a bright rainbow. Where the rainbow met the red earth, elephants ambled through a luminous curtain of light. In that moment of bright clarity the parched bush seemed suddenly as green as

Ireland: saltbush, palmetto, thorny acacia, all wet and slick and as green as emeralds. Then the rain came for real, and sky and bush dissolved in a wash of gray. Time was passing, and the short rains were coming on, and we were still waiting for to go. *Hakuna matata,* I thought, watching the play of light over the bush, praying that rain was falling farther north as well, around Turkana, and that people there too were watching rainbows rise over green land.

HOME AND AWAY

When we returned to Nairobi, Mr. Sheth awaited us with good news. A vehicle had been found and even now stood in the parking garage under the UTC office building. Together we descended to the garage.

"That is not a proper safari vehicle," Mr. Sheth said when an attendant brought forth our extra-long, extra-tall, shiny new brilliant peacock-blue air-conditioned Toyota diesel Land Cruiser. His face fell. "It is a target! You will need good fortune to drive out of Nairobi without being carjacked."

"Yes," I said, opening the back door to peer inside. "And look here. It's a motel."

As it turned out, the vehicle had been custom built for the chief financial officer of Toyota Kenya, a man apparently bent on advertising that he lived better than his average countrymen. (In Nairobi, that is not smart.) He had installed a kind of den in the back of the Land Cruiser. Behind the driver's seat, facing the rear, there stood a plush high-backed couch. Opposite the couch—in the rear of the vehicle, facing forward—were two matching plush lounge chairs, perfect for watching television, although the TV set was not included. There were twin pedestals for a table too, though no table, and a special outlet to plug in a fridge, which was also missing.

Despite the absent amenities, the vehicle was posh and clean, and it came with little paper doilies on the floor to protect the carpet. Later, after a trip to an auto-parts store to buy essential tools—high-lift jack, shovel, tire levers, pump, wheel spanner, wrenches—I hid them behind the driver's seat because they looked so out of place, so untidy, in the lounge. The second spare tire I had requested was the only eyesore. It couldn't be hung on the back (since that's where the first spare hung) or bolted to the roof or hood (since that would mar the vehicle's brilliant peacock-blue paint job), so it lay on the carpet in the "parlor," filling the space between couch and lounge chairs like an oversized hassock. The fancy furnishings left little room for our gear and us, but for the next few months, this overstuffed motel room would be our home.

At the time, I couldn't quite take it in, woozy as I was from taking Lariam to prepare myself for camping in malarial areas. Some travelers avoid Lariam as a dangerous drug with nasty side effects, but malaria gets them in the end—as it got Muggleton on the first leg of this expedition. So I was taking Lariam despite the known possible side effects, liver damage being among the least of them. An article I'd read in a medical journal listed one possible complication of the drug as "death," but the most significant symptoms were mental: depression, paranoia, disorientation, memory loss, anxiety, panic attacks, and the wooziness I felt as I watched Mr. Sheth paste big yellow UTC stickers on the shining peacock-blue immensity of the Land Cruiser.

At last we shook hands all around, and Caro and I climbed into the front seat, with me behind the wheel. "Oooh," Caro said, "it's got a tape deck." It was, however, missing some promised spare parts, which I intended to collect at once at Toyota Kenya. That meant driving out the Uhuru Highway, a local speedway punctuated by traffic circles, which Kenyan drivers use to crank up a good running start on the straightaway. The prospect was terrifying since we might not be killed outright in a crash but dispatched with injuries to a Nairobi hospital. As I inched out of the parking garage on Muindi Mbingu Street, Caro reminded me, "Keep left!" We were in the heart of downtown Nairobi in the midst of rush hour, just as it was growing dark. Rain poured down in sheets. Umbrellas scurried in and out of traffic. I was on the wrong side of the vehicle on the wrong side of the road on the wrong side of the world in a torrential downpour in a Land Cruiser so fancy it screamed "Steal me!" to Nairobi's ambitious carjackers—and night was coming on. From someplace deep inside me a strange half-strangled shriek emerged.

"Don't worry," Caro said. She had made a career of directing complicated films in remote places with half-trained crews. She was always cheery. Unflappable. "It's the Lariam," she said.

. . .

Two days later, we were ready to leave Nairobi. Celia showed up at dawn carrying a duffel bag, a cooking pot, and a big bottle full of the ashy water that Kenyan women use to tenderize tough green vegetables. Close behind her came her brother Joseph, breathless, waving the certificate of yellow-fever vaccination she'd left behind. Clinging to Celia's skirt were her two daughters, four-year-old Honey and two-year-old Joleen. Our first stop would be in western Kenya at Celia's home place, where most of her family still lived. There Celia would entrust Honey and Joleen to her mother, Mama Robai. A strong woman of great dignity, Mama Robai was the daughter of one of the ten wives of a powerful Luhya chief, and Mama Robai's mother as well was the proud daughter of a chief. It seemed only fitting that we should pay our respects to this royal lineage as we set out in search of the Queen of the Lovedu.

Still, I was nervous about this plan, because to reach Celia's home place we had to drive the main Nairobi–Eldoret highway, one of the most notorious death traps in Africa. Thousands had died on this road—including, two years earlier, Celia's own husband. But by the time we reached the edge of the escarpment, an hour west of Nairobi, and saw below us stretching to the horizon the flat volcano-studded floor of the Rift Valley, I was getting the hang of it. We crossed the valley, passing through Naivasha and Nakuru and catching sight in the distance of soda lakes ringed with pink flamingos. We climbed the western escarpment and the hills gathered around us, patched with fields of cabbages, tall rows of maize, plots of beans and greens and carrots, and stands of exotic eucalyptus trees raised for firewood. The landscape was perfectly domesticated and tended, and a peculiar beauty arose from this orderliness. But the farther west we went in Kenya, the smaller the patches became, for each generation produces too many children for too little land.

I remembered another time, a few years earlier, when I'd ridden out of these hills across the vast tawny grasslands the Masai call the Mara, moving among herds of long-faced wildebeests and natty zebras, on a horseback safari led by my friend Tristan. Each day as we rode we came upon Masai settlements, such low-lying, unassuming assemblages of sticks and mud and cattle dung that they were nearly invisible. As we passed by in our dusty breeches and tee shirts, glorious women emerged from the enclosure of thorns encircling each settlement. Tall and silent, they were resplendent in layers of brightly printed batiks, broad collars and chokers of beads, and tiaras dripping with cowrie shells and bits of tin. Their ears, lacy with holes, held ornaments of leather and dangling beads. *"Soba!"* We called out the Masai greeting, and they broke into laughter. *"Soba,"* they called back, laughing and waving. Almost all those women carried babies, and toddlers clung to their knees. The birthrate in Kenya was among the highest in the world, and the Masai population alone had tripled in the space of three decades. By tradition the Masai are nomadic herders, following the new grass just as the migrating wildebeests do and living on milk and blood drawn from their precious cattle. But the spreading farmlands and *shambas* of other Kenyans—Kikuyu, Luhya, Kalenjin—push the Masai, with their grazing cows and close-cropping goats, westward onto the high plains and into the hills. The Masai never hunt the wild grazers—"God's cattle," they call the gazelles—but increasingly Masai cattle compete with God's for the same grass.

Now we too drove westward, and beyond Kakamega we turned the Land Cruiser into the yard of Celia's brother Morton, a minor civil servant in the district, and his wife, Gladys, a schoolteacher. We would sleep in our tents there—the only flat place on the Muhonja hillside—but first we walked across the *shamba* to the home of another brother, Ebenezer, who was also a teacher and farmer. (They were all civil servants or teachers, these Muhonjas.) Recently Ebenezer had lost his beautiful young wife, Rose, to cancer and buried her, after the Luhya fashion, in the front yard. We stood beside the flower-covered mound while brother Morton intoned a Swahili prayer to a Christian God.

Out of respect for Rose, we were to dine in her house. In the small mud-and-thatch kitchen out back, Celia sat on a low wooden stool, her skirt hitched between her legs, and fed sticks into the fire burning under a pot that balanced on a tripod of stones. Four little nieces helped her as she stewed a muscular chicken, then a big pot of *managua* (greens), and finally prepared *ugali,* the staple of Kenya. She built up the fire, poured maize meal onto the boiling water, and stirred the thickening mass with a long-handled wooden paddle. After a long time, she turned it out onto a plate and paddled it into a dome shape. I too sat on a low stool in the dark smoky kitchen, keeping Celia company, watching as she worked. I leaned back against the side of the milk cow's pen and scratched the cat who came to beg scraps. The cow watched too, and a white rabbit peering from his hutch on the wall. The firelight shone in their eyes. Later we gathered at the long table in Ebenezer's front room to dig our fingers into the *ugali* by the light of the kerosene lamp. The little girls flitted in and out of the darkness, bearing cups of black tea from the kitchen.

In the morning we drove on toward the family home place near Chakavali, not many kilometers down the road. There a radiant Mama Robai waited for us in the front yard, her head wrapped in a beautiful red scarf. *"Mirembe,"* she said, clasping our hands. *"Mirembe, mirembe."* Peace, peace. Brothers Mudachi and Gideon were there too, teasing Celia, who was already well settled in her Toyota TV chair, strewing banana peels and peanut shells about the lounge, making a home away from home. (Riding in the front seat made her nervous, but she was happy to make the "parlor" her own.) And Celia's father, Mzee, the gentle patriarch, was there, dignified in the black suit he had learned to wear as a young man assisting missionaries in colonial Kenya. With his Bible in hand, he was just setting out on his own ministerial rounds—a kindly man, still giving his life to others. Mama Robai ordered platters of *matoke* (stewed bananas) to be served to us in the front room of her little house, and she threw open the shutters so that we looked out upon the front yard, where her son, Caro's lover and Celia's brother Lazarus, lay under a mound of flowering plants. No one is ever alone in this family, I thought. Not even in death. To be a Muhonja, to be an African, is to be embraced. Afterward we gathered in the yard at Lazarus's grave and Mama Robai prayed for him and for us. Then quietly she enfolded Celia's weeping children as we drove away toward Tanzania.

Late in the day we came out of the hills above Kisumu and descended the escarpment to the broad flat plain and Lake Victoria stretching to the horizon like the sea. Ahead lay another country.

AFRICAN TRAVELER

Most Africans don't travel much on their own continent. Rail and road transport can be erratic, flights expensive; and as a rule, Africans are exceedingly attached to their homes. Most African women don't travel at all, save where their own feet take them. So for our African friend Celia, leaving Kenya for the first time in her life, this expedition was a very big deal. For me too, for I began to learn about Africa from the African inside my vehicle. Not that Celia gave out much. Like most Africans, generally dismayed by the confessional style of conversation so popular among "friendly" Americans, she wore that practiced mask of reticence and impassivity. She rarely revealed her opinions, and never her feelings. She deferred to Caro and me as her elders and never challenged our decisions. But for the sake of survival— a very popular concept in Kenya—she was not above fiddling the truth. On her passport application she had listed her marital status as single rather than widowed for the very good reason that as a widow she was required to get permission to leave home from her father-in-law. He in turn would have consulted his sons, the brothers of her late husband, any one of whom was entitled to marry Celia without her consent and might jump at the opportunity to make her property his own. At the border she looked the Kenyan immigration official in the eye and handed over her single woman's passport. He turned over every page, studying the document with painstaking care.

"You know what I want!" he said sternly.

"I know what you want," Celia said, producing a letter. It was an official letter releasing her from Kenya, signed not by her father-in-law but by her boss, the minister of health. Without it her passport was worthless. The immigration official turned his attention to the letter, studying every word. At last he handed it back, stamped the passport, and handed that over too, with only the faintest trace of a smile passing over his mask of official ferocity. *"Safari njema,"* he said. Good journey.

Then we drove on into Tanzania, with Celia sitting in the back in her Toyota lounge chair, taking in the scenery, keeping a tight grip on her excitement. She was a formidable study in self-control, her feelings perfectly masked. Implacable. Stolid. Unlike the land, which seemed almost to groan with relief from the pressure of overpopulation once we crossed the border from the hills of western Kenya to Tanzania. The patchwork of tiny *shambas* dissolved into bush, dry flaxen grass studded with leafless shrubs and thorny acacias, broken only here and there by clusters of crumbling mud-and-wattle thatched houses. Herds of dusty cattle—white, dun, and black—plied the roadside tended by Masai children.

"How do you like Tanzania?" Caro asked.

"I don't mind," Celia said.

Caro turned to me and said, "She really likes it."

Driving along the empty highway, we overtook a long procession of Masai men riding their bicycles, their bright red plaid blankets hitched up around their thighs. They might have been a bicycling club on an outing, but their machetes were slung across their backs, newly sharpened and gleaming. Knives and heavy-headed *rungus* (Masai batons) bristled from their belts. Spears were strapped to the handlebars.

"What is your news?" Celia called in Swahili from the car window. "Where do you go?"

The Masai glared at us and pedaled fiercely through the dust. "They have taken our cows," one warrior answered. The anguish in his voice scarcely needed the translation Celia provided.

"Who stole their cows?" I asked. "Are they going to fight to get them back?" I imagined a story of cattle rustling and revenge. Greed. Lawlessness. Murder. Muggleton would have loved it. "Is it a war party?"

"No, no," Celia said. "They had to sell some cows, although they like their cows very much. Now they are going hunting."

"Hunting!" I said. "But this area is a nature reserve."

"Yes," Celia said patiently. "That is why they had to sell their cows. They are no longer permitted to graze them here. But they must eat. So now they must go hunting. Do you understand?" Like any catch-22, it was simple, really.

Late in the afternoon, just as we began to think of looking for a place to pull off the road and camp, the clouds opened. We'd stopped in a village called Bunda for a Tangawezi (ginger soda), and when the downpour started, we were still parked in front of the shop beside the highway. It rained so hard and fast and thick that the air seemed liquefied. Water suddenly filled the ditch beside the road. It swamped the parking lot. It covered the steps of the shop and inched up the sides of the Toyota. Celia stuck her head out. "We are now standing in a river," she said.

"Don't worry," I said. "We'll float."

"Ah," Celia said. "That is very fine. I am not a swimmer."

For half an hour the rain continued, and then, as though someone had shut the tap, it stopped. People emerged from shelter and sauntered again down the road, the highest ground, but all around lay swamps of red mud. We did the only prudent thing. Like an amphibious craft, our Land Cruiser rose from the water and waded down the road to the HiWay Hotel. It was an African hotel: bare simple rooms, each equipped with one hard bed, one clean gray sheet, and one rope dangling from the ceiling where once a mosquito net had hung. It was built Swahili-style, with rooms opening off the sides of an open courtyard. At the back were toilets and bathing cubicles complete with pipes and faucets, from which no water emerged. The trick was to fill a bucket from one of the newly replenished rain barrels in the courtyard. We went across the road to get a plate of rice and greens at Yankees Restaurant, a hole-in-the-wall with three tables under a battered Coca-Cola sign. When we returned, Caro emptied out her pink shoulder bag, a capacious container that held every needful thing except the key to her room. "It must be in the room," she said. It was the only key, and the window was barred. "I must have forgotten it," Caro said. "These things happen all the time, don't they?"

"Do they?" I said.

Then while Caro, Celia, and the hotel manager lamented the lost key, I fetched some tools from the car and removed the door from its hinges. I took the key from the bed where Caro had left it and handed it to her. Then I put the door back and stowed away the tools. "Camp-

ing is a lot easier," I said. After dark the HiWay Hotel fired up a generator to power a big TV in the garden out front, and most of the men of
the village gathered to drink beer and watch soccer far into the night.
Camping is quieter too.

The next night we were in the Serengeti Sopa Lodge, a luxurious
tourist hotel with spacious suites and breezy balconies looking out from
a hill across the vast plain of the Serengeti. (Mr. Sheth had asked us, as a
favor, to visit three lodges affiliated with UTC in northern Tanzania's
national parks, and we could scarcely deny his request.) All the lodges
in the Sopa Hotels chain in Tanzania were designed by an Indian architect inspired by a peculiar fantasy of African village life. He was heavily
into bricks and soaring spaces and meandering steeply canted ramps
and king-sized bathtubs and odd-shaped swimming pools. So it was
imposing and cushy, if not authentic. Celia, who had never before
stayed in what she called a "posh lodge," adored it precisely because it
was nothing like a real African village at all. She donned her best *kangas*
to go to the dining room.

"Celia," I said, "don't get too accustomed to posh lodges. This really
is a camping trip, and *this* really is not camping."

"Anna," she said, in her stern voice. "Be quiet, please. Let me enjoy."

The distance between the HiWay Hotel and the Serengeti Sopa
Lodge could be figured in light-years. But to get from one to the other,
we had driven across the Serengeti, from the rolling bush-covered western hills to the grassy eastern plain. All day we watched the animals that
thrive on this wild expanse: lions, baboons and monkeys, bat-eared
foxes, jackals, hyenas, impalas, gazelles, topis, kongonis, Cape buffalos,
giraffes, zebras, and great streams of wildebeests moving north in their
endless migration. The wildebeests came in long lines, racing to cross
the road ahead of our vehicle, running in lopsided circles when we
rattled past, then closing ranks again to charge across the road and
catch up. They were not clustered in one great herd but strung out like
streamers, converging strand upon strand, braiding themselves into
a single thickening rope of wildebeest, swinging north to the Mara
trailed by predators and back again, following the grass in the annual
unrelenting round of birth and death and rebirth that is nature's best
performance and last word.

·   ·   ·

The next day as we neared a village I pulled to one side of the skinny washboard road to make room for an oncoming truck, but I failed to see a jagged boulder lurking in the grass. Bam! The Land Cruiser tilted sideways, and I knew at once what had happened: two high-priced radial tires slashed at one shot.

"Ohmygod!" Caro said, pacing in the road.

Even Celia's mask slipped slightly, revealing momentary panic. "We have broken two tires," she said.

"Ohmygod! What can we do? What can we do?"

"For starters," I said, "we can change the tires."

I moved a pile of luggage in the back of the Land Cruiser and dragged the heavy "hassock" out of the lounge. Using a wrench, I detached the other spare tire from the back door and dropped it on my foot. I took a lug wrench to the lug nuts on the dead tires and found I hadn't the strength to loosen them, but when I stood on the wrench and jumped up and down, they came free one by one. Then I dragged out the jack, jockeyed it into position, and by swinging my full weight over the handle, I managed to raise the vehicle. I paused to tie a bandana around my head to keep the sweat out of my eyes and then squatted down by the front tire to remove the lug nuts, shimmy the tire off the hub, exchange it for the spare, and screw the lug nuts back in place. All the while Caro and Celia and a little crowd of curious villagers stood in the road and watched me work. Then I repeated the process on the back tire, but before I could replace the lug nuts on the newly installed spare, a young man stepped forward and gently nudged me aside, saying something in Swahili I couldn't understand.

"He says a woman must not do such work," Celia said. I made an effort to help him with the lug nuts, but he pushed me aside again. "He says it is a man's work, and because he is a man he will do it."

"Asante sana," I said, and stepped aside with what I hoped was a gracious invitation to the young man to be my guest. "Where were you half an hour ago?" Late though he was, his brand of gender discrimination worked in my favor, for changing tires was—as Muggleton so often said—"bloody hard work."

"You see," Celia said, "it is as my mother said: cars are not for women." Celia's mother had been astonished when we drove up in the Land Cruiser without a male chauffeur. That three women could go down the road without a man to drive them defied her imagination, though to her credit the actual mind-boggling spectacle, in which her daughter seemed to star, made her laugh with delight.

The young man worked up a manly sweat finishing the job. Then he guided us to another man in the village who could insert tubes in our slaughtered radials, making them serviceable as spares in the event of another flat. In the sun-blistered open yard of his "garage" I helped his workmen pry the tires from the rims, and after the tubes had been installed, pry the tires back on. It was one of those long, hard frustrating jobs, straining to ease things into position only to have them pop out and make us start all over again; but at last, with the last of my energy, I hoisted one of the reincarnated tires into position on the back door and bolted it down, and I dragged the other into the back of the vehicle and restowed the luggage. The men laughed and shook my hand and clapped me on the shoulder and laughed some more when an overenthusiastic congratulatory backslap nearly knocked me down. I was worn out—sweating under the stunning sun, swatting at squads of glue-footed flies—and furious that I alone seemed to be responsible for the vehicle. Caro and Celia had long since grown weary of watching and retired to a cool cafe, like two grand ladies awaiting their laggard chauffeur. Why was I the one who did all the bloody work? Why was I the one who calculated distances and times and gas consumption, who washed windows and checked tire pressures and fluid levels and changed oil? Why was I the one who daily checked the engine—or at least such small parts of that closely encased diesel contraption over which an amateur might have some influence? I sank down on the steps of the garage with a shock of recognition: This must be the way Muggleton felt about me. But now we were all women, in this together, share and share alike. How had I come to be saddled with Muggleton's role?

"I'd forgotten we had extra tires," Caro said when she and Celia emerged, refreshed and smiling, from their pleasant sojourn in the cafe. "Wasn't that lucky?"

"Luck had nothing to do with it," I said. "Don't be stupid." I seemed to have fallen into Muggleton's mind-set as well, and his vocabulary. My better judgment told me not to be so mean. Didn't I know perfectly well that neither Celia nor Caro was quite herself—Celia at sea in strange new experiences, and the normally independent and capable Caro distracted by grief that often shook her suddenly to tears? Screw that, I thought. I'd been slaving for hours at this "man's work." I was past reasoning with myself—in a rage. "Where the hell were you?" I said at the top of my voice. "You two might have given me some help, you know. This is damned bloody hard work." What was happening to me? "Who cares," I snapped when they started to explain. "It's probably too hard for you ladies anyway." Was it the Lariam? The discomfortingly posh lodges? The new burden of responsibilities for which I knew I was ill-equipped? Or could this simply be my true character— this surly macho bully? Goddess, help me, I thought. I am becoming a monster.

We drove on through Olduvai Gorge, pausing to pay our respects to common ancestors, and then climbed up a long slow incline to the rim of Ngorongoro Crater and crept over the precipice to the crater floor, fifteen hundred feet straight down. By sunset we were high on the other side, on the terrace of Ngorongoro Sopa Lodge, looking back on the great round bowl that cradles so much life. As the floor of the crater fell into shadow I could just make out the fold of hills where the road lay that we had descended that morning to the salt lake. Even as I watched, a vehicle wrapped a curl of dust along the floor of the crater, just where we had driven, skirting the edge of the lake and the forest of fever trees where elephants browsed. Tomorrow we would leave this idyll, heading south. But tonight, I thought, Celia was right: we should just enjoy. The air turned cool, and a strong breeze blew. The surrounding hills grew gray, and the crater floor threw back a dun-colored afterglow as the sun disappeared and the world before me slipped away. Out of the darkness came Celia's stern voice. "Anna," she said. "Go pack your bag. Tomorrow we go camping."

The next day we stopped along the road to talk with a group of Masai women who were selling baskets and mats made from palm leaves. Celia wanted to buy a basket to hold our fruit and vegetables, and Caro wanted to film some women doing what so many women in Africa do: selling goods beside the road. The Masai women agreed. Out came the camera and the tripod. And out came Celia, proud to be wearing for the first time an outfit she'd chosen in Nairobi for her new life as an international tourist and film assistant: a bright red Toyota baseball cap, dark shades, a tee shirt, and sleek blue jeans. Normally Celia dresses in a modest blouse and tailored skirt (in the city) or wrapped *kanga* (in the village), so she was a little self-conscious about her internationally hip new outfit. Nevertheless, everything was going smoothly—Caro filming, Celia playing the role of shopper—until a Masai woman in the back of the little crowd that had gathered to watch called out to Celia, "Why are you putting on trousers? Are you not a woman? Do you not have a woman's shame?" She made loud clucking noises to indicate—in any language—that Celia's dress was shameful. She turned to her neighbors and threw up her hands. What was the world coming to? Caro and I were wearing trousers too, but we were weird *wazungu,* without shame, past redemption. Nobody cared what we wore, but Celia was a real woman, an African. And this apparently was another side of African communal life, this public humiliation of the nonconforming woman. My own bad temper pained me with secret guilt, but how much heavier for Celia was this public shaming?

"Leave her alone," shouted another woman in the crowd. "She can put on what she pleases."

"Ndiyo!" called another in Swahili. "Yes! You Masai think you are perfect. You think all the world must dress like you. But the modern world is different. She can put on whatever she pleases."

"Shame," the Masai woman called again. "Shame!"

Some of the others muttered condemnation, but the women on the side of the modern world shouted them down. Without a word Celia folded the tripod, returned the microphone to its case, picked up her new basket, and with the palpable dignity only an African woman can muster, walked slowly across the road and stepped into the vehicle. She shut the door and took her seat in the big lounge chair at the back, staring straight ahead, stolidly awaiting her *wazungu* drivers—a proud African woman on the move into the modern world.

TWO CAMPS

Not long after we passed Mount Kilimanjaro, shrouded as it nearly always is in cloud, we turned off the main road and started looking for a place to camp. We had left the posh lodges of the game parks behind and now at last could pitch our tents in the bush of Tanzania. On a dirt track leading into the hills, we found a likely spot—deserted, miles from nowhere. We stepped out of the vehicle to take a closer look, and suddenly a woman burst out of the bush and rushed toward us, brandishing a gigantic machete. She swung it in circles, slicing the air within inches of the faded red scarf tied round her head. She shouted something in Swahili, but I couldn't make it out over the sound of my heart pounding with a rush of adrenaline. I froze in my boots, but Celia marched straight into the woman's path as if she were prepared to die. But no, the woman was smiling—and she was calling out a Swahili greeting. Then I realized that the weapon she waved was an ordinary machete that appeared gigantic only because the woman herself was so small and slim. Her name, she said, was Hadijah.

"Welcome," she said in Swahili. "You are welcome to make your camp here. I myself will inform the neighbors so they won't be afraid that you have come to steal our land."

We could see no neighbors, but in fact we were surrounded by poor squatters like Hadijah who had come to the hills to grow a little maize and chop firewood to make charcoal. She was a widow, she told us, and she had to get money for her children. She had borne eight, but only three survived. They lived many kilometers away with her mother in the village where the school was. But Hadijah lived most of the time alone in a mud hut no bigger than a garden shed. She slept on the dirt floor and spent her days chopping firewood. She was strong and lithe and swung the machete with an easy grace, but this was back-breaking work. Sheepishly we unloaded from our sumptuous vehicle more earthly possessions than Hadijah and all her neighbors combined would own in their lifetime, and we set up our camp.

Celia wanted to do the cooking. Caro and I did all the driving, she said, and in fairness she wanted a similar essential job. Secretly I thought she figured it was the only way she'd get a decent meal. Caro had queer tastes, like cheese and banana sandwiches for breakfast, and I was likely to cook something Celia found truly disgusting, such as pasta. When Celia first requested a job, she and Caro looked to me for direction, as if I were the commandant, and I'd given her the task of taking care of the water. That meant filling jerry cans and the solar shower at clear streams, and using the small hand pump to purify some of that water and transfer it to special jerry cans reserved for our drinking supply. Celia went at it with a will, but our fancy camping gear proved no match for this big strong African woman. Equipment that had served Muggleton and me for six months without complaint now gave up the ghost. First the shower bristled with unpatchable holes. Then the pump fell to pieces in her hands. What did it matter? she asked. Even when she managed to purify some water, she didn't bother to keep track of which container she put it in. Why should she? She didn't mind drinking river water, which tasted much better to her than all those poisonous chemicals anyway. So why go to all this trouble? I couldn't explain. Lacking the facility to purify water could have been disastrous in the remote regions of central Africa; but here in East Africa, where we were never far from towns with potable water, what was the point? Celia wanted a meaningful task. So I labeled the jerry cans clearly and filled and dispensed them myself, and Celia took over the cooking.

She bought vegetables from women in the markets or at the road-side, and she drove a hard bargain. We were no longer allowed to have red bananas. Too expensive. But green leaves for *sukuma* were a bargain. *Sukuma* is short for *sukuma wiki*—literally, "push the week"—and many an East African family pushes the week along with greens until, if they are lucky, they get to some meat at the weekend. In their market state *sukuma* leaves come with a lot of dirt and small creatures attached, so Celia started picking them over in the back of the vehicle as we drove along, flicking bugs and worms out the window, making preparations for cooking. Then she stewed the leaves with onions and shredded carrots and chopped tomatoes into a dish so heavenly we didn't mind eating it over noodles, as we had to do at first because I had bought the wrong kind of maize meal. Ignorant *mzungu* that I am, I bought meal for chapatis when what was wanted was meal for *ugali*.

Ugali. Kenya's staple and Celia's specialty. *Ugali* is like grits cooked to the consistency of Play-Doh—an acquired taste. Caro had lived in Kenya long enough to become addicted to the stuff. But me, I was a lesser enthusiast. Besides, *ugali* took forever to cook, which meant that when we pulled into camp, tired after a long day on the road, and I wanted nothing more than a quick light snack before crawling into my bedroll, I had to wait and wait for dinner to be served. I'd suggest a vote and nominate a nice tomato salad, but there were always two hands raised on the other side, for *ugali*. *Ugali* made the menu every night. Yet Celia was unhappy about the way they made *ugali* flour in Tanzania. They mixed it with wheat. That made the final dish lighter, less glutinous, more like mashed potatoes than silly putty, altogether less robust and certainly not, by Kenyan standards, anywhere close to the real thing. Luckily for us, Celia managed by inexplicable means to acquire on the road a very large supply of authentic undiluted Kenyan *ugali* flour.

Celia was not happy with our American camping stove either. She was used to cooking on a Kenyan tripod: three big rocks in the midst of a wood fire. She could manage on an electric hot plate in the apartment she shared with her brother in Nairobi, but real cooking called for a real fire. The camp stove produced only fake fire. It produced a super-hot flame, I explained, and consequently could cook food fast. But *ugali* took a long time, Celia said, and quick-cooked *ugali* was not *ugali* at all. Besides, the stove was far too complicated. You had to push the little plunger thirty-five times. Keep your normal big human-sized thumb over that teeny tiny little hole. Turn the little lever up. Then turn the little lever down. Push the little plunger again. There was scarcely time to stir the food. Any African cook would want to finish off this diabolically complicated contraption. Celia did it with *ugali*. The heavy-duty fare was just too much for the sophisticated self-igniting two-burner unleaded-fuel-only and please-keep-free-of-dust American stove meant for a bland backpacker's diet of prepackaged dehydrated two-minute meals. *"Ugali!"* it seemed to sigh. Even the name was heavy. The stove began to heave and cough. It sent up a burst of flame in one final salvo, then sputtered into silence.

"Damned wimpy American stove," I burst out when I had tried everything I knew to fix it. (Here was another part of my Muggletonian role: fixing busted equipment, of which we seemed to have a lot.) I slammed down the cover in an angry clatter of tortured tin. "This damned thing is just not up to cooking *ugali*."

"Don't worry," Celia said, always calm and philosophical. "Be thankful. It has cooked the *sukuma*."

In the morning a man wearing trousers and a velveteen sport coat came to greet us formally with many rhetorical flourishes of Swahili. He would have come the night before to pay his respects to the honored visitors, he said, but he returned to his home too late. He was Hadijah's neighbor, the husband of her friend Amina. We walked down the hillside with him to their homes to say goodbye to the women. They were working outside Amina's hut, pounding maize kernels in a wooden mortar with big wooden pestles the size of fence posts. Rhythmically they raised the heavy poles and brought them down again and again while half a dozen men lounged on the big sacks of maize meal the women had already prepared. This is the standard arrangement in Africa, where women do something like eighty percent of the work and produce something like seventy percent of the food. (The statistics vary from study to study, but the basic arrangement is clear.) It's not that men do nothing, now that so many of their traditional tasks have slipped away. They supervise. They make decisions. They accumulate the fruits of women's labor. They hold the capital: the goats, the cattle, the machines. And since Hadijah had sent word to her neighbors about the strangers camping on the hill, all the men were duty-bound to gather and pass judgment on the visitors. After I gave Hadijah and Amina a Polaroid photo of themselves, the men let it be known that they collectively were prepared to pose for such a portrait. One raised his *panga* in salute. Another unwrapped one carefully saved cigarette and put it in the corner of his mouth at a rakish angle. A third dragged his goat into the picture. A fourth held up a little portable radio. They stood up proudly—the menfolk. They had the goods.

· · ·

We made our way south along the shoulder of the Usambara Mountains, passing great vacant expanses of bushland and baobab forest interrupted by huge plantations of sisal—mile after mile of straight spiky rows rolling to the horizon. (Like coffee in Kenya, sisal was Tanzania's monocrop in colonial days, when it was Tanganyika.) One night we made camp on a sisal plantation, a good safe place, far from the road. The next night we asked permission to camp at another plantation, but this time the foreman said no. Instead he directed us down a muddy track to a village in the bush. The headman came out to greet us, a tiny wizened elder wearing an embroidered Tanzanian pillbox hat and a once-white shirt. "You are human beings," he said in Swahili. He shook our hands warmly. "We must take you in." He led the way to a small hut. Other men surrounded us, ushering us in. We three took seats on a low bench opposite the headman. Other men crowded in at the door and leaned in at the window. A young man took out a pen and held it at the ready, though he had no paper to write on. He sat next to the headman and seemed to speak for him.

"Where do you come from?" he asked. "How did you come to this place?"

Celia leaned forward earnestly and answered the questions softly in what even I could tell was extremely polite Swahili.

"What is your purpose? How long will you stay here?"

A woman slipped onto the bench beside me and seized my hand. *"Rafiki!"* she cried. "My friend!" She clutched my hand in both of hers and worked her way up my arm. She was small and wiry and very strong. She snuggled against me. She turned her face up to mine with a radiant gap-toothed smile. *"Rafiki!"* She was very drunk. All at once I remembered what that peculiar smell was that filled the room. Home brew. Which in Africa is high-octane stuff. Another young man took the floor, offering an opinion of us that clearly was unfavorable. We were not welcome. We would get them in trouble with the government. Other men chimed in on his side. I tried to catch the eye of the kind, welcoming, fellow-human headman, but it was glazed and sightless. That's when I noticed the bows that hung on the wall over his head, and the quivers of short arrows, the points sharpened and discolored by some toxic herb designed to finish off the victim. I turned again to the men standing in the doorway and noticed for the first time the machetes dangling from their hands. Then it came to me that we had delivered ourselves and our bright blue Land Cruiser laden with precious objects into the hands of a village tripping through a ritual drinking ceremony on the high road to violence.

"I'm leaving now," I announced in what I hoped was a cordial tone. I got up and extricated my arm from the grip of my *rafiki,* who slumped back on the bench singing "Bye-bye" in English. I stepped toward the door as if the crowd would part, and reminded myself to keep breathing. Caro and Celia were right behind me. In the center of the doorway stood a grim-faced man who held his machete at his side in an easy backhanded grip that turned the keen edge of the blade toward me. If he doesn't move, I thought, I'll split my leg wide open. But if I stop now, we're in trouble for sure. I kept moving and felt him fade backward and dip to the side like a dance partner gracefully following my lead. The crowd behind him stepped back as well, like a wave curling in upon itself, and I walked forward briskly to the Land Cruiser before the wave could break and sweep us under.

"Thank you so much for your very kind hospitality," I said to the village in general.

"So terribly sorry to rush off like this," Caro was saying. "*Asante sana.* Thank you. Thank you. Another time perhaps. *Kwaheri.* Goodbye."

I started the vehicle and edged forward toward the wall of the crowd. For a long moment it held firm, and we stared through the windshield at faces that stared back at us. Then the wall cracked in the center and slowly slowly opened to let us go. When we hit the highway and sped away, Caro made an effort to be jaunty. "I didn't quite like the look of those machetes," she said brightly.

Celia whispered, "Did you see the bows and arrows?"

Farther down the road, as darkness fell, we came upon a recreational compound maintained for the army. There'd be no question about trouble with the government here. This *was* the government. They let us pitch our tents inside the fence.

In the morning we packed up slowly slowly, as usual, for Caro and Celia still had not quite got the hang of camping. I'd suggested some time- and energy-saving tips, such as minimizing laundry by wearing no underwear, which in tropical Africa only makes you hot and sweaty and liable to bizarre infections. But the idea shocked them. I'd suggested that they bring only one small bag and only one change of clothes, thereby minimizing bulk, laundry, and bothersome decisions about what to wear. But each of them had brought one exceedingly large bag jam-packed with stuff, plus a lot of odds and ends. So every night there was a lot to unload, a lot to unpack, a lot of little blouses and little bras and cute little flowered panties to be laundered and strung up on the clothesline. There were faces to be washed too—a long process of buffing, rinsing, cleansing, rinsing, and toning that consumed jerry cans of precious water. And dishes, for preparing the nightly *ugali* enlisted every bit of equipment in the kitchen. After the demise of the cookstove, there was firewood to be gathered in embarrassingly huge amounts, since proper preparation of *ugali* required forty minutes' cooking time and not a minute less. In the morning there was another fire to be built and coffee to be made and moisturizers and sunscreen to be applied and purses to be searched for hairbrushes and just the right tube of lip emollient with vitamin E and aloe vera. And then everything had to be gathered up and packed away and loaded once again in the vehicle. By the time we pulled away from a campsite it was nearly noon and I was in a surly mood.

"Do you really need all this stuff?" I'd snap at Caro. "Why do you have to take such good care of yourself?" And to Celia: "Why can't we just have some bloody bananas?"

We went on in this way until one day Caro and Celia summoned me to a meeting. They told me that I was always angry and bossy and just no fun at all. Why had I gotten so mad that time we had the flat tires and they went to the cafe? Didn't I know that they were only trying to be considerate and not get in the way? Why had I spoken so sharply to Celia just because she got the river water and the drinking water mixed up? No disgusting parasites sucked our brains or drilled holes in our livers, did they? We didn't even get sick, did we? And why was I so snappish about my precious equipment? What did it matter that the stove and the water-filtration pump and the lantern didn't work anymore? Didn't we get along perfectly well without them? Or the shower—didn't we have another one? Or those dumb little tent stakes and poles that had gotten themselves lost? Who needed them? And what was wrong with waiting for laundry to dry? What difference did it make if we left at six o'clock or nine o'clock or noon? In short, why was I in such a snit? And when did I plan to get a grip on myself and get over it?

I tried to talk a little about safe and efficient camping, about having a system so fast and foolproof that you could find anything in seconds in the dark.

"Why would you want to do that?" Caro asked.

"Well, you know, in an emergency."

"But we haven't had an emergency," she said.

"Having a system also saves time," I said, trying a different tack. "On a daily basis, you don't have to spend so much time hanging about."

"What's wrong with hanging about?" Caro said. I knew it was hopeless. Poor Muggleton, I thought. Only weeks ago I'd called him a macho monster. Now that I had become one too, I missed him. Maybe I could send a wire: *Please come back all is forgiven.* But what had come over Caro? What had reduced a brave, creative, capable woman to this state of seeming ditziness? The enforced intimacy of traveling in an overland vehicle, a hothouse on wheels, could drive anybody crazy. But what was there about our particular situation that wrenched us from our true selves—independent women together—and recast us as macho and bimbo cartoons? Was this all there was to personality: the ineluctable acting out of roles into which our circumstances had thrust us? If this was the human comedy, why wasn't I laughing? And if we were doomed to play these stupid roles, why couldn't I at least fight for myself as I had fought toe to toe with Muggleton? The grief that Caro and Celia shared seemed to envelop them in a crystalline bubble. "Fragile" was written all over it, and I found it impenetrable. United in their league of grief, they lived together beyond my reach. I was looking for a land where women rule, and once again in my own vehicle I was outnumbered and on my own. I was looking for a way to rule myself, yet resentment ruled me as though my overheated brain, like a pot of *ugali,* had been set on long-term boil. When I reminded myself of the values of the great Queen of the Lovedu—tolerance, compromise, peace— they seemed far, far beyond my reach. Yet what good was it to find the Queen at the end of the journey if I could not at least try to live by her ideals along the way?

"Look, you're right, I'm sorry," I said. "I'm just used to operating a very tight ship. This kind of sloppiness—well, it drives me up the wall. It just doesn't seem like camping to me."

"You can be overcoming this habit," Celia said.

"Yes," Caro said. "Lighten up. This *is* camping. This is the way we camp."

UJAMAA

Once Tanzania was a beacon, and President Julius Nyerere the Mwalimu (teacher) of his people, the conscience of black Africa. Nyerere was a teacher by profession, educated at Makarere University in Uganda and the University of Edinburgh. When he returned to Tanganyika in 1952, he took up politics as well, working with the Tanganyika African National Union for independence from the United Kingdom. When it came, Nyerere won the presidency (in 1962) with ninety-seven percent of the vote, and he soon merged Tanganyika with Zanzibar to form the new nation of Tanzania.

He became a teacher in a larger sense: a statesman and a leader of enormous moral force who envisioned a great egalitarian United States of Africa. He reminded the people that "the very origins of African democracy lay in ordinary oral discussion—the Elders sat under a tree and talked until they agreed." Within Tanzania, he tried to build a democratic African socialist state based on the traditional family and comprising small-scale communal villages engaged mostly in traditional agriculture. (To Westerners, the traditional African family is an "extended" one; Africans see the nuclear family of the West as unnaturally "contracted.") *Ujamaa* was the word Nyerere used to describe his brand of African socialism: "familyhood." It was opposed to capitalism, he said, because capitalism tries to build a society based on the exploitation of one person by another, "the relentless pursuit of individual advancement." But *ujamaa* was also opposed to doctrinaire socialism, which tried to build a society around a belief in inevitable conflict between one person or class and another. To the true African socialist, all people were kin. Familyhood extended throughout a village, a country, a continent: the United States of Africa.

It wasn't just talk. Nyerere constructed a state apparatus to enlarge traditional African familyhood into a unified nation. He established a school system that made his country literate in a decade. He established the best health-care system in Africa and increased Tanzanian life expectancy by twenty years. He established Swahili—not English—as the national language. He lived modestly, declining to make himself rich as president; and he made rules to keep other official hands out of the till. He set the precedent for humanitarian intervention when he sent his army across the border into Uganda to bring down Idi Amin. He retired from office voluntarily in a peaceful transfer of power, but he continued to serve the pan-African cause. At the end of his life, even as he was dying of cancer, he was mediating the conflict in Burundi— as Africa's greatest statesman. But these achievements didn't seem to count for much with those who measure a nation's success by its gross national product. Measured in Western economic terms, Nyerere's idealistic national experiment was not a success—perhaps because its socialist aroma offended the capitalist nose, or perhaps because its African accent threatened white ears. Or perhaps because the country had no real resources but its sisal plantations. Who knows what might have become of Nyerere's dream if Tanzania had possessed Nigeria's oil, the Congo's minerals, or South Africa's diamonds and gold? But Nyerere was gone now, and as we drove across the country we could see that the people, like Hadijah, were still poor, the roads rocky, the village houses of mud and wattle shabby, the capital seedy, the phones out of order, the dreams of Mwalimu deferred.

Caro and Celia hoped to sail off into the Indian Ocean to the island of Zanzibar. Was it a bad sign, I wondered, that after only weeks on the road they wanted to go to the beach? It was Caro's wish. Little more than a year before, she'd flown to Zanzibar with her boyfriend, Lazarus, for a romantic holiday, just before he passed into the shadow of terminal illness. Returning with Lazarus's sister would be a descent into the underworld of remembrance and grief from which she might emerge with more impulsion for the years ahead. I would again be an outsider, a straggler tagging along on a path laid out for two. Yet how could I say no? I shouldered the Land Cruiser through the gridlocked streets of Dar es Salaam to the waterfront, and we caught the hydrofoil for Zanzibar.

It's a place with a magical name and a terrible history. On this island the Sultan Sayyid Said of Oman set himself up in 1832 as the world's greatest trader in ivory and slaves. He dispatched an emissary to the United States in 1840—to make contracts with slaveholders and to shop. With his sons, he built a grand palace on the seafront with broad verandas high up to catch the breeze, and filled it with finely carved furniture from India, porcelain from China, and wives and concubines from Persia, Nubia, Turkey, and Abyssinia. (The sultan's daughter, Princess Sayyida Salme, sized up the value of women in this world and fled to the arms of a German merchant, who established her in Hamburg as a respectable *Hausfrau*.) Slaves worked the great clove plantations of Zanzibar, and more than fifty thousand of them passed through the port each year at the height of the human export trade. They were marched to the coast from as far away as Lake Tanganyika, bearing the tusks of slaughtered elephants, and shipped out, mostly to America.

Here in 1857 Richard Burton and John Hanning Speke prepared to search for the source of the White Nile; and in 1866 in a tall shuttered house on the seafront, missionary David Livingstone planned his last great trek on the continent, the one marked by the famous meeting with Henry Morton Stanley at Ujiji in 1871, when Stanley, fearful of displaying emotion before Africans, suppressed his urge to run to Livingstone and embrace him, and instead merely uttered the famous salutation. That was the trek that ended two years later in fever and the burial of Livingstone's heart under a *mvula* tree at Chitambo's village, far inland, and the long walk of his loyal porters, led by Susi and Chuma, bearing his body to the coast and beyond to England.

In the tiny library of the Zanzibar museum Celia came upon a letter Stanley wrote to Sir John Kirk, the British envoy in Zanzibar, four years after Livingstone's death. Stanley asked that money be sent to pay Livingstone's porters, who were still waiting for their wages. The Foreign Office had sent silver medals for the men, engraved with the slogan "Faithful to the End." Stanley wrote that he would present the medals, but what the men wanted—and had earned—was money.

"My father named two of my brothers for this man," Celia said. "The first-born son is Henry. And after comes Morton."

"Why would he do that?" I asked, surprised.

"He liked the sound of the names," Celia said. "But I'm happy to see that Stanley was a good man." It wouldn't do to tell her that the euphonious Henry Morton Stanley later went to work for Leopold, King of the Belgians—Leopold, Curse of the Congo. Or that as Stanley led his "Anglo-American Expedition" (1874–77) from Zanzibar to the Congo, he sacked twenty-eight large towns and "three or four score" villages, according to the account he kept in his journal. Richard Burton complained that Stanley shot Africans "like monkeys."

We headed for the village of Nungwi, at the far end of the island, aboard a *dalla dalla,* a truck with benches in the back for passengers. We rented a tiny bungalow by the sea and spent our days carelessly, swimming in the crystal clear water. Too modest to wear a swimming suit, and too frightened to enter the water, Celia appeared on the beach wearing a tee shirt and *kanga* with a ruffled petticoat underneath. Little by little Caro coaxed her into the sea—up to her ankles, her knees, her hips. I gave her my blue swimming goggles, and Caro induced her to put her face in the water. By the third day she was floating on her back: a big buoyant space lady surviving at sea.

"You must take a photo now, Anna," she called out. But when I approached with my underwater camera she said, "Wait! Wait!" because she couldn't stop grinning, and it would never do to be caught on film showing rows of bright teeth. She composed her face and I composed the photo. "An African swimming!" she said, beaming again. "Me, Celia Muhonja, swimming! My mother will never believe it."

Sometimes we watched groups of women wade fully clothed into the sea and walk back and forth, up to their necks in water, seining for fish. Sometimes we walked into the village and talked with women who sat under the trees in the square, weaving grass fibers into beach mats and sun hats for the few tourists who found their way to this far corner of the island. They thrust the materials into our hands and laughed at our clumsy attempts to twist them into shape. "It's a tropical paradise," Caro said, "and all the women do is work."

Much later, when our trip was over and Caro had returned to

England, she sent me a clipping from a London newspaper about the future of Nungwi. The *Guardian* reported that several British companies planned to undertake a $4 billion "tourism development" project there. The complex of fourteen luxury hotels, several hundred villas, a cruise-ship harbor, three championship golf courses, and a world trade center will be "East Africa's biggest holiday resort." But what will become of the fisherwomen, the weavers, the owners of our little bungalow—the twenty thousand Tanzanians who *live* in Nungwi? According to the *Guardian,* the plans announced by the British-owned East Africa Development Company (like those of King Leopold a century before) "seem to suggest that the area is uninhabited."

Sometimes when we went out to dinner in the open-air restaurants of Nungwi, we ran into vacationing *wazungu,* recuperating from their work with international aid organizations elsewhere in Africa. Doris was a born-again Christian who one day heard the voice of God speaking through the radio. God said, "Why not train to be an aircraft engineer?" Now she was working for the mission of her evangelical church, fixing medevac planes. She and her friends made me think of the aid workers I'd seen in Nairobi just before we set out on our travels. Weary and bedraggled, they milled about the lobby of a five-star hotel, newly arrived from Goma, in Zaire, and Kigali, in Rwanda. How confused they must be, I thought at the time, to have started for Africa to "do good" and finished as proprietors of refugee camps that provided room and board and operational headquarters for Hutu Power troops carrying out genocide against Tutsi and moderate members of their own tribe. That fall—1996—elements of the Rwanda People's Army moved into Zaire with the rebel Congolese forces (the ADFL) of Laurent Kabila, and Zaire's Banyamulenge rose up to defend themselves against Hutu *génocidaires* and their Mobutu allies. Rwandan refugees, who had been little better than hostages in the Hutu Power–controlled camps in Zaire, fled toward home. Thousands upon thousands walked the roads to Rwanda as Zaire exploded. Before it was over at least ten African nations would aid Kabila in the first pan-African intervention to overthrow a despot. (Nyerere would have approved.) But at the time, with the outcome in question, I saw only those dazed out-of-a-job aid workers and the terrible footage on CNN—gaunt, miserable Zaireans battling one another, pushing women and kids aside, to claim a package of food flung from an aid truck manned by black African drivers after all *wazungu* had fled. I'd seen those people in person, only months before, when Muggleton and I traveled among them along the muddy canyons of Zaire. The lean men pushing bicycles laden with bananas and palm oil. The women bearing jugs of paraffin. The wayfarers who stopped to smile, to sell us pineapples, to dig out our vehicle, to help us rebuild a bridge to let us pass. The villagers who welcomed us to their huts for a bowl of porridge, a glass of water. The Bantu workers at Epulu. The Pygmy hunters. Pastor Nyete at the Monga mission and his assistant, Mr. Tongbo. Simon the Monga schoolteacher. Kimbanguist Pastor Patrick and Ana, his wife. Dear sweet gentle Pastor Alphonse. Katina and the Chief. The Italian priests. Where were they now?

At last we dragged Celia from the sea and returned to the mainland. Soon we hit rocky roads again—the typical Tanzanian road surface— and the screws of the battery housing shook loose for the umpteenth time. The first time this happened, on the corrugated roads of the Serengeti, the battery came loose from its moorings, beat itself sui- cidally against the engine housing, and smashed its cells. I battened it back in place with duct tape, but for days, until we reached Arusha, where batteries were sold, we turned off the engine only on a downhill slope and hoped for the best. Now our recently acquired replacement battery began the same tap dance of death against the side of the vehicle and impelled us onto the premises of Malawi Motors Ltd., a Nissan dealership just over the border in Mzuzu. Peter Nazombe, the head mechanic, didn't have the right screws to secure the battery housing, but he had a better idea. Within five minutes he had welded onto the housing another little arm that made the battery sit down and stay put. The Nissan dealer said, "You have to wonder: Why didn't Toyota think of that?"

We sent out for coffee before hitting the road again, and sat with the mechanics in the back room of the garage, exchanging stories, sipping from tiny cups. Looking around the circle of friendly faces, black and white, I was struck by the difference between this journey and the first, Muggletonian leg of the expedition. What had become of adventure? Confrontation? Near disaster? Narrow escapes? For one thing, we were traveling in a much more "developed" part of Africa, well used to inter- national visitors. Governments, whatever their problems, were more stable, and the people generally better off. We had a much better vehicle, and far better roads. True I'd turned into a bloody Muggleton clone, often reducing Caro to a state of semihelplessness, but at least as women together we were more or less content to accept the world we found. To Muggleton Africa was a challenge, an obstacle, a battleground, an arena for the performance of exploits that sprang full-blown from his itchy imagination. To us Africa was the home of people we were pleased to meet. We moved through our days more slowly, though we felt our pace was still too fast. None of us would ever entertain a barroom crowd with tall tales of challenge and victory, or tempt Death by bragging how nearly we had escaped his hand. Death already sat too near us in our vehicle—no theoretical challenge but a real presence, bringing every day to Caro and Celia sighs and sudden tears, and to me memories of friends made and now lost in Zaire.

Often I missed the heady adrenaline rush of Mugglemania, though I was grateful for the slower, steadier pace—the chance to look about and begin to see. But if this journey was not a bold adventure anymore, what was it? What was our mission now? Caro and Celia hoped for peace, surely: for life after Lazarus. As for me, I still hoped to meet the Queen, but I felt rewarded by the journey. That's the lesson I'd learned as a child from all those road trips with my dad: it's not where you're going that matters, it's the ride. I had hoped to find in Loveduland that a people who believed it worth doing could live in harmony, and the evidence lay all around me here in Tanzania. *Ujamaa.*

The Mzuzu mechanics directed us to the street market to find screws for the battery housing—just in case—and while we were at it, we found a cobbler who sewed up Celia's newly purchased pseudo-hightech sandals with palm fiber and made them better than new.

"I will be wearing my sandals to the beach," Celia said proudly as we drove away.

"Would you like to go swimming again?" I asked. I glanced in the rearview mirror and caught her grinning.

"I don't mind," she said. And then: "To say the truth, I am looking forward to it."

WHAT YOU SEE

When we drove across the border from Tanzania, the immigration officer said, "Malawi is a very poor country. You will see." But we didn't see. Not really. Not at first. And when we did begin to notice what lay behind appearances, it only brought home to me how little of this immense continent I had seen, and how much less I understood. We drove south almost nine hundred kilometers down the skinny corridor that is Malawi, and what we saw was the beauty of the land—the windswept grassy hills of the high Nyika Plateau, the rolling surf of the great inland sea of Lake Malawi, the steamy lushness of the Shire River valley where the lake drains away into the forest. One day I parked under a tree and we made camp on a beach at the lake. During the night mangoes bombarded the Land Cruiser and arranged themselves on the hood in a breakfast buffet. Who would not be captivated by such a place?

But as we drove south, we realized that what was important about the country was what we didn't see. Wildlife, for example. In the uplands of Nyika National Park, where great herds used to roam, we spotted only a few animals—mountain reedbuck, eland, bushbuck, roan—all running scared. Three-quarters of the park's animals had disappeared long since into the cooking pots of hungry people in Malawi and Mozambique, just across the border. Trees had disappeared too, felled to make room for people and fields of cassava and sugarcane, and thrown into the fires that heated those cooking pots. There were about ten million people in Malawi, most of them clustered in the south, and as we drove southward we could measure the rising population by the disappearance of the trees. The hardwoods—ebonies and Natal mahoganies—had gone to woodcarvers, and the rest were for sale along the road in great stacks of firewood and giant bags of charcoal five feet tall. "Why do you cut down all the trees?" I asked a woodsman we met along the road. "We have too many trees," he said. "In New York is no trees. New York is modern. When trees is gone, Malawi is also modern." As we talked, a slight stirring of the air lifted the bare red earth around us in clouds of dust. When the rains began it would pour down the hillsides into the rivers and into the lake, where it would turn clear waters to deep brown muck.

We saw fishermen go out each night in their dugout canoes, working in teams with lights to lure the fish into nets and encircle them. We saw them again in the early morning, sitting on the beaches with their nets spread on the sand, making repairs. But their nets had come up empty again. In a small grass hut that served the fishing camp as a restaurant, men nibbled on cassava, a tasteless white tuber of no known nutritional value, the crop they felled the trees to grow, the staple of the Malawi diet. They drank tea—hot water poured over a few soggy leaves and four or five heaping tablespoons of sugar. That's what passed for a meal when they had only small fish in their nets and nothing in their pockets.

We saw modern universities, but invisible to us was the disease that plagues graduates who postpone marriage while getting an education—and substitute casual sex and prostitution. AIDS strikes hardest at the educated classes. Ten physicians graduate from medical school, and within a year three of them are dead, some of the others ailing. By the year 2000, in this tiny country, AIDS had made orphans of a million children.

But the roads were good, the beaches beautiful; the weather was fine and the surf was up—the perfect setting for a heedless holiday. It was enough to make us all lighten up a little and reach a tentative détente. We worked our way down the lake, camping on the beach, feasting on mangoes that lay all over the ground and still rained from the trees. One day as we walked up the beach after a swim, we were suddenly struck by the appearance of our camp. "Do you think we've overdone the blue?" Caro asked. The centerpiece of our camp was the Toyota Land Cruiser, with its distinctive monochrome paint job: peacock blue.

Every time we crossed a border, officials emerged from cubbyholes to admire it. "There's nothing like this in Tanzania," they said. "Nothing like this in Malawi." Toyota Land Cruisers were everywhere in East Africa, but none quite so ostentatious as this. Now it stood far up the beach, surrounded by three small dome tents of peacock blue. "It looks like the car gave birth," Caro said. Three promising blue lumps—a litter of baby Land Cruisers—might grow with proper feeding into three full-grown vehicles so handsome, so peacock blue, as to make Toyota proud. There was something serendipitous about the color. Nobody planned it. The tents were sent to me from the States. From London Caro brought camp chairs striped in magenta (rather like her pink purse) and peacock blue. All three of us—three women from three different continents—packed shirts or pants in this peculiar blue shade. We'd sit down to dinner looking as if we'd been costumed and accessorized by a set designer. Then I'd crawl into my tent and don my satin pajamas: peacock blue. I hesitated to ask what Caro and Celia wore to bed. At that moment, walking up the beach, Caro and I were wearing blue bathing suits. Celia, fresh from an intensive swimming lesson, was wrapped in a blue *kanga,* my blue goggles still perched on her forehead. We paused to admire our tidy blue homestead.

"It does look weird, doesn't it?" I said.

"A bit over the top, do you think?" Caro said.

"I am enjoying it," Celia said. "It is very fine." That settled it.

Thousands of kilometers still lay between us and the Rain Queen, but we began to feel that we were closing in. When the skies darkened over Malawi and a fierce wind whipped sheets of rain across the road, I thought it might be Modjadji at work. The windshield wipers whooshed back and forth whispering, "Rain . . . Queen . . . Rain . . . Queen . . . Rain . . . Queen."

We tried to imagine what it might mean to be a queen in Africa. All around us, all along the way, we saw women doing nothing but work. Caro had been filming women at work, and she had footage of women hoeing, planting crops, weeding, harvesting, gathering wild edibles, shucking maize, pounding maize, grinding maize at the mill, carrying maize meal home, chopping wood, gathering firewood, carrying firewood home on their heads or on their backs, building fires, cooking, serving food, washing dishes, scouring pots, making clothes, buying clothes, washing clothes (after first carrying the laundry to the river, or carrying the river water home), selling clothes and food and baskets in the marketplace or beside the road, building houses, painting houses, gathering thatching, preparing mud plaster, polishing floors with cattle dung (to keep out insects), scrubbing floors, weaving palm fibers, making mats, making baskets, making hats, dying fabrics, sewing, knitting, embroidering, making pots, minding children, doctoring children, teaching children, feeding children, washing children, dressing children, plaiting hair, milking cows, feeding chickens, butchering chickens, shopping, making brooms, sweeping houses, sweeping yards, cleaning churches, cleaning wells, planting trees, and keeping accounts. So far she had no footage at all of women being queens. What would a queen *do*?

In Nkhata Bay we met Margaret Mazembe. Celia wanted to buy some good fabrics to sell in Kenya when she went home, and many people told us that Margaret produced the best. (Although Celia was a civil servant in Kenya, she had to "make business" on the side, like most Kenyan women, to make ends meet.) Margaret showed us two lengths of cotton, tie-dyed in all the subtle colors of a Lake Malawi sunrise: rosy pink and purple and soft gold overlaid with palest blue. But that was all she had to offer. "My business is not go well," she said. The two rooms of her little house and workshop were almost bare. She said that she had dyes on hand, but no money to buy cloth. "What has happened?" Celia asked, and bit by bit the story came out. Margaret got her start by making and selling *mandazi* (doughnuts) in the market. She used the profits to buy a sewing machine, and she took a course offered by a government agency in making tie-dye, batik, and screen-printed fabrics. Soon she had many handmade fabrics for sale, and money to reinvest in her business. She bought six sewing and knitting machines. She employed five tailors to make men's shirts and ladies' dresses to sell in big markets as far away as Mzuzu.

Then from nowhere, she said, her husband came and took away four of her machines and most of her supplies. Margaret went to the police, and they called in her husband to ask him why he had taken Margaret's property. The property was his, he said, because Margaret used it in *his* house. The police agreed. The husband sold the machines and went to live with another woman. "The government had sent me to a training program to learn to make fabrics and to manage a business," Margaret said. "But without money to get started again, the knowledge is useless." Margaret asked the government for seed money, saying she had already proven that she could operate a business. The government turned her down, saying she had already failed. Margaret went back to selling doughnuts again in the street. "It's where I started," she said quietly.

Margaret's story made me think again of the way Celia filled out entry and exit permits at border crossings, always checking the box for "single." When the average African woman had no right to her own property, or even to herself, how could we visualize an African queen?

We eased on down to Makuzi, where a white Malawian named Jane was building a perfect little beach lodge on a perfect stretch of beach. The local Tonga villagers had given Jane the beach in gratitude for her years of voluntary help in developing a school and clinic. (They made her promise only that if she tired of them, as the Livingstonian missionaries had, she wouldn't tear down the buildings for spite when she ran away, as they had done.) Jane invited us for dinner on the deck of her new lodge, overlooking the water. When we had finished dessert and pushed back our chairs to gaze at the gauzy moonlit breakers that seemed to drift dreamily toward us on the breeze, Jane told us the story of Manake's airplane. She'd been explaining why the missionaries had abandoned the Tonga people with such calculated malice. "The missionaries kept getting malaria and moving their church farther and farther from the water," she said. "Finally they tore down everything—the church, the school, the clinic—and carried the bricks up onto the plateau to work on another tribe. They said it was the malaria, but it's plain they simply got fed up with the Tonga. They'd spent forever trying to convert them, and the Tonga—not the least bit interested—went right on practicing witchcraft." Jane clearly admired the intractable Tonga, and they liked her so much they not only gave her the beach but also told her a secret. They told her about an enormous airplane that belonged to Manake, a man of the village. It flew only at night and carried only men—up to one hundred of them—who stripped naked and zoomed away to distant cities. Jane went to Manake's house and was shown a replica of an airplane, the size of a matchbox, woven entirely of pubic hair. And then illiterate Manake, who had never read a newspaper or seen television or traveled beyond the next village, told Jane all about the things he'd seen in Paris and New York.

"It's some kind of astral travel, I think," Jane said. "I can't explain it."

"Malawi Gold, more likely," someone else said.

"The Tonga people believe that the stars in the night sky are other countries," Jane said. "England and France and America. Their theories of the universe, and our place in it, couldn't be more different from ours." She looked out over the water, perhaps pondering the arcane cosmology of the Tonga, which she was privileged to understand. "When you see a falling star," she said, "that's Manake's airplane coming back."

A few days later we drove to Lilongwe, the capital, to obtain the visas we needed to pass through the Tete Corridor of Mozambique. Then we drove across the border. Malawi had been a deceptive paradise, its problems washed by tropical breezes and mango rain, but the troubles of Mozambique were written large across a landscape long ravaged by war and newly ravaged by wood choppers. Around us the rolling hills lay naked and exposed, the trees mowed down like stalks of grain, the red earth bare and parched. Stacks of firewood and feed bags full of charcoal lined the roadside. Flimsy huts made of reeds and grass—the houses in which people lived—leaned into the hillsides as if swept by high winds. People wandered down the road wearing clothes so tattered we wondered why they bothered to put them on. In a clump of thick bush, a team of workers from the United Nations High Commissioner for Refugees patrolled with bomb-sniffing German shepherds, searching for land mines. When the workers had cleared the mines, woodcutters would clear the bush. Next would come floods, rolling unimpeded over the treeless land. It was only a matter of time. We fell silent, saddened to be driving through such distress.

What chance had the people of Mozambique ever had? Enslaved by the Portuguese, condemned to illiteracy and forced labor, they fought thirteen years for freedom, led by Frelimo, the Mozambique Liberation Front. After independence in 1975, the new Marxist government of President Samora Machel called upon them to sacrifice. It put them to work in nationalized companies, state farms, and collectives. In their name it supported freedom fighters in neighboring countries: the

African National Congress in South Africa and the Zimbabwe African National Union in Rhodesia. The white supremacist governments of South Africa and Rhodesia retaliated by organizing the Mozambique National Resistance Movement, a force that destroyed villages in Mozambique, executed leaders and skilled workers, sabotaged schools, clinics, workshops, and transport, and swept up the people in ceaseless war—a "civil" war in which one side was sponsored entirely by other countries. In 1992 peace came at last, and in 1994 UN-supervised elections—which Frelimo won. But how long does it take a people to recover from thirty years of war? How long does it take the land?

At a roadblock at the long bridge over the Zambezi we fell into conversation with the drivers of a UNHCR truck loaded with portable kennels housing bomb-sniffing dogs. "There are still at least a million land mines in Mozambique," one driver told us. A million land mines ready to kill or maim a woman going to the stream for water, a child minding a cow, a man taking a shortcut home. Long years after the official peace, it was as if the land still waged war against the people.

We crossed the bridge over the Zambezi and drove slowly through the seedy streets of Tete, where once-lovely Portuguese villas stood among ruined gardens. "How do Africans do it?" Caro said. "They have such troubles." How little we know of those troubles, I thought; and of the beliefs that sustain the people. Caro turned to Celia. "Where do you think they get the spirit to carry on?"

Celia shrugged. "These people must be very strong," she said.

Later that night we stood near our tents and searched the dark sky, wondering which of the bright stars above was Zimbabwe? Which was South Africa and which was Loveduland? And where, when so many people could have used it, was Manake's airplane?

AFRICAN HERITAGE

After we crossed the border from Mozambique to Zimbabwe, Celia sat quietly in the back, taking in another dramatic change in the landscape. Well-tended fields spread around us, green and prosperous, and in their midst like monumental sculptures enormous *kopjes* stood—big bald granite mountains made smooth and round by wind and weather, and crowned by huge boulders balanced so precariously one upon another that it seemed they could only be sustained by the hand of God. The highway itself was excellent: well paved and well marked. Thoroughly modern service stations sold Coke, and it was ice-cold. "I am enjoying this very fine drink," Celia said, impressed.

We drove into Harare, the capital, through lush garden suburbs. When we reached the city center, we found it clean, modern, orderly, and scaled to human proportions like a pleasant country town. In the public garden at African Unity Square, well-dressed Zimbabweans, black and white, strolled under flowering jacaranda trees. The shops along Robert Mugabe Road were bright and busy. The National Gallery bloomed with a show of stunning contemporary Zimbabwean arts. In the park, vendors were selling spectacular flowers and crafts of remarkable quality—batiks and printed fabrics, pottery, intricate wire sculptures, and elegant Shona stone carvings. On the radio we caught Thomas Mapfumo and Oliver Mtukudzi and the upbeat rhythms that once inspired Zimbabwean freedom fighters.

Celia was dumbstruck. "Nairobi used to be like this," she said. "Then everybody learned how to grab." This was Celia's political theory. "The British grabbed," she said. "That's how we learned." Like so many other Kenyans, Celia was cynical and resigned. Without hope.

Like Kenya, Zimbabwe was ruled by an authoritarian ruler: capitalist President Moi in Kenya, socialist Prime Minister Robert Mugabe in Zimbabwe. Both countries had seen economic troubles, political unrest, government corruption—the familiar panoply of neocolonial African problems. Both rulers used power high-handedly to control the press, quash dissent, and cling to office. There'd been plenty of grabbing in Mugabe's Zimbabwe too, if scandals reported in the international press could be believed. Yet Zimbabwe seemed altogether different—as if we had passed from the Third World to the First. Almost everything worked, and the citizens, both black and white, seemed to enjoy their city and take pride in it. "This country is still young," Celia said. "When Kenya was young, Nairobi was like this."

Zimbabwe (formerly Southern Rhodesia) came late to independence—in 1980—because as the wave of liberation swept Africa, Southern Rhodesia's white population dug in their heels. In 1964, when Northern Rhodesia became independent Zambia, white Southern Rhodesians refused to give the United Kingdom the assurances it demanded as a precondition for independence that they would work toward eventual majority rule. Instead, in 1965 Prime Minister Ian Smith and his Rhodesian Front Party unilaterally declared independence. Most of the world joined an economic boycott against the renegade white-supremacist state; but with the help of apartheid South Africa and some Western corporations, white-run Rhodesia prospered and built a strong, self-sufficient economy by diversifying agriculture and manufacturing. It was black Rhodesians who brought the government down. The relentless guerrilla war they waged as the black nationalist Patriotic Front, led by Mugabe and Joshua Nkomo, proved too costly in lives and money for the Smith government. Rhodesia reverted to colonial status in 1979, and the following year became independent black-run Zimbabwe, with Mugabe as prime minister. Whites feared Mugabe's vengeance because he'd spent ten years as a political prisoner of the Smith government; but like Jomo Kenyatta in Kenya, Mugabe encouraged white settlers to stay and work for the good of the new nation—though twenty years later he would turn against them. Ian Smith himself stayed on to farm and criticize the Mugabe government and give embittered interviews to visiting foreign journalists. Elsewhere—

in the offices of UTC, for example—former Rhodesian adversaries worked together in apparent Zimbabwean harmony. Speaking one day about the independence struggle with a black UTC mechanic, a former guerrilla with the Patriotic Front, who was working on our vehicle, I said, "I'm amazed you didn't shoot Smith or boot him out of the country." I was always dazzled by the African capacity to forgive and, without forgetting, go on, exemplified so well in the character of Nelson Mandela. "Why in the world did you allow Smith to go on farming?" I asked. The former freedom fighter seemed surprised by my question. "Why not?" he said. "He is a good farmer."

One day, when we were driving our conspicuous blue vehicle aimlessly around downtown Harare, taking in the sights, the police stopped us; but they didn't want a bribe. They wanted to know if we needed directions or assistance. To Celia, who was already reaching for her purse, it seemed a revolutionary concept—the police in the service of the people. Kenyan police routinely collected bribes from drivers at roadblocks all over Nairobi, and often shot down "suspects" in the streets. Celia retreated into silence, a stranger in a strange land. Traveling through Tanzania, Malawi, and the wasteland of Mozambique, she had proudly pointed out all the ways those countries fell short of the standard set by her native Kenya. But now she seemed shaken by what she saw in Zimbabwe, shaken by scenes of a better life. "Pray they don't learn how to grab," she said.

Throughout our journey Celia had clung to Kenya through the radio. Caro had brought a shortwave to listen to the BBC, but Celia quickly claimed the radio as her own. She carried it around with her in her palm-leaf pocketbook. She placed it beside her plate on the table at meals. She carried it to her tent at night, where it was the last thing we heard as we fell asleep and the first thing we heard on waking. But it wasn't the BBC she listened to. It was Radio Kenya: official news of the official doings of President Moi. He spoke to a conference of dentists. He issued a report on maize production. He advised women to dress decently. Celia took it all in, not because she admired what President Moi did but because, like so many Kenyans, she longed for the day when he would be done. Her favorite program was the death notices, half an hour every morning and evening devoted to a recitation of the names of the day's deceased and all their many survivors earnestly grieving. The announcer's voice droned on, reciting the list of familiar-sounding names—Kikuyu names, Masai names, Luhya names. As we traveled farther from Kenya into Tanzania and Malawi, the signal faded. The Swahili voice dissolved in static that poured from the radio like audible suds. "Have you lost the signal?" Caro would ask brightly. That was her gentle indirect suggestion that we might switch off the noise and listen instead to the evening chorus of the bush. But Celia would say firmly, "It is there," and go on listening. Somewhere in the crackling froth of static curled a fine bright strand of Swahili, like a delicate ribbon tying her fast to home. Then somewhere in Zimbabwe, she turned the radio off.

Soon the time came for Celia to go home to her daughters. We took her to the street market to buy dresses and shoes for them. Caro bought her a new bag and helped her pack the gifts she had bought for her family, and then we took her to the airport. "How do I get my bags back?" she asked Caro when she surrendered them at check-in. Flying was new to her. But she was a world traveler now, wearing smart new sneakers and thinking who knows what brave new thoughts. We embraced her, and she turned and disappeared through the gate alone. Caro and I waited until the plane took off and then walked out to the parking lot in silence and climbed into the Land Cruiser, which seemed to have much more room now that Celia and all her things were gone, more empty space.

Caro and I wanted to explore Zimbabwe. But we were on the track of the Rain Queen now and eager to meet her. Phone calls sputtered back and forth along uncertain wires between Zimbabwe and South Africa. Through contacts in South Africa I had come up with an address for the Lovedu Tribal Council—and a phone number. Exploration not being what it used to be, we telephoned the Tribal Council and asked for an appointment with the Queen. "Call back tomorrow," said the man who answered the phone, and we did. The answer was yes. Her Majesty Mokope, Modjadji V, reigning (and raining) Queen of the Lovedu, granted us an audience, and the date was set. First thing Monday morning. It would be a formal visit, the Lovedu spokesman said, giving us to understand that the courteous thing to do afterward was to leave. What could I say? "I've schlepped half a million miles through sand and mud to get here, and I'd really like to hang around"? What was the point? I'm no anthropologist, and if I were I'd be embarrassed to lurk about studying a "primitive" tribe in which—if they were anything like other African people—the average member speaks four or five languages. And what did it matter? Hadn't I already had my vision of Africa along the way? Hadn't Africa already crept into my conscience? Caro and I packed up and sped south.

We had just enough time to make one stop along the way—at Great Zimbabwe, the greatest ruin in sub-Saharan Africa, a monument to black culture. I was interested on other grounds: hints I'd found in the scanty literature about the Lovedu that Princess Dzugudini, presumed founder of the Modjadji Dynasty, may have been a refugee from this place. If there were such a connection, and if it were true that Lovedu society, under the rule of the Rain Queen, valued "female" ideals—cooperation, appeasement, compromise, tolerance, generosity, peace—would we find these ideals also represented at Great Zimbabwe?

"Shona people settled the hilltop in the eleventh century," Caro said. I was driving, and she was reading aloud from a book we'd picked up in Harare. "In the twelfth century they began to build in stone." The Shona people were farmers who still made up three-quarters of the population of Zimbabwe. What they built was walls. "Cattle seem to be the key," Caro said. She read: "People with many cattle could obtain more wives and so have more labour to cultivate more lands."

I said, "I guess those 'people' obtaining wives are male 'people.' "

Caro went on reading: "Large herds and distant grazing lands can only be managed properly if there is a single powerful leader."

"Ah, yes," I said. "Hierarchy. Private property. Traffic in women. Does this system ring any bells?"

Caro read on: "The leaders who controlled the herd lived on the best young beef. Their grain was largely consumed as beer." She groaned and snapped the book shut. "Beef and beer. It's a paradise for good old boys," she said.

"Does it say anything about football?"

"No wonder the princess ran off. It's too depressing."

We camped near the ruins and made our way at first light to the Great Enclosure, an immense circular wall embracing a space where crowds must have gathered on ceremonial occasions. Within the space were several other curved walls forming smaller enclosures. We recognized the Great Enclosure as a gigantic version of the sort of compound that many African villages build, usually of rough branches placed upright, like palings. Such enclosures have many names—*kraal* or *boma* or *manyatta*. In Shona the word is *"zimbabwe."* This Great Enclosure was a monumental *zimbabwe* made of stones, piled up centuries ago in irregular courses without mortar, and now gilded by bright lichens. The great circular curtain wall, more than sixty feet high, was stunningly beautiful, the patterns made by the undulations of the stones enthralling. Like Stonehenge or the pyramids, it was something to see.

For decades after Great Zimbabwe was rediscovered, Europeans tried to prove it had been built by people other than black Africans. Modern interpreters seemed to have something else on their minds. "The guidebook says this tower is meant to be a phallic symbol," Caro said as we came upon a conical structure within the Great Enclosure. "How do they know that?"

"It looks like some of the pots the women made," I said. "Maybe it's meant to be a pot. Or a spindle."

"It could be maize," said Caro, always a prodigious eater. "Perhaps they worshiped grain."

"It could be just a tower."

We walked to the small museum nearby to see the carved-stone birds that once stood on the hilltop. In the museum was a case full of small stone objects: one that looked like a large bolt, another like a small thimble, and many nondescript fragments in between. The case was labeled PHALLIC SYMBOLS. Caro was exasperated. "These anthropologists!" she said. "Can they think of nothing else?"

We made the long climb up a path of ancient stones to the hilltop, a huge granite *kopje* crowned with immense boulders that were laced together with stone walls to form a series of rooms and passages and circular enclosures. These structures were a great feat of human engineering, yet they were so perfectly entwined with the hilltop that from below they were nearly invisible. To the sides of the path lay the stony vestiges of terraces once occupied by the huts of twenty thousand people who were the citizens of Great Zimbabwe. This was a place of busy international trade; shards of Chinese celadon still turned up among the stones. A place where pottery was made, and sculpture. Where great stone birds gazed from the western wall. We climbed atop a boulder that formed the upper level of a hilltop enclosure and looked out over the walls and terraces, over the green valley below where the Great Enclosure stood. We tried to imagine how lively it must have been— the terraces full of people, and the paths leading up the hill and down to the peaceful valley.

Great Zimbabwe struck us with amazement. It wasn't the place we were looking for—the place where women rule. But neither was it the sort of place you think of when you think of Africa. The peoples of Africa built their capitals with mud and sticks and grass, biodegradable cities that disappeared, leaving little trace upon what we call history of the civilizations that once flourished within their precincts. But at Great Zimbabwe, and other sites scattered in southern Africa, another architecture—another Africa—remains visible: stone walls that give durable form to human endeavor, social order, art, and culture. African culture.

THE RAIN QUEEN

We crossed the bridge into South Africa just as a red sun slipped into the brown wash of the Limpopo, and on the morning of the day appointed for our audience, we circled through the Drakensberg Mountains toward Loveduland. Fog rose from the valleys, and mist cloaked the hillsides where spectral plantations of eucalyptus stood. Planted for timber, the fast-growing eucalyptus drank up Drakensberg waters, leaving the once-productive plains below parched by thirst that even the Rain Queen couldn't quench. Nothing in Africa was simple, it seemed, and every "improvement" held the seeds of loss. In my mind's eye I riffled through the snapshots of African life we'd gathered in the past year, both Africa's best and her worst. I'd set out on a lark and passed through a gallery of unimagined richness. That's something, I thought—just knowing how various the continent is, how abundant in fact and possibility. Journalists and experts of one sort or another seemed so often to write off Africa as unstable, hopelessly impoverished, maniacally violent, backward beyond redemption. They were wrong. That much I'd seen for myself. Somehow their reportage left out the people: their strength, their resiliency, their music, their laughter, their boundless capacity to move on. (Was it merely a geological fluke that the African continent, as Graham Greene noticed, is shaped like the human heart?) Now I was to meet the woman—the afterthought—who had served as a justification for my journey. Almost there, I said to myself, and felt a stirring—too soon to name it joy.

"Do you think this audience with the Queen will change your life?" Caro asked. She was going over the directions again and watching out for road signs.

I laughed. "Do you mean, will it make me any easier to get along with? I doubt it."

"No. Seriously. You've come all this way to see her, but you've never actually talked about your expectations. Do you imagine a revelation? Will you come away as a new person?"

"Sorry, Caro. I think I'll just be content to see her. Anyway it's Africa itself that changes people. Look how it has changed your values, the way you live: made you chuck 'success' and live with your heart."

"Maybe it was my heart that brought me here," she said, "to find a home. How does one ever know?"

How does one ever know? Whatever changes Africa was to work in me must already have been wrought. They didn't show. Yet they were there, I thought, simmering under the skin. Snail eggs, working their way into the system for good or ill. Whatever the Queen might tell me, I held my images of Africa in my mind. It was the journey, not the destination, that counted in the end.

Travelers are tested by the land they travel. In Africa we had traveled often through a landscape of pain—the legacy of colonialism, neocolonial corruption, development, and globalization. Yet I had been struck daily by the beauty of the people, their kindness and generosity, their hospitality, their infinite patience and politeness and good humor, their boundless dignity. Africa moved me, though I couldn't imagine then—as we drove toward our rendezvous with the Queen—that it would actually make me shake off my old ordinary American life. Later, when I went "home," I would find I couldn't bear the wealth of goods that seemed to be everywhere in America, and the way people worked so long and hard to get things. It was stifling. As stifling as once again being shut up indoors with central heating and air-conditioning and windows impossible to open. (Years later President Museveni of Uganda, describing a visit to the United States, would say to me: "You Westerners consume all the world's resources—except air. That you trap inside buildings and force people to breathe it again.") I left my job and my apartment, gave away most of my things, and flogged the remains at a yard sale. I drove west with my cat and my old horses and came to rest in a one-room adobe house in the desert. I threw open the doors and windows and let the dry winds blow through, bringing heat and dust and birdsong, and when the monsoon struck, toxic toads. But at night the coyotes yipped and set to barking all the German shepherds and

Dobermans that lurked behind the walls of my neighbors' houses, guarding their acquisitions. My neighbors built gated housing developments and golf courses, consuming the flowering desert at the rate of an acre an hour and draining the aquifers. They came closer, but they did not become better neighbors. One day I loaded the horses on the trailer, and moved on.

All that lay ahead. But that day, as we turned a corner into the valley of GaModjadji—into the realm of the Rain Queen—the fog suddenly lifted and the factory forests gave way to a human landscape of huts and gardens and ordinary-looking black people walking toward us in the road. All across Africa I'd seen the ingenuity and resourcefulness of African villagers such as these. It wasn't just that they made do with what they had. What they had was not the center of their lives. Always they gave time to one another. Always the long formal greetings, the offered gift of hospitality—a few groundnuts, a bit of parched maize, a glass of water. Always the sitting together, the sharing of tasks and even of children. The sense of decorum: the quiet, observant children, the deference to age. All of this seemed to reflect the purest kind of social coherence. Western individualism contends that this social life is gained at the expense of the individual, though I could see that villagers lived easily with individuals we would have sent to an old-age home or an asylum or jail. I could see a dark side too in the deference of women to men—yet women gathered together and lived their hardworking lives with great spirit, manifest in the boisterous parties they threw to raise money for their mutual-help societies, the work teams singing together as they hoed their *shambas,* the laughter rising from the marketplace.

Here in the valley of GaModjadji, women in bright blouses and skirts gathered at bus stops and gangs of men hiked toward the crossroads where trucks would collect them. It was as if the whole valley were emptying out, dispersing Lovedu people over the length and breadth of the lowveld, checkered with white-owned plantations and farms. But only for the workday. Theirs was a daily diaspora, but in the evening the Lovedu people would return to the valley again, retreating to the reserve from the lands that had once been theirs, the lands where now they labored for small wages. Long ago their freely cooperative farming life had given way to the coercive cash economy of the white man, who had stolen their lands. Yet here they were still. What held

them together? Was it the Queen and the traditional culture she represented? Or something more profound: the collective memory of
Lovedu power and freedom?

We swung off the main road and climbed a long winding gravel
track that led up the mountainside to a small storefront. This was the
tribal headquarters of the Lovedu, or as they spell it now, Lobedu.
There waiting for us were Nerwick Molokwane, a teacher who would
serve as translator, and Victor Mathekga, a member of the royal family
and the Queen's Council. Both men were lean and handsome and
smartly dressed in sport shirts and trousers. They looked thoroughly
Westernized, but we had long ago learned that in Africa, where half the
population is dressed in the hand-me-down tee shirts of Europe and
America, Western dress does not mean Western thought.

Nerwick and Victor got into our vehicle and directed me to drive to
the top of the mountain. There they said we would visit the Sacred Forest, entrusted by the gods to the particular protection of their great
Queen. "Wouldn't you know she'd be an environmentalist," Caro said.
We left the vehicle at the summit and entered on foot a dark maze of
towering twisted prehistoric plants, their stout trunks and flaring
crowns bristling with palmy spikes. They didn't grow straight up like
more familiar trees but lunged down at us like scaly green dragons,
twisting their necks to get a look at us. "Incredible," Caro said, recognizing them from tropical Australia. "They're giant cycads." These
ancient seed plants that once covered the earth, long before the
dinosaurs came and died, survive now only by the handful in a few
remote tropical pockets around the globe. Yet we followed our guides
on and on through the fabulously contorted foliage of the Jurassic Age:
perhaps the last such substantial stand of cycads on the planet, pre-
served only because they grew here in Loveduland, venerated as Queen
Modjadji's Sacred Forest. This extraordinary example of botanic preser-
vation seemed to me reason enough to value the monarchy of Queen
Modjadji. Yet I imagined that the Queen herself must be as endangered
as her cycad forest—both relics of another world, clinging to the same
mountaintop while the seas of global development rose around them.

Our guides led us back down the mountain to an iron gate marked
MODJADJI HEAD KRAAL. Caro shot me a look that said she hadn't a clue
what to expect next. But I remembered my visit with Muggleton to the
Palace of the *fon* of Nkwem, he of the twenty-four wives. I wasn't

expecting grandeur. A fat young woman in a short red skirt shuffled to the gate and opened it. The Queen's daughter, Nerwick said. We drove into the compound and parked in the mud under a huge mango tree. Below us the land sloped sharply away, affording the tenants of the Head Kraal a royal view of the realm. Princess Dzugudini couldn't have chosen a better spot than here, where the prevailing winds from the sea met the tall barrier mountains, to set up shop as a rainmaker. Just above us stood a modern building reminiscent of a fast-food stand, but smaller and incomplete. Paper was still attached to the dusty window glass, and plywood was nailed over the door frames. "That's the new reception room," Victor said, catching my gaze. "We hope to find the funds to finish it soon." Both the Queen and the Tribal Council were short of cash.

Nerwick and Victor led us through an inner gate and through the ceremonial *boma,* a large enclosure of tall wood palings. We followed them along narrow paths through the royal compound, crowded like any African village with closely built *rondavels* of sticks and mud. The paths and courtyards were empty, the members of the Queen's family inside their huts, out of sight. Our guides took us into a large house of mud brick and let us gaze upon the ceremonial drums. They led us to a gnarled and leafless tree nearby and bowed their heads in portentous silence. This tree, Nerwick explained, was a Sacred Tree—one of three sacred shrines at which the Queen carried out the rainmaking cere-mony each October. Here the Queen poured a bowl of beer upon the earth, and important men, including Nerwick and Victor, knelt upon the ground to lap it up. Then the Queen beat the Sacred Drums, which we had just been privileged to see. Everybody danced. Nerwick said slyly that Victor was an exceedingly fine dancer, and Victor swiveled his slim hips to give us a glimpse of the ceremonial dance he did so well. "The Queen led the ceremonies as usual in October," Nerwick said, "and now as you can see the rains fall."

At last our guides led us to a modest thatched *rondavel* surrounded by a cement platform upon which slumbered a dozen yellow dogs. On the step rested a heavyset dark-skinned black woman of indeterminate middle age. She looked like any other African woman—an older, wea-rier incarnation of Celia, I thought. But she rose and padded barefoot into the hut while our guides bowed and shuffled out of their shoes. By the time we removed our sandals and followed our guides into the hut, the woman had seated herself on a red leatherette La-Z-Boy recliner, which still bore its original label. Our guides fell to their knees and crept toward her with their heads bowed and their eyes downcast, and I found myself—still standing—gazing directly into the eyes of Mokope, Modjadji V, Queen of the Lovedu.

"Your Majesty," I said. I cast down my eyes and launched some clumsy gesture—part curtsey, part bow—in awkward imitation of something I must have seen in movies. Caro undertook a more graceful deferential move that involved also an elaborate swoosh of the long scarf she wore. To her credit, the Queen did not laugh. Instead she masked her face with a look of perfect implacability. Obviously she was a woman who had done this many times: sat stolidly on her throne and watched a parade of clownish visitors. That's when it struck me: *This* is a queen. All this time we had wondered what a queen would do. But a queen needn't *do* anything. It is enough for a queen to *be*.

Queen Modjadji V was dressed for the occasion in a navy blue polo shirt and a wrap of leopard-patterned cotton. She wore big gold earrings and a bright red print scarf about her head. But though her dress seemed casual—no fancier than the outfit any of her female subjects might wear to work—that implacable look on her face was deadly serious and powerfully intimidating. "Fierce!" Caro whispered. Despite the absence of grand trappings, Queen Modjadji V was the real thing.

Our guides prostrated themselves before her and then crept backward across the floor to seat themselves on grass mats on either side of her La-Z-Boy throne. They gestured to us to be seated on a couple of overstuffed vinyl chairs on the far side of the room opposite the Queen. We sat—just a little too far away to make out the logo on her polo shirt. Surely not Ralph Lauren. In the ensuing silence, we were at a loss. We'd rehearsed for this moment, planning an effusive greeting, but in the presence of the implacable Queen our protocol fell apart. Caro and I had prepared a gift: a rainproof flashlight (Caro's idea) wrapped in a royal purple *kanga* from Kenya. Atop the bundle I'd tied the small blue velvet beaded pouch that I'd worn around my neck throughout my long journey, and inside the pouch I'd tucked a pair of gold earrings. Clutching our gift, Caro and I scurried across the room and bowed deeply. Without looking at it, Queen Modjadji placed the bundle on a chair beside her.

Splendid, I thought—that simple gesture of royal indifference. Why should the Queen take an interest in our gift? Why, come to think of it, should she take an interest in *us*? She was a queen, after all, doing dispassionately the work of a queen, and we were blundering *wazungu* merely being intrusive, as *wazungu* will do. Nerwick explained that the Queen, being a queen, did not speak directly to her subjects and certainly not to guests. Nor were we allowed to address her. We could, however, direct our remarks to Nerwick, and he would convey them to the Queen, who in turn might or might not condescend to direct to Nerwick a reply for him to convey to us. Caro recovered her manners and asked Nerwick to thank the Queen for receiving us and to explain that we had come from the United States and Australia especially to pay our respects to her. When he finished translating, the Queen said something in Sesotho that made Nerwick and Victor laugh. They didn't repeat her remarks to us, and I realized with a sinking feeling that we were all in the hands of the bilingual men who would translate what they chose of the Queen's words and tell her only what they wanted her to know. Language is power.

"You may ask your questions now," Nerwick said.

"Do we find the Queen in good health?" I asked.

In response, once the question had been translated, Queen Modjadji made a sort of humming noise that we took to mean, "Yes."

"Is the Queen responsible for the current rains?" Caro asked.

"Hum."

"With all due respect," I said, "would Her Majesty kindly explain the reasons for the drought of recent years?"

"Hum."

Clearly, the Queen was a woman of few words—though she had Nerwick and Victor chuckling at sotto voce remarks they kept to themselves. The Queen waved a hand at Nerwick, making a circular gesture as if she were winding him up, and Nerwick took it upon himself to elaborate upon Her Majesty's terse answers. The drought, he said, was caused by the fact that the cemetery had burned. Such an insult to the ancestors always brought trouble. The Queen had nothing to do with it. I recalled from the pages of the anthropologists' work that in the old days it was Christian converts who burned the cemetery to discredit the Queen. I wondered if Loveduland, like the United States, was troubled these days by mean-spirited right-wingers prone to dirty tricks, but I feared the question might not translate well and kept it to myself.

"Did the Queen take action to end the drought?" Caro asked.

"Hum."

Again the Queen prompted Nerwick to elaborate, and as he spoke she sat back in her recliner and let her steady gaze pass over us, inspecting us without curiosity. He told us more about the ceremonies she had performed in October and of the immediate salutary change in the weather. The Queen wondered that we had not noticed the rains increasing daily as we drove toward GaModjadji.

"Indeed we did notice," I said, thinking of the incessant swish of our windshield wipers. "We were very impressed." Caro backed me up, and Nerwick translated our remarks for the Queen, who seemed to settle more deeply in a satisfied way into her throne.

"Is Her Majesty a Christian?" Caro asked, with a nod at several large pictures of Jesus that hung beside portraits of the Queen herself on the walls of the audience chamber.

The Queen laughed out loud at this question, and Nerwick explained that she had hung the Jesus pictures to please the visiting Christian missionaries who had given them to her. That's just the sort of thing a Lovedu queen *would* do, I thought, remembering what I'd read about the traditional values of Loveduland. I thought again of Lovedu queens of the past who refused to fight with would-be conquerors, who invited them instead to settle down, get a wife, a little land, a little beer. Make love, not war. Make friends, not converts.

"I have read that Lovedu people place a high value on appeasement, compromise, reconciliation, and tolerance," I said. "Would the Queen kindly tell me if this is true? Does Her Majesty still hold those values?"

"Hum," the Queen said. She smiled slightly and gave a little nod of recognition as if she were pleased that we actually knew something about Lovedu culture. Then she added something more. As if to illustrate the value of tolerance, the pagan Queen told Nerwick to ask us to convey her Christmas greetings to the people of the West.

Encouraged, I dared to ask: "Is it true that the Queen has many wives?"

"Hum," she said, and although her face was in shadow, I swear she smiled again, ever so slightly, as she gestured to Victor to tell us more.

"Plus or minus twenty-five wives," he said. They were given to her by the *indunas,* or headmen, who governed the villages. They lived in the huts we had seen within the royal compound, together with their children, and they served the Queen. Certain men of the royal family saw to it that the Queen's wives bore plenty of children. "It is my duty," Victor said proudly. Victor the dancer of the slim swiveling hips. He wrestled with the grin that crept across his face. He explained that the Queen herself had given birth to two daughters (one of whom had died after giving birth to a daughter of her own: a beautiful young girl who had followed us through the compound) and a son—although of course she had no husband. The Queen continued the proud tradition of Dzugudini, the tribe's founding single mother, who fled her father's kingdom in Zimbabwe so very long ago. But that story—the saga of the exodus of Dzugudini and the foundation of Loveduland—was a long one, which the Queen could tell only during the passage of many days and only with the help of her learned counselors.

"We would especially like to know," Caro said, "how the Queen rules men." Nerwick laughed. Victor laughed. Neither of them translated the question for the Queen, who sat back and watched us, expressionless, as the men provided answers of their own. Nerwick said that women were very highly respected among the Lovedu—although a woman's first duty was to care for her home and her husband. This answer was meant to set us straight lest we conclude from the deference they showed the Queen that she actually ruled the land, or that the average woman ruled anything at all. Did not England have a queen as well? And did women rule over men there? It seemed that the average Lovedu woman, unlike the Lovedu Queen, had a husband whom she served just as the Queen's wives served her. Like most other African women, the average Lovedu woman was busy looking after a man as well as her children and tending her *shamba* and commuting to a job or "doing business" of some moneymaking kind on the side. (Hadn't we already seen that the average Lovedu woman sitting by the roadside was waiting for a bus to take her to work as a domestic laborer in some white household?)

So the valley of GaModjadji these days was not, after all, a land where women rule. Nor was it an egalitarian paradise for liberated women, or a sensual garden of delights for sexy old women, irresistible to young men. Where relations between the sexes were concerned, the old topsy-turvy customs of Loveduland seemed to have been set straight by the patriarchal cultures that had overwhelmed them. Modern Loveduland seemed to be, like the rest of Africa and much of the rest of the world, a land where women lacked the power even to rule themselves. Why was I not surprised?

Yet Loveduland was no paradise for macho men either. Aggressive individualism was still not welcome in this "feminine" domain where harmony was the highest ideal. What held the power to make life different in GaModjadji even now was not the rules of daily gender relations but the fundamental "feminine" values of the culture, shared alike by women and men. Those values—cooperation, compromise, tolerance, mutual helpfulness, forgiveness—are among the values Nelson Mandela alludes to when he speaks of the "natural socialism" of Africans, and they still seemed to be stirring in Loveduland.

I wondered if Modjadji V and Mandela saw eye to eye. "Does the Queen enjoy good relations with President Mandela and the new government of South Africa?" I asked.

"Hum," the Queen said with some enthusiasm, and she went on to explain.

President Mandela had paid her a state visit, and now his government was bringing electricity to her villages, Nerwick translated. But she had enjoyed good relations with the old apartheid government of South Africa too. She would enjoy good relations with *any* government, Nerwick said, for only a fool fails to find peaceable compromise. High on her mountainside in GaModjadji, what should Modjadji V care who rules the country that encompasses her Queendom? (Or who comes to visit, for that matter.) Her job was to look after her people.

She was not an educated woman, she said. She grew up in the small hut we had seen in the compound where now her own wives lived, and she succeeded her mother, Makoma, Modjadji IV, who reigned from 1960 to 1980. All the land of GaModjadji was hers, and so was responsibility for the welfare of the people who lived upon it—perhaps fifty thousand of them, perhaps five hundred thousand. No one was quite sure of the numbers. Her *indunas*—all male—managed daily affairs in their respective areas, carrying only the problems they couldn't solve to the Queen. Here in her modest *rondavel*, seated upon her La-Z-Boy, wearing the royal leopard skin about her shoulders, she told the *indunas* what to do—or helped them figure it out, more likely—probably with the same curious mix of reticence, tactful evasion, implacability, and humor she brought to our audience. In her spare time, Nerwick said, Her Majesty enjoyed watching wrestling on TV, but her responsibility as the hub of Lovedu civilization was to bring the rain and keep the peace. If one can believe the meager evidence of history and legend, she and her predecessors have done so for hundreds of years. When you think about it, that's no small achievement.

"One last question, please, Your Majesty," Caro said. I glanced at my watch, amazed to see that two hours had hummed away. "Is there anything the people of the Western world could learn from you, Your Majesty, and the women of your culture?"

The Queen drew her brows together in thought. "Hum," she said. She added something else that made both Nerwick and Victor laugh, and this time they both translated at once.

"Her Majesty says she could teach you to dance."

She dismissed us then with a wave of her hand, and our guides signaled that it was time for us to crawl backward out of the audience chamber under the splendid mango tree and take our leave. The Queen's remark seemed enigmatic and profound. But what did it mean? On my hands and knees, I looked up and caught the Queen's gaze and held it for a moment; and I thought I understood. Dancing among the Lovedu is ceremonial, performed by the Queen's wives and the women of her court, or by the men of her council. It honors the gods and the ancestors and brings on the rain. It is the purest expression of the cohesion of society: the beneficent balance of authority and general well-being. The dance, physical and spiritual at once, is a metaphor for the intricate relationships of society. What the Queen meant, I thought, is that she could teach the people of the West to live in peace and harmony with others, just as her people had done for hundreds of years.

Then I was outside, blinking in the bright sunshine, among the Queen's sleepy yellow dogs. Wasn't I grasping at illusions, reading into the Queen's remark overblown implications of my own invention? Wasn't I leaping to meet literary conventions that demand, at this point in the proceedings, major insight? One of the Queen's dogs raised his head and lifted a leg to scratch his ear. Then he stared at me with just the trace of a smile on his face, waiting for me to figure it out. "Do you think she meant it literally?" I asked him. He blinked lazily and stretched out again with a sigh. Maybe what she meant to say was as simple as that: "Hey, give it a rest. Lighten up. Get down. Boogie. *Dance.*"

We didn't stay long in GaModjadji. Our hosts escorted us back through the royal compound toward the reception area and tactfully let us know that the time had come to end our visit. We walked slowly back to the car, prolonging the moment, but one great lesson I'd learned in Africa was to let things be. When we reached the car and turned to take a last look, we saw that Queen Modjadji had emerged from the rondavel and was seated in a white plastic lawn chair under the mango tree with several of her grandchildren and her yellow dogs around her. She was listening to Shangaan pop music on a boom box. Around her shoulders, like an alb of office, she wore the purple *kanga* that Caro and I had brought from Kenya. We bowed and waved from our vehicle as we drove away toward the big iron gate, but she didn't acknowledge our salute. She stared after us, but she didn't wave. She didn't smile. She was implacable. She was a queen.

Not long after we visited Queen Modjadji, she granted an audience to a reporter from the London *Daily Telegraph,* and the following year to a reporter from the *New York Times*. Both men wrote clever features, full of wry comments about El Niño and modern weather forecasters and South Africa's efforts to improve potable water supplies, all of which were cutting into the Queen's rainmaking "business." Apparently knowing little of Lovedu social order and values, or the centrality of the Rain Queen to the culture, the reporters seemed to think the Queen's rainmaking was a commercial enterprise. And based on foolish hocus-pocus at that. (She made the *Times* man pay $50 for the audience, and $40 more to take her picture—which goes to show that she *can* run a business, though rainmaking is not it.) The Queen herself left the reporters unimpressed. What was she to them after all but a curiosity that just might fill the weekly quota of column inches? One described her as a "dumpy old woman," and both said she was "sullen" and stared at the floor. I suspect their skeptical attitude tried her patience. She is, after all, a queen—and who are they? She made them sit on the floor, feigned ignorance when asked about Nelson Mandela, and wouldn't say a word about how she made rain—only that she *could* do it. Getting nowhere with the "cult" Queen, the *Daily Telegraph* man tried another story formula: changing times. The Queen is "fighting to keep her status," he wrote, as modern youth lose respect for old traditions; but high school students he interviewed said that if they were to see the sequestered Queen, "they would go down on their knees." Neither reporter wrote anything about Lovedu culture, or beliefs, or values, or what would impel thoroughly modern young people who must have met meteorological explanations of rainfall to go down on their knees before an aging woman who said she made the rain herself.

Chinua Achebe argues that Africans must redefine themselves and make amends for betraying their African heritage, but Queen Modjadji has never left her post. She is no idle modern royal, breaking vows, trimming duty to suit the company she keeps, but a true queen who trims her own freedom to advance the welfare of her people. She is a woman in thrall to the circumstances of her life; but by giving herself to those circumstances she acquires authority, power, purpose, identity. Her duty gives significance to her life and in turn to the life of her people. Nevertheless, it's true that the forces of change (capitalism, development, modernization, globalization) are sweeping over the land in a kind of twentieth-century "overwhelming" that may in fact cause Queen Modjadji's young subjects to betray their Lovedu heritage just as Achebe's father betrayed his Igbo traditions when, under the influence of foreign invaders who defined his culture as misguided, he became a Christian and repudiated the faith of his fathers. Then the Queen will become in truth what she already seemed to the *Times* reporter to be: a tourist attraction, a curiosity, a charlatan perhaps, and surely a vestige of the old benighted Africa that Europeans came—and still come—to civilize. The Modjadji dynasty survived the Zulus, the Boers, the British, the missionaries, the anthropologists, the apartheid regime, and the African National Congress. The next onslaught will be tourists. Queen Modjadji V was recently written up in a guidebook, and one day her forbidden image, imprinted on tee shirts, may be for sale—like the beer that once flowed so freely in Loveduland—in a souvenir stand in the heart of the Sacred Cycad Forest.

Still it's not wise to wax sentimental about the general loss of old traditions. What stands to be lost with Lovedu culture is a certain set of values the modern world could use, and forms of social life in which those values inhere. Other African cultures have other "traditions" the world could well do without, slavery and genital mutilation of women being only the most obvious examples. Consider this: In Zimbabwe, the land from which Princess Dzugudini supposedly fled so long ago, men "make amends" by turning back the clock to some imagined pre-colonial time. After independence in 1980, Zimbabwe recognized women's roles in the long fight for freedom by establishing equal rights for women in the new Constitution. The government also passed a law to guarantee women's rights and signed several international human rights treaties that outlawed gender discrimination. That body of law provided the basis for Vennia Magaya, a fifty-eight-year-old seamstress, to sue her half brother for her rightful portion of their deceased father's estate. In April 1999 the Supreme Court of Zimbabwe ruled against her on the grounds that women are *not* equal to men, especially in family relationships. The five male justices based their unanimous decision on unwritten precolonial African "cultural norms" that dictate, they said, that women "should never be considered adults within the family, but only as a junior male, or teen-ager." Overnight women's rights disappeared and they were returned to ahistorical "precolonial traditions": that they could not own land, inherit property from their deceased husbands or fathers, choose their own marriage partners, lay claim to their children, or object to their husbands' polygamy. Welshman Ncube, Zimbabwe's leading constitutional scholar, commented: "Basically, there's nothing left of the gains women's rights have made in the past twenty years. It's a full-bench decision. . . . There is no appeal. They meant to settle this question once and for all."

All right. So my long quest did not lead me to a utopian land ruled by women, and Zimbabwe has suddenly become just the reverse. I found instead a tiny land where a woman rules, after a fashion, under economic and political constraints of more powerful neighbors and the new world market—where a woman rules on sufferance, really, and probably only temporarily, and where most women lack the power and freedom to rule themselves. Even the Queen is bound by the rules and rituals of her office and compelled to maintain the aura of power by living in seclusion. To outsiders she might seem to be a prisoner in Modjadji Head Kraal, a pawn of her people, trotted out to perform for visiting journalists, her image (once sacred and forbidden) for sale to the foreign press. But the same could be said of Elizabeth II, though she enjoys a higher pay scale. "I am not happy," Queen Modjadji V said, "not unhappy. I am just a person of my people." This unfreedom seems the antithesis of feminism (or women's self-rule), for feminism is all about choice, the very thing that most traditional societies cannot afford—a luxury of those for whom survival is no longer the first concern. For Modjadji V, Queen of the Lovedu, choice—other than the one she has made—is surely an impossibility. Upon her consent to unfreedom everything depends.

In all of Africa I met no woman, except Caro, who possessed a freedom of self-determination and a wealth of privileges equal to my own. None who was free, as I was, to be an *inspecteur du monde*. Yet I envied the African women I met their deep human connections, their valued places within their families and traditional societies, even as I could see those societies changing before my eyes. Take Celia, who lives two lives: educated urban English-speaking civil servant in Western dress, and when she returns to her village, farm woman in African dress at the heart of a close-knit Swahili- and Luhya-speaking extended family. During the week she sits at a desk in an office in a modern building in the capital. When she visits the village of her birth, she carries buckets of water uphill from the stream or squats beside a tripod cookfire or polishes a floor at the home place with a fresh coat of cattle dung. And what will be the life of her daughters, whose childhood already encompasses the two worlds of their mother?

After our audience with the Queen, Caro and I drove south to Cape Agulhas, the southernmost point of the African continent, and there we parked on the beach and stepped into the sea. For me it marked the completion of the journey from one end of the continent to the other. I put my camera on a timer and called to Caro, "Come up on the roof." I wanted to shoot a commemorative photo of the two of us atop the ridiculous blue Land Cruiser. I hopped up, but Caro circled below. "How do you get up there?" she said. I extended a hand to help her, and she climbed up, still toting her pink purse. Together we stood on the roof of the blue vehicle with the blue sea behind us, and the camera took the picture. Then Caro reached deep in her purse and brought out a kite her sister had sent from London. She tipped it into the wind and it soared into the blue sky like a bird.

A few days later we drove to Lesotho. We wanted a break—a time out of time to take in what we'd seen and learned. We hired a couple of

Basotho horses and rode to a tiny village high in the Maluti Mountains. There, having left our tents behind, we rented a stone hut that seemed as old and sturdy as the earth itself. That night in the Lesotho village high in the mountains we sat side by side in the doorway, both of us missing Celia, and I missing Muggleton, who at that moment was again defying death in the Sahara, on a motorcycle this time. In silence Caro and I watched the full moon slide onto a distant ridge and roll off the edge, a bright coin coasting skyward. Soon it slipped among fast-moving clouds. Then lightning came, stabbing the mountainside across the deep valley. And then rain. It poured on the thatch of our hut and rolled from the roof as a glittering silver screen through which we still gazed out at the world beyond our doorway. The rain poured on the villagers' steep and tidy fields. It poured on the pale cows huddled in the stone *kraal* just below our hut, and on the innocent horses, tethered out there in the dark. It poured as though it would wash the whole world clean.

"That Modjadji," Caro said. "Does she never rest?"

DAISY BATES IN THE DESERT
A Woman's Life Among the Aborigines
by Julia Blackburn

In 1913, at the age of 54, Daisy Bates went to live in the deserts of southern Australia. She meticulously recorded everything—from the songs of the kangaroo and dingo people to detailed inventories of her possessions. In this riveting work of investigation and imagination, Julia Blackburn reconstructs the life of this intriguing, mysterious adventuress and allows us to feel what it must have been like to be a middle-aged European woman staring out across a red desert, surrounded by the remnants of a dying culture.

Travel/Women's Studies/0-679-74446-0

TRACKS
A Woman's Solo Trek Across 1,700 Miles of Australian Outback
by Robyn Davidson

When Robyn Davidson set out to cross the deserts of Australia, alone but for her dog and four camels, she was called a lunatic, a would-be suicide, and a shameless publicity seeker. But *Tracks* reveals her to be a genuine traveler driven by a love of Australia's landscape and an empathy for its indigenous people. Enduring 130-degree heat and fording swollen rivers, fending off poisonous snakes and lecherous men, chasing her camels when they got skittish and nursing them when they got injured, Davidson emerges as a heroine who combines extraordinary courage with exquisite sensitivity.

Travel/Adventure/0-679-76287-6

SAMBA
by Alma Guillermoprieto

Samba—that sensuous song and dance marked by a driving, rapturous beat—is for the people of the villages surrounding Rio de Janeiro their most "intense, unambivalent joy" in the face of poverty, violence, and racism. Every year, each of the villages sends a samba school to compete in Rio's Carnival parade. Alma Guillermoprieto lived for one year in Mangueira and joined its famed samba school. *Samba* is an exuberant account of her experiences and a cogent, lucid examination of the history and culture of black Brazilians.

Travel/Sociology/0-679-73256-X

SHOOTING THE BOH
A Woman's Voyage Down the Wildest River in Borneo
by Tracy Johnston

When Tracy Johnston signed up for a rafting expedition down the Boh River in Borneo, she had no idea that it had never been fully navigated, and no one had warned her about the swimming cobras and swarms of sweat-eating bees. But perhaps the most frightening discovery that Johnston made was what she learned about herself. A thrilling, touching, and densely instructive book, *Shooting the Boh* is also a frank self-portrait of a woman facing her greatest fears—and triumphing over them—with fortitude and unflagging wit.

Travel/Adventure/0-679-74010-4

TWO IN THE WILD
Tales of Adventure from Friends, Mothers, and Daughters
edited with an introduction by Susan Fox Rogers

Trudge through Australia's muddy outback with Sara Corbett and her childhood chum, go fishing with Holly Morris, kick back with Pam Houston at a Denver ranch, bike with Diane Ackerman, and climb the Himalayas with 54-year-old Jean Gould and her 70-year-old travel partner. Whether you are an armchair adventurer or a thrill seeker in your own right, these exhilarating essays will inspire you to dust off your bicycle, lace up your hiking boots, fill your gas tank, and take your dearest friend along for the time of your lives.

Travel/Women's Studies/Anthology/0-375-70201-6

VINTAGE DEPARTURES
Available at your local bookstore, or call toll-free to order:
1-800-793-2665 (credit cards only).